ARABULA;

OR,

THE DIVINE GUEST.

CONTAINING

A NEW COLLECTION OF GOSPELS.

BY

ANDREW JACKSON DAVIS,

AUTHOR OF SEVERAL VOLUMES ON THE "HARMONIAL PHILOSOPHY."

"Within thee is the all-wise, ever-loving Arabula."

DEATH AND THE AFTER-LIFE, p. 88.

THIRD THOUSAND.

BOSTON:

WILLIAM WHITE & COMPANY,

158 WASHINGTON STREET.

NEW YORK:

BANNER OF LIGHT BRANCH OFFICE, 544 BROADWAY.

1868.

INTRODUCTORY.

THIS volume is, to some extent, a continuation of the author's autobiography, entitled, "The Magic Staff." But, chiefly, it contains a faithful record of experiences which, it is believed, are far more *representative* than exceptional. The exceptions occur in that private realm where the individual differs, as each has an undoubted constitutional right to differ, from every other.

A new collection of living Gospels, revised and corrected, and compared with the originals, is herein presented to the world.

The alternations of faith and skepticism, of lights and shades, of heaven and hades, of joys and sorrows, are familiar to the human mind. The causes of these mental states are considered.

May the Arabula be unfolded in the heart of every reader.

A. J. D.

NEW YORK, *Nov.* 4, 1867.

INDEX TO THE GOSPELS.

CHAPTER L.

CONTAINS INSPIRATIONS FROM THE FOLLOWING NEW SAINTS:

THE ARABULA.

CHAPTER I.

THE LAMENTATION.

OH, the heartless contradictions in human nature! Man, in his present state, is only a tamed savage. His best development of civilization rests upon a broad and ever-enlarging basis of brute instincts and savage attributes. All his monumental labors for the world's advancement are mixed with the unsubdued and undisguised propensities of selfishness. Civil society is but an entangling medley of antagonistic self-interests and immoral expedients.

Therefore no man is happy. Selfishness, the primal instinct, drives happiness out of the temple. The perplexities and contradictions of selfishness generate excessive laws in the tyrannical intellect. O, the deathless anguish of the wounds inflicted by man's struggling passion for wealth and power! His blunders and blindness are forgiven; but his lynx-eyed, self-justifying, willful intellect, which would crush millions to gain power and wealth, is anathematized and forever excluded from heaven.

And what is man's knowledge? Who believes that

it is wise? The millions walk in the false and hollow thoroughfares of ignorance and priest-supported superstitions. Mammon-serving myrmidons crowd upon the paths of selfish knowledge. Ignorance first builds light-excluding palaces, and then dedicates them to the mysteries of an impracticable religion. And man, in the plenitude of his shameless inconsistencies, prides himself upon his devotion to mystery. With commanding dignity, he styles his religious mystery, "Knowledge of God's Will." Wherefore, in the boundlessness of his ignorance, he assumes the possession of rare intelligence. The slanting rays of science, a sun that has not yet risen, he applauds as the full blaze of absolute truth.

Moralists disappoint their intimate acquaintances. Their virtues are best seen in the shrouding profundities and hair-splitting distinctions they exhibit in the science of morals. They exhaust themselves in preaching and expounding the laws of virtue; they consign the duty of practicing morality to the uneducated multitude. The profoundest theorist in morals is impelled, by an ever-increasing tendency, to transgress, in daily dealings, his fundamental maxims of justice, truth, and virtue. The primal instinct of selfishness surmounts and crushes the holiest proclamations of eternal truth.

The contradictions of human nature cover the earth with a blighting, desolating darkness. A man who preaches the precepts of peace is not often a comfort to his family. His wife is a great skeptic in his theory. Her eye is upon the manifestations of the eloquent expounder's life. Peace-laden principles flow out from his word-skilled tongue, and the tender glances of pure and undefiled religion fall from his heaven-lifted eyes;

yet his family, sailing in the weather-beaten bark of a selfish society, compounded of conflicting interests, longing for love to direct the helm, can remember the trials and wounds of fierce wars at the fireside.

If you want Justice, do you appeal to robed and ermined power in the State? If you seek Religion, do you adopt as final the magnificent mummeries and cabalistic ceremonies of the Established Church? If you seek consistency, do you take as its embodiment the man of civilization; only a tamed savage, with positive selfish instincts, and the profoundest intellectual disregard of others' rights and liberties?

Crucify the redeemers of the world; put them through nameless miseries; banish the reformers into interminable mountains of frost, desolation, and sorrow; kindle the fagots of wrath about the pioneers of infinite benefits; condemn to dungeons the brave heroes who have resisted the organized selfishness of powerful governments; starve the saviors of slaves, who have, during a sad lifetime, toiled without reward, under the blistering lash of crime-promoting task-masters; turn deafened ears to the sighs of fallen women, who have, under the magnetic touch and bewildering persuasions of hypocritical love, erred within the burning passion of some self-gratifying human savage; cover, with inextinguishable contumely and misrepresentations, the fearless teacher, who would overthrow the world's errors in religion, bring a rational conception of God, and initiate principles of higher degrees of existence. O, intelligent, selfish, tyrannical, savage, contradictory man! What shall increase your capacities for consistent, benevolent, magnanimous living?

Most vulnerable is he who makes boast of his high impregnability. No man is more cowardly than he who prides himself upon his valor. The immeasurable fool is self-sustained with the sweet consciousness of being the wisest man in town. The richest merchant in the city cannot afford the luxuries common in the household of his chief clerks. The inimitable comedian, whose simplest speech and gesture convulse with merriment an audience of two thousand intelligent people, is the epitome of independent and incurable melancholy. The infinitely happy lady, whose street habiliments and evening-party deportment are unapproachably perfect, carries a heart well-nigh bursting with wounds and disappointments. The honest citizen is unjustly living upon heavy profits filched from the daily toil of hopeless men and women. The virtuous trader gratifies his savage rapacity by overpassing the boundaries of justice in every bargain with less keen, but really honest men. The pious preacher, whose voice is for the extermination of sin and every other form of evil, is profane when anathematizing the enemies of his creed. The politician is the faithful servant of the State so long as the emoluments and accruing fame are commensurate with his magnanimous selfishness. The physician's interests are inseparably allied with the pecuniary health of his patients. The family of a professional philanthropist is most threatened with visitations of poverty and inhuman neglect. An eloquent champion of the equal self-ownership and political rights of women, was a tyrant at home, trampling upon the personal liberties of his resistless wife, and giving his sons an education superior to his daughters.

O, the contradictions of human nature! Might is mistaken for right; brute force is made to do the work of love; folly is substituted for the hints of wisdom; hypocrisy is more fashionable than innocent virtue; whited sepulchers attract thousands of worshipers, who habitually neglect the temple of the spirit; wealthy vice is more courted and sustained than poor virtue; a bold robbery is sparingly punished, while the half-famished outcast is imprisoned for petty larceny. A crazy actor is murderously executed for a single assassination, while an intelligent plotter of a nation's destruction, in whose war-prisons loyal soldiers are dying inch by inch, with the unutterable pangs of hunger, and with the nameless agonies of disease, is granted the freedom of the world; while the rich are growing richer, in the very heart of a so-called Christian civilization, the poor are becoming poorer; and crime and misery prevail where peaceful industry and progressive happiness might exist.

CHAPTER II.

REFLECTIONS.

Inquietude pervaded my thoughts—feelings freighted with concernment, not for myself—a holy seriousness full of prayer, to learn the causes of man's universal selfishness.

Is selfishness a fundamental principle of human nature? Is the foundation of man's mind composed of incurably self-seeking and savage instincts? The bloody wars—do they originate in principles of war in human nature, or do these cruelties crop out of conditions and circumstances? Does man err only; or, as some affirm, does he sin? He acquires knowledge through reflection and experience; but why does he employ his knowledge to accomplish his selfish ends? If the selfish instinct is the basic law in man's mental constitution, can the originator of such a crude and cruel constitution be revered as a power of perfect wisdom and perfect goodness? What are called man's innocent and rational amusements? Such as baiting the hook and jerking from their native element the beautiful fish; or hunting to death the affrighted hare; starting savage dogs after the foxes; slaughtering the graceful and harmless deer; shooting the singing robins and the playful squirrels; running horses until the innocent animals drop dead; or brutal men fighting with each other like goaded beasts; or men of this breed training dogs and cocks to enter the ring and to fight until one or the other dies, applauding meanwhile with howlings and profanities too fierce and maddening to be repeated.

Distressing and disgusting as all this is, yet the depth of man's brutality is not reached until he tramples upon woman; when, taking diabolical advantage of her weakness and timidity, he bends and breaks her upon the wheel of his ungovernable lust. No theorizing or philosophizing can mitigate the unutterable treachery of such a man. He covers his nature with the corrupting blight of an unpardonable sin. The beasts of the field and the fowls of the air are spotless angels compared with him.

Man's injustice to children, too, is unspeakably detestable. They are born from the unseen world of causes, are gentle as evening music, bringing into embodied life the infinite possibilities of deathless existence; but selfish man treats them as interlopers and unwelcome servants, whips them instead of reasoning with their intuitions, stifles their sobs with his fist, and fills the heaven-life of the little angel with lamentations too sad for the long-suffering heart of woman to bear.

Are these accumulating evidences of man's inborn selfishness insurmountable? Can you give any relief to your doubts? The construction and capabilities of his mind—its immense breadth, its grasp of thought, its intellectual abilities to meditate, plot, elude, attack, retreat, countermarch, counterfeit, decoy, capture, imprison, assassinate, burn, rob, murder, and end in suicide; all this, taken together, apparently gives an overmastering weight of evidence deplorably against the redemptibility of human nature.

CHAPTER III.

THE PRAYER.

With thoughts and feelings overwhelmed and intertangled by the foregoing reflections, and fatigued with waiting for responses to interrogatories so earnestly put, I entered the secret closet of the more interior, and prayed—

"Heavenly Father! Hear, I beseech thee, the spirit of the words I would breathe in thine ear.

"O, Fount of Eternal Good! Lift from before mine eyes the vail of mysteriousness, which shuts out of my understanding the *light*, by which I would behold, divested of errors and uncertainties, the unbroken beneficence of thy government.

"Spirit of Infinite Truth! O, breathe upon my mouth once more, and aid my tongue to utterance; inspire my bosom with the myriad tendencies of wisdom; make my blood instinct with thy universal laws; and impart, O, I pray thee, to my brain the balance whereby truth can be weighed as by the hand of Justice; and to my heart, whose chambers are filled with thy love, an insight that shall discern thee at all times and in all things.

"Father of All! O, let me fearlessly approach thee, as a son would in reverential love draw nigh unto his earthly parent, and ask for divine light and unselfish knowledge. Humbly I would ask—*Is the universe perfect in thy sight?* Was the universe any less perfect millions of centuries ago? Will it be any more perfect millions of years hence? Answer, I beseech thee, O, Fountain of Knowledge! Didst thou foreknow all things from the beginning? And before thou filledst the world with forms and animation, didst thou foresee the selfishness of mankind? Didst thou make man to follow the impulsions of passion—to grow in intelligence and in experience, and to profit by both in devising ways and means to overreach and cruelly to trample upon the rights of his fellows?

"Reveal thy Truth, O, Eternal Source of All things! Enlighten man's reason with thy reason! Give of thine abundance. Shine like a sun of everlasting righteousness. Let, O, let mine eyes behold the *consistency* of thine attributes. Make me to see how *perfect* Love could consent to fill the world with suffering; how *perfect* Goodness could originate a being so savage and selfish as man; how *perfect* Wisdom could have justified itself in constructing a nature apparently so imperfect as man's; how *perfect* Justice could institute a fixed government in which the strong is permitted to crush the weak; how *perfect* Truth could ever be triumphant in a universe where hypocrisy is fashionable, and false professions succeed on every hand; and finally, I pray, O, Father of All! to comprehend how *perfect* Power can exist in thy nature, and, with thine other perfect attributes, suffer to be perpetuated, year after year and age after age, the innumerable evils and miseries which afflict the human race.

"O, help me to bear my part of life's work. Strengthen my heart with increasing love toward earth's wretched millions. Guide to my side the feet of some angel mind, so that I may be taught the lessons of infinite truth. Help all who struggle into the light; and bless, with the fullness of an everlasting blessing, all thy children everywhere."

CHAPTER IV.

LIGHT IN DARKNESS.

MANY days and nights have I waited, overshadowed and darkened in spirit—waiting for some response to my prayer. I look with dismay on the dense and stifling atmosphere pervading the wretched and suffering world of human nature. I behold the dark breathings of universal selfishness—poisoning the very air with evil emanations—blinding, polluting, degrading, and filling with torment and consuming anxiety all human hearts.

The gates of wealth are closed against the poor and desolate. Sin and error walk abroad hand in hand. They enter the temples of religion, and worship openly the crafty supporters of superstition. Ignorance, selfishness, grossness, materialism, sensuality—the evil spirits of civilization, dressed in the bright livery of wealth and fashion—reside like princely demons in every human habitation. Dwarfed and deformed, and burdened with the mournful consciousness of living unworthily, appear the people of every clime and country.

My inmost heart, I feared, was, with its latent energies and fond affections, rapidly withdrawing its sensibilities from mankind. For days did this heavy weight rest upon my mind. What a mournful gloom! I began to imagine that every person meditated mischief to promote selfish ends. It seemed to me that craftiness and over-reaching keenness of perception were the chief characteristics of my fellow-men. I felt miserably hopeless! The world was so crowded with sin, error, disease, wretchedness. Hell was not so bad, after all! The saving ordinances and fiery doctrines of the most fanatical adherents of orthodoxy seemed less offensive. Without a shudder, I cried "fire!" "fire!"—the fire which burns as an oven—the burning hell of God's consuming vengeance—not too hot a fate for the beasts and brutes and demons that make up the human race.

At length, after so long a night, blacker than Egyptian darkness, a grayish morning light streamed into my soul's wilderness. For days and days I had but feeble and shadowy gleams from truth's altar-fires. There was no depth, no breadth, no vitality to my thoughts. A miserable irresolution, an uncontrollable chaos, a feeling of vague foolishness, and a dreary faithlessness, not to say worthlessness, pervaded and possessed my entire consciousness. Wails of grief, suggestions of indescribable despair, indifference toward my dearest friends, an irresistible impulse to fret and quarrel with my circumstances—these, and unnumbered other psychological states and temptations, accompanied the approach of light.

My prayer was still unanswered. But "*the answer will surely come!*" I will possess my soul in patience. A mysterious presence, like a divine and immortal essence, floats in upon the whispering air. Surrounding forms and familiar objects seem more interesting. Trees and shrubs in the garden, little flowering vines by the window, the grasses on the lawn, the plumage of birds in the cherry-trees, and the faces of my associates—all things, both present and distant, seemed touched and bathed with a sweet and tender light as from the morning stars.

The refinement and beauty of this experience surpass the power of language. Slowly, day by day, during weeks of waiting and searching, the transforming light crept in—so stealthily, at times, and so exquisitely sensitive did it seem to be to the least interruption, I was many times troubled with fear lest it would be withdrawn. It came upon me as sunlight gradually works its way into the buds of little flowers in early springtime. My blindness was almost imperceptibly removed. The vast void of space was being filled with the light of innumerable worlds. It rolled over the earth like the enkindling breath of God. The watch-fires in all human hearts burned with melodious effulgence. Men's minds seemed to bloom with a holy significance, and the life of the whole humanity emitted a fragrance that suggested the celestial and everlasting. The effect of the *light* was like enchantment. The whole world was pictured as in a mirage; lakes, groves, forests, castles, oceans, cities, delightful landscapes, villas, beautiful mansions, and the peoples of all lands walking by streams, or working in green pastures, toiling in fields and in stores and factories, cultivating the hills, gardenizing the islands—all came up by the mirage-law of reflection, and seemed as perfect in the immediate atmosphere as the same delightful sceneries and human beings would appear were they presented in an extended landscape within reach of your ordinary sight.

CHAPTER V.

THE CONFLICT.

UNDER the enchantment of the Light, which I have so imperfectly described, the whole world seemed a fruitful and ever-blooming land of inconceivable beauty and immortal delights. I yearned to dwell forever in the magnetical radiance of that celestial Light. My inmost feelings glowed responsive to that incomprehensible golden illumination. And yet, I was not at rest; was far, far from the happiness I sought.

True, my feelings, which had grown misanthropic and indifferent toward humanity, were lifted from their dark and dismal dungeons of doubt, to a youthful love of every thing human. But my intellectual principle, which had covered my soul with a shroud of wintery clouds, had not been answered. By its cold, accurate perception of facts, I realized that men are selfish, false, crafty, hypocritical, brutal, diabolical. With Shelley, I acknowledged that "War is the statesman's game, the lawyer's jest, the priest's delight, and the hired assassin's trade."

Thus, while in heaven's holy radiance which shone upon my heart, my intellect continued in painful darkness. The insignia of death appeared along the blood-covered pathway of empires. Cupidity and ambition, with robbery and death, looked out from every throne. Crowned heads, inspired by pride and thirst for power, the root of which is selfishness, forcing millions of men into opposing armies, intent upon each other's destruction; while the kings and emperors, safe in strong castles above the work of death, look exultingly down upon the smoky scene of young men, husbands and fathers, struggling, shrieking, bleeding, slaughtering, cursing, despairing, dying! With my intelligence I perceived these unspeakable calamities all through human history—the manifestations of man's selfishness, savage cruelties, and brutal instincts.

'Tis said that there is a joy in grief when peace dwells in the breast of the sad. "But sorrow wastes the sorrowful," said Ossian. "They fall away like the flower on which the sun has looked in his strength, after the mildew has passed over it, when its head is heavy with the drops of the night." And such consuming sorrow was mine, day by day, although the Light with peaceful radiance continued to shine upon every thing around me. Have you not had a conflict between your heart and head? Has not your bosom said "yes" to what your brain said "no?" Had I believed in "faith," as thousands in the world's pagodas unquestioningly do, how easily could I have reposed my restless intellect. But I could in principle surrender no part of my consciousness to the bewitchments of sentimentality and hopeful faith. Once, yea, often, I had clearly seen, as I thought, the solution of the problems now beclouding and acidulating my being. Perhaps, methought, my bodily condition is unholy. This reflection recalled the saying of Pythagoras: "That whatsoever obstructs divination, or is prejudicial to the purity and sanctity of the mind, to temperance, chastity, and habitual virtue, should be shunned; also that which is contrary to purity and defiles the imagination at any time. That the juvenile age should make trial of temperance—this being alone of all the virtues, alike adapted to youths and maidens and women, to all of advanced life; and that it comprehended the goods both of body and soul, and also the desire of the most excellent studies. He thought boys were especially dear to divinity, and exhorted women to use words of good omen through the whole of life, and to endeavor that others may predict good things of them." Again, one of his disciples has said: "Our first duties go abreast, comprehending the care of the mind along with the body. Parents are protectors of families and States; they stand for comfort, for nobility; for earth-husbandries and man-culture, not as Cattle Gods and Pantry Providences only; but for State and family interests largely considered and beautifully combined; for temperance, for thrift, humanity, and the future." Investigation, however, assured me that the conflicts were not caused by my habitual drinks and foods; but that I would find the true causes of my trouble in the selfishness and limitations of intellect.

CHAPTER VI.

THE TRANSFORMATION.

The conflict continued, day by day, until the Light had almost gone! The fierce war of selfish intelligence and unselfish intuition. The preponderance of intellect was massively on the side of debasing selfishness and all-absorbing personal interests.

Yet, thanks to Omniscient goodness! under the sunlight stealthily slipped the supernal star-shine of impersonal purity and unmixed justice. It flooded the fields *under the sunlight*, so to speak; it lifted the colors of flowers; it flowed, like a river of liquid jewels, over the wavy bosom of streams; it made music in the careless songs of wild birds; it spread a carpet of velvety gold under the living green grasses of field and lawn; it loaded the air with holy, healing fragrances, like the breathings of unnumbered flowers; it cushioned, with bright green mosses, the cold stones by the roadside; it diffused a sacramental wine through all the waters of well and spring; it poured a glorious Sabbath through the hours of every day; it emitted marvelous music through the Æolian harp of wide-spread elms, and dark, tall pine-trees; it imparted an indescribably loving tenderness to the voices of my friends; it filled with a beautiful gladness the laughter of children; it invested domestic animals with attitudes and expressions more wondrous and varied than was ever imagined by Phidias; it changed all manhood into Apollos of matchless grace and beauty; and all womanhood it transformed into Minervas of wisdom, love, freedom, truth, purity, and harmony. And I prayed—

"O, Omniscient Father! I beseech thee to let this Light become part of my soul's possessions. With words, my soul can neither approach nor worship thee; with thoughts, I cannot tell the boundlessness of my tearful, joyful gratitude. Translate, O, I pray thee, all these wonder-working living lessons into my reasoning faculties. Permit me, very reverently, to perceive intellectually the plenitude of the truth within this Light."

CHAPTER VII.

WEIGHED IN THE BALANCE.

The blissful hour lived in that world-lifting Light made the succeeding hours—when Intellect was pre-eminently positive, politic, active, and selfish—exceedingly dark and dismal.

O, the memory of the pain of that reaction! What despairing disappointment, when, coming out of the enchantments of that holy Light, I realized that my thoughtful brain was *not* nerved anew, as I had so fervently prayed and hoped, for the impending conflict of the Right against the Wrong.

Indeed, I was alarmingly proud and willful. To the Truth I had no objection, *if it only came as I wanted it; if it was not inconvenient; and if it did not command me to sacrifice any worldly possession or personal comfort.* And thus I reasoned:

There is no disguising mankind's groveling and revolting selfishness. Prominent influential men—capitalists, monopolists, slave-dealers, money-changers—are heartless, cruel, villainous. What care they for the divine Light? "Practical righteousness," in the opinion of such stone-hearted oppressors, consists in systematically worshiping the "almighty dollar," and constructing a Parthenon of aristocratic nabobs, by which the poor working classes shall always be kept poor, and all through the strong arm of the church and government.

If I turn *reformer*, I must BREAST all this mighty array of money and interlaced power. In place of "money" I must offer *Man;* in place of "falsehood" I must present *Truth;* instead of "fashion" I must preach *Freedom;* I must substitute for "lust" the holy principle of *Love;* instead of "war," my voice must ever be for *Peace;* and in place of "parties" in government and "sects" in religion, I must insist upon unmixed *Principles*, and the familyhood and equality of all members of the human race.

"What!" indignantly exclaimed I—"Does the reformer's work require me to breast this stupendous opposition? Am I called upon by an incomprehensible, an unreasoning, a mysterious 'Light' to take a public stand, like a living monument of sacrifice, or like a target, inviting the arrows of every popular pimp of church and government, and receiving the bitter scorn and unconcealed contempt of every urchin, because he is safe in the fortifications of established society?"

The prospect was becoming darker and darker every moment. And the Light! Alas, *that* was GONE; and, what is worse, I scarcely remembered it; my intellect was keen, and so logical! So capable of philosophizing on the question of duties and consequences! My understanding of men, and my knowledge of the fate meted out to the world's saviors, cautioned me. "Don't make a sacrifice of the best years of your life, Jackson," wisely whispered my bright and practical intellect. And thus it continued, looking every moment more and more like the sovereign pontiff of worldly sagaciousness.

"Now examine the question in all its bearings. Of course, being benevolent, you love humanity, and wish it well, and all that. Sentimental young men usually experience impulses of generosity, and ofttimes long to engage in deeds of disinterested benevolence, but a few years of contact with the solid facts of the world effectually dissipates their reformatory propensities. In fact, if you can but wait ten years, he who was an ardent reformer at twenty-five, will unblushingly decline taking an open, active part in unpopular questions. In substance he will confess, thus:—

"'True, I love freedom; I think slaves are human beings, and therefore ought not to be held in bondage; I am progressive in sentiment—but, but, but I can't act with you; indeed, I am deeply engaged in the church; I am very much engrossed with our political party; I am absorbed in business; in other words, *I have taken unto myself a wife, and therefore cannot come.*'"

"Why, my dear Sir," continued the wise-headed magistrate, "your common sense of what is prudent and *expedient* will convince you that your demand, that educated, professional, and business men should be reformers, is, in the extreme, *absurd.* They are involved in new interests, have taken unto themselves wives, and have devoted their talents and energies to new responsibilities. This is about what the best of men, once warmly engaged in reforms, will, with some sarcastic mortification, privately confess: 'Oh, I cannot but think favorably of your reforms, although I dare not publicly avow my favorable opinion. Yet I am so absorbed in what the world calls religion; so intent in looking after God's interests and glory, I cannot attend to man's wants and interests; and inasmuch as I have sold myself—soul and body—to my party, sect, and business interests, together with my desire to attain wealth and social position, I cannot engage in that which is unpopular, and which requires earnest thought and manly action.' "

CHAPTER VIII.

BECOMING AN ATHEIST.

THE Light! The Light! Where is it? O, where is that river of celestial amber which flowed like music through the meadow slopes; which so illuminated and pictured the earthly solitudes; which wreathed willowy groves and pond-lilies in dreamy beauty; which brooded over the boughs of trees, like the golden haze of autumnal splendors; where—O, where is the Light that filled all the world with clusters of eternal love and beauty? O, soul-enchanting Light! O, kindling, unfolding, floating, flooding, pleading, saving Light! Where art thou? Without thee I am covered with a thick cloud of intellectual selfishness—verily, I am plunged in a bottomless vortex of "outer darkness," where naught is heard but the fiendish conflict of human passions, the murderous antagonisms of strong men against strong men—an outer world of woe and hopelessness, with "weeping and wailing and gnashing of teeth."

I have prayed—with my whole intellect and heart, I have prayed. Why am I not answered? If there is a God, if, in the far-off immensity, there is an intelligent Omniscient brain, called God, *why*, in God's name, *does not that brain answer my brain's questions?* Why does not God's heart give rest to my painful heart? Truly has it been said, "by searching none can find out God." Why not, if there is a God? Is it not true that the most strenuous God-believers confess that it is only a belief with them; that they really *know* nothing on the subject? Where shall we search for the existence of God? Enter the material world; ask the Sciences whether they can disclose the mystery? Geology speaks of the structure of the earth, the formation of the different strata, of coal, of granite, of the whole mineral kingdom. It reveals the remains and traces of animals long extinct, but gives us no clue whereby we may prove the existence of a God.

Natural History gives us a knowledge of the animal kingdom in general; the different organisms, structures, and powers of the various species. Physiology teaches the nature of man, the laws that govern his being, the functions of the vital organs, and the conditions upon which alone health and life depend. Phrenology treats of the laws of the mind, the different portions of the brain, the temperaments, the organs, how to develop some and repress others to produce a well-balanced and healthy condition. But in the whole animal economy —though the brain is considered to be a "microcosm," in which may be traced a resemblance, or relationship with every thing in Nature—not a spot can be found to indicate the existence of a God.

Mathematics lays the foundation of all the exact sciences. It teaches the art o combining numbers, of calculating and measuring distances, how to solve problems, to weigh mountains, to fathom the depths of the ocean, but gives us no directions how to ascertain the existence of a God.

Enter Nature's great laboratory—Chemistry. She will speak to you of the various elements, their combinations and uses, of the gases constantly evolving and combining in different proportions, producing all the varied objects, the interesting and important phenomena we behold. She proves the indestructibility of matter, and its inherent property—motion; but in all her operations no demonstrable fact can be obtained to indicate the existence of a God.

Astronomy tells us of the wonders of the Solar System—the eternally revolving planets, the rapidity and certainty of their motions, the distance from planet to planet, from star to star. It predicts, with astonishing and marvelous precision, the phenomenon of eclipses, the visibility on our earth of comets, and proves the immutable law of gravitation, but is entirely silent on the existence of a God.

In fine, descend into the bowels of the earth, and you will learn what it contains; into the depths of tho ocean, and you will find the inhabitants of the great deep; but neither in the earth above nor the waters below can you obtain any knowledge of His existence. Ascend into the heavens, and enter the "milky way," go from planet to planet to the remotest star, and ask the eternally revolving systems, Where is God? and echo answers, Where?

The Universe of Matter gives us no record of his existence. Where next shall we search? Enter the Universe of Mind, read the millions of volumes written on the subject, and in all the speculations, the assertions, the assumptions, the theories, and the creeds, you will find that Man has stamped an indelible impress of his own mind on every page. In describing his God, he delineated his own character; the picture he drew represents in living and ineffaceable colors the epoch of his existence—the period he lived in.

It was a great mistake to say that God made man in his image. Man, in all ages, made his God in his own image; and we find that just in accordance with his civilization, his knowledge, his experience, his taste, his refinement, his sense of right, of justice, of freedom, and humanity,—so has he made his God. But whether coarse or refined; cruel and vindictive, or kind and generous; an implacable tyrant, or a gentle and loving father;—it still was the emanation of his own mind—the picture of himself.

It is pretended that God made man perfect. But after he pronounced the world "good," which included the human pair, he suddenly found that *man* was desperately *wicked!* Then it is pretended that God invented different plans for the redemption of man. He first tried the universal flood-process; but the human world was not one whit improved. Then he was forced to resort to the last sad alternative of sending "his only-begotten son," his second self, to save mankind. But alas! "his own received him not," and so he was obliged to adopt the Gentiles, and die to save the world. Did he succeed, even then? Is the world saved? Saved! from what? From ignorance? It is all around us. From poverty, vice, crime, sin, shame, and misery? They abound everywhere. Look into your poorhouses, your prisons, your lunatic asylums; contemplate the whip, the instruments of torture, and of death; ask the murderer, or his victim; listen to the raving of the maniac, the shrieks of distress, the groans of despair; mark the cruel deeds of the tyrant, the crimes of slavery, the suffering of the oppressed; count the millions of lives lost by fire, by water, and by the sword; measure the blood spilled, the tears shed, the sighs of agony drawn from the expiring victims on the altar of fanaticism;—and tell me from what the world was *saved*. And why was it not saved? Why does God still permit these horrors to afflict the race? Does omniscience not know it? Could omnipotence not do it? Would infinite wisdom, power, and goodness allow his children thus to live, to suffer, and to die? No! Humanity revolts against such a supposition.

Look around you, and confess that there is no evidence of intelligence, of design, and consequently of a designer? I see no evidence of either. What is intelligence? It is not a thing, a substance, an existence in itself, but simply a property of matter, manifesting itself through organizations. We have no knowledge of, nor can we conceive of, intelligence apart from organized matter; and we find that from the smallest and simplest insect, through all the links and gradations in Nature's great chain, up to man—just in accordance with the organism, the amount, and quality of brain, so are the capacities to receive impressions, the power to retain them, and the abilities to manifest and impart them to others,—namely, to have its peculiar nature cultivated and developed, so as to bear mental fruits, just as the cultivated earth bears vegetation—physical fruits. Not being able to recognize an independent intelligence, I can perceive no design or designer except in the works of man.*

* The foregoing is the substance of a Lecture by Mrs. Ernestine L. Rose, delivered in Boston, Mass., 1861. It is an able and eloquent statement of the argument for Atheism.

CHAPTER IX.

PARTS AGAINST THE WHOLE.

EMBODIMENT of all wisdom, is the human Intellect! Its conceits are stupendous, its grasp is gigantic, its sublimations of argument truly marvelous, its self-importance—ah, that is greatest of all!

Intellect, knowledge, is, after all, but *one-third* of that wondrous organization called the human mind; and it is also the *poorest* third of the conscious mentality; and, for this reason, probably, it is the most pedantic and self-asserting. The roots of intellect [Knowledge, see Gt. Har. vol. 4, *et seq.*] start from Experience. The trunk, branches, and fruit of the knowledge-tree, constitute Memory. Of itself destitute of vitality. Its possessions are acquired from the realm of things without. Much knowledge in a man's mind—the details whereof have no existence save in Memory—is like much furniture in his house. It may serve him, and promote his selfish interests, or it may oppress and stultify his entire nature. Unfashionable knowledge is as mortifying to pride as are unfashionable clothes, or furniture in the mansion out of date.

The highest discovery of intellect is fragmentary and fleeting; the hour-fact rooted in the hour-experience; the rest is the *chance* that, through memory and judgment, the individual may be profited. Only a higher faculty than intellect in man can discern the limits of the powers of his intellect. The voice of the whole nature can alone reveal what the whole nature yearns to possess. The whole can alone sit in judgment upon the testimony of the parts. The intellect can in its own right freely criticise, condemn, or justify the instincts; but the instincts have the advantage of being radicals (or roots), while intellect is nothing but the furniture and accumulated trappings of sensuous experience. The instincts naturally rise, like birds of paradise, into the mind's higher imponderable atmosphere; and there they rapidly change from "creeping things" into angel-winged INTUITIONS, with clairvoyant powers and boundless aspirations. The policies and limitations of intellect shrink away from the higher powers like affrighted fowls beneath the lofty courage of the soaring eagle.

These reflections disturbed my atheistic conclusions, but these reflections did not come until I had passed through what is described in the next chapter.

CHAPTER X.

THE ARABULA.

For a few days I was mentally plethoric with the intellectual negation of atheism. While puffed with this self-satisfying conviction, that I had argumentatively annihilated the stupid superstition of a God, I enjoyed my mind comfortably. The idea of seeking "Light" out of the usual course was given up forever; and with it went the correlative idea of sacrificing my personal interests to promote the interests and happiness of others. My conclusion was, "I will do what I can for others' benefit when it does not cost me more than others bestow; in other words, I will do all I can *consistently* with my idea of the opportunities and abilities I may have for doing." In short, my philanthropy was narrowed down to *thinking benevolently* and acting as selfishly as any Turk or Christian in the neighborhood.

Alas! what darkness settled upon my feelings. Wretchedness was my lot. One day I walked away, far away up the mountain—a godless and hopeless mortal; and there, away from the world, and forgetting my profound atheistic arguments, I bowed my spirit in prayer!

"Light, more Light!" was the burden of my supplications.

My temples throbbed with birth-throes; and my unhappy heart, weighed down with feelings of unfaithfulness to truth, seemed to lose its pulsating power; my breath was suspended, and a holy silence reigned.

Lo, the Light! In a moment it seemed to flood the mountains with an indescribable glory. Through green meadows, overflowing waters, between the overhanging branches of forest-trees; everywhere it floated and tremblingly baptized the world.

My intellect was for a brief period marvelously enlarged, or, rather, *lifted* into a new perception of things. I thought of resisting, but my will was not with my thought, and so, like a bird in the viewless air, I sped away *into the light*—INTO THE LIGHT!

Strange to relate! My thoughts roamed over passages in different books, in which the expression "light" occurs, and with the expression I instantly comprehended an impressive signification. "The *light* of wicked men shall be put out." The truth of that I had tested; for when I was selfish, I was in darkness. "To the upright ariseth *light* in darkness." That was my experience then. "Thy *light* shall break forth as the morning." I prayed that it might be so. "Let your *light* shine before men." My intellect said, "No;" but the remaining *two-thirds* of my being said, "Yes." "What communion hath *light* with darkness?" I thought there could be no intercourse between the two states. "God is *light*, and in him is no darkness." I prayed to dwell in Him for evermore.

While occupied with these passages and meditations, and breathing joyful thanks for my deliverance, I heard a voice, saying, "I am *Arabula*; I am the *light* of the world; he that followeth me shall have *light* and life; he that loveth me keepeth my commandments."

CHAPTER XI.

THE MYSTERY.

THAT night I could not sleep. A new problem was pressing for solution. O, that low, sweet voice! That still, small voice! Was it spoken by the tongue of some personality? What angel-lipped being was it that said, "I am the light of the world?" As I heard it I seemed to be sitting by the ancient fountains of inspiration. The infinite presence of an indefinable intelligence brooded lovingly upon all around me. The distance-softened music of the human world, like the breathing whisperings of gently waving pine-trees, floated through the trembling air, and filled my receptive soul with brave and faithful love toward the family-hood of man.

Delightful and chastening as was my experience, and fresh and youthful and new-born as were my feelings, yet the problem—"Did that low, sweet, still small *voice* come from the mouth of a person?"—prepossessed my thoughts. It did not sound like a human voice, nor like the voice of any spiritual personage, but rather like the voice and language that one's imagination might give to flowers; or like, in your fancy, making the air to think and speak as though it were a person. There was in that voice the vagueness I have described, but in no other respect or quality. By association of ideas, very naturally, my mind could not but think of "Jesus." Sacred history records that such a personage made use of many of the words I heard.

But the expression, "*I am Arabula*"—words which seemed, like the others, to have spontaneously formed themselves in my mind as the true definition of the *quality* of the Light—started the whole train of questions now under review.

Can a person be everywhere at the same moment? Is it possible for a person to flood the whole world with Light? Can a person be omnipresent in history? Could a person have taught the primeval Greek intelligences, Socrates and Plato, intuitively to know all wisdom? When Prometheus lay chained to the rock, and the Muses were instructing the gods, and the colossal Sphinx of black basalt in the Libyan Mountains was being sculptured to represent what is inscrutable and inexorable in the universe, was all the Light in the brains and bosoms of men derived from one person?

The serious-hearted world is yearningly praying for Light. "I am the light of the world," says the Arabula. "He that loveth me will keep my commandments." This Arabula is the world's religious mystery. It appears in the philosophical, moral, and spiritual teachings of Persians, Indians, Chinese, Jews, Greeks, Romans, Christians. It is peculiar to no people; to no religion; to no sect of believers; to no epoch or era in human history. It invariably enters the world by birth of a virgin state of mind; it performs wonders in healing the sick; it is powerful in overthrowing kingdoms; it everywhere dies upon the cross; and it, for a time, leaves the world by ascending above the world. It is worshiped as a God by some; is denounced as a Devil by others. It is practically peaceful; yet it divides families, sunders States, and destroys governments. It loves the companionship of the down-trodden and wretched; yet it enters the temples of rich priests, and holds controversies with the chief dignitaries of the empire. It is powerful with words; preaches sermons on mountains and in cities; fearlessly rebukes sin, forgives the lost women; stills the tempest, brings the dead to life; and, lastly, having no power over evil chieftains of the State, it falls into the hands of executioners, and dies, forgiving its enemies and blessing every thing human.

Is this mystery a person? Do you not perceive its presence in all the *good* men do, and in all the *truth* they speak? When a volume of Light shines into the world, regardless by whom or by what it shines, do you not discern the *same qualities*, though differing in quantity according to person, circumstance, condition, or country? Verily, in all this there is a mystery; which demands research and further elucidation.

CHAPTER XII.

MOUNTAIN MEDITATIONS.

From wanderings long and wild, from society and its mockeries, from selfish thought and bitter speech, I come, like an over-wearied child, to live forever in the Eternal Life of God. The soft, low voice, that still whispering witness in my heart, calls me, and—I come, I go, I am thine.

Henceforth, whatever is selfish will be visited with my fiercest anathema. The soul that would live for itself alone, is a libel on God's noblest work. The stagnant pond is typical of selfishness. It is still and slimy, and gathers to itself from earth and sky, giving nothing freely but disease and death. Selfishness is morbid and evil-thinking. It generates misfortune and diffuses the seeds of desolation.

But hills and lakes and mountains are typical of benevolence and boundless hospitality. They welcome the world. The smiles of unnumbered suns lie upon their honest faces. Their palpitating bosoms are filled with the divine life. The winds breathe upon them. They tenderly touch every bending leaf and drooping flower. The songs of the day dwell among the hills. The ineffable melody of mountains is akin to the majestic anthem of ages. A sweet and pensive sadness floats into the listening soul. The ethereal music of harmonious dreams pervades the hills and the mountains. Like the incense of true worship from a thousand hearts, like the holy music of the world of celestial stars, are the sacred sounds of the everlasting hills.

O, beautiful and grand is the vesper song of Nature. Let my spirit flow into thy spirit—my life and thine blend—my heart and thy heart be one through eternal ages. I would pillow my head upon thy bosom. My soul would inhale the immortal fragrance of thy bright and beautiful flowers. Amid thy grandeur my soul feels its divine origin, and holds unspeakable communion with immeasurable things. The breathings of the mountains are like the soundings of the distant sea. My soul catches the inspirations of long-departed ages, and my thoughts tenderly touch the thoughts of angels, who, with the light feet of dancers, tread the celestial mountains of light away in the clear blue. The sweet freshness of their breath comes like the gentle ministrations of fields. The ringing brook and the singing bird come over the hills. The green arches of the woods are full of heavenly music.

But the charity of mountains is vast and unsympathetic. Snow lingers long on their summits. Cold and frosts dwell with them. They breast the winter tempests, and keep the warmth of summer long waiting in the valleys. The sun smiles genially upon gentle slope and verdant vale, while the mountains catch few of his golden blessings. Yet the world without the templed mountains would be poor and mean. Overwhelming symbols of God's omnipotence are the earth's mighty masses of rocks, towering heavenward, clad with trees, and set amid lakes and fields of eternal beauty and abundance. They teach that nothing lives for itself.

They elevate man's soul to heavenly heights. Lowlands and murmuring brooklets receive their verdure and music from the mountains. Rain descends from lofty places. The gentle dew is distilled upon highest slopes. The teeming harvest-fields owe their wealth to the high lands and sterile peaks.

Go upon the mountains, O my soul, and learn of God —the Universal Father and Friend—and of Nature—the Mother and Lover of countless hosts. Speak to me! Tell me the sublime story of your origin. Lift my reason in gratitude to its divine source. Cause the lessons of infinity to occupy my thoughts. I would dwell with ye, O holy mountains! There is grandeur in the expression of your significance. In the wildness and freshness of your unchangeable leisure my soul takes ineffable delight. Heaven's repose is symboled forth by your immovable stillness. The beautiful sky bends lovingly over ye—like the spiritual heights, with their unmeasured opulence, spanning the fields of Paradise. The realms of the mountains, with their everlasting tranquillity, attract the lovers of wild woods and untraversed ravines. Earth's savage beasts cling to the mountains. The Father gave them his grandest forests. They roam amid waterfalls and roaring cataracts, sleep upon the shoulders of beetling cliffs, build their beds amid craggy gorges, on the sides of mountains. And wild fowls scream, while gentle birds pour forth their harmonious melodies in worshipful gratitude to the Infinite Father. They live and sing among the mountains, to help on the world of matter and mind. Not one lives for itself. The lesson of charity—of free and boundless benevolence—is taught by every thing.

O, my soul, look up and learn of the mountains. Go upon the hills of God.

CHAPTER XIII.

HAPPINESS NOT COMPLETE.

For many days after the interview with the mysterious "Arabula," my whole nature seemed light as the air and thoughtless as an innocent child. Every thing was "good"—the *night*, for it brought out the holy stars—*pain*, for it unfolded the infinite blessings of pleasure—*selfishness*, for it revealed the divinity of benevolence—*briers*, for they shielded and protected flowers while blooming—*skepticism*, for it compels the soul to search and learn the lesson of fundamental principles—*darkness*, for it brings out the spirit's inherent love of everlasting Light.

And so I was exultingly enjoying religion! I had a bewildering, dreamy, luxurious "faith in God," which, methought, nothing could disturb or darken. The familiar rills in the meadow laughed with joy. The abundant weeds in the garden were performing a hallowed mission. With new eyes I looked upon human wretchedness. I was not troubled, although battle-arrayed men were that moment fiendishly slaughtering each other in bloody war! Trustingly and lovingly, like a child led by its fond and faithful mother, I walked with God in the flowery garden of all-harmonizing truth. And day by day I rejoiced exceedingly, was light and glad beyond expression.

But, alas! one morning I came from my slumbers with a heavy, cloud-covered heart. I could not account for it. "Am I not happy?" thought I. "Have I not beheld the flowery mount of God's inextinguishable wisdom? Do I not trust all his ways, and walk therein unquestioningly?" And thus, in my unexpected wretchedness, I complainingly interrogated for the causes of the change in my feelings.

Before the evening of that day, I had found the secret of my unrest and depression. It was this (and the confession is made with reluctance and mortification): *I was not cured of intellectual selfishness.* Now, look at my case: I was happy, was comfortably and contentedly situated in my daily circumstances at home, was knowingly surrounded with the heavenly influences emanating from angel realms of life; and thus (I fain would think), all unconsciously to myself, I was like a sordid and piratical miser, selfishly subordinating and appropriating the whole to my *individual* benefit and gratification.

Concerning the world outside, I said: "Let the world take care of itself. It's all about right as it is. What's the use of fretting about what others say, or think, or do? Take care of yourself! If every one would but take care of one, and that one himself or herself, the world would get along comfortably, and everybody be contented and happy. Now, Jackson, don't disturb yourself about other folks' welfare. They don't care a farthing whether you live or die. Every one lives and dies on his own hook! This effort of yours, to liberate by education the children of indifferent parents, who don't half protect and care for themselves, is a mistaken benevolence. You can do better by looking after your own children. If you've got money to spare, spend it all on your own family; make your garden beautiful and your house elegant; indulge in a first-class horse and carriage; wear plenty of the best jewelry; and dress yourself and family in silks and fine linen, and eat and drink the best you can get. Yes, you've got 'the light' now; you are now happy; now *let well enough alone.*"

CHAPTER XIV.

THE DIFFERENCE.

My patient and thoughtful reader, doubtless, already understands my state better than I myself did. It must appear manifest that "The Arabula" had entered with truth's amazing splendor, and lifted my intuitions and affections far above the bonds and ties of the world; had disintegrated my personality from all entangling terrestrial associations; and had put me in sacred communication with the Divine Principle, which is THE CENTRAL GOOD of all persons, places, times, institutions, religions, states, observances, impressions, convictions, and inspirations.

But is it necessary to record that my Intellect—the third, poorest, experience-rooted part of man's mental structure—was not correspondingly unencumbered and enlightened. In that quarter I was not *saved;* was still atheistic and selfish; was local in my perceptions, temporal in my tendencies, and individual in my appetites and desires. Intellectually I could hold no rational communication with the rest of my consciousness. Therefore, as quick as the Arabula's low, sweet voice was still, the loud-mouthed words of pompous Intellect sounded authoritatively in my thoughts. In substance he said:

"Be not deceived. Instead of solid argument beneath

you, and deductions based upon the experimental demonstrations of science, you go headlong into sentimentality. Poetry is all well enough in its place; so are painting and music—and the Fine Arts generally—very good pastimes; but, man! what can they give to satisfy your skeptical Intellect? Come, stand up for yourself; look facts in the face, and confess there is no God."

Thus Intellect, wily and unprincipled *per se*, perplexed, pampered, and harassed me; and O, how fearfully did its protests damage the touching, impressive teachings of Arabula!

The depredations and intimations of Intellect were fatal the moment I lost communication with the interior illumination. It seemed to me that this conflict was unnecessary; that it was attributable to lack of balance; but, in this respect, I found that I had, in the world about me, plenty of company.

And these counterparts, strange to say, were mostly in the churches. I noticed that there was so much of the world in the churches, it was impossible that the churches should ever improve the world. Selfishness had invaded the sanctuary. Every member was anxious to secure *his own salvation*, from the machinations of an imaginary personal devil (the personation of wily selfishness) and from an everlasting hell—the fabled conservatory of what was too bad to be redeemed by omniscient goodness.

I noticed, furthermore, that the churches were supported by men, who, bent on their own salvation, habitually shut their ears to the pressing wants of the world's working and hell-going millions. The churches claim to be the reservoir of all private worth, of all public virtue, of all sinless charity. But behold! The broad, comfortable pews are loaded with the heartless devotees of hot-house aristocracy; with commercial gamblers; with the villains of speculation; with languid, listless, indifferent, godless dyspeptics; with cloistered, convented, lip-serving dogmatists; with atonement-seeking cowards of traditional piety, who *dare not* imitate the example of Jesus—the public physician, the unconventional preacher, the associate of publicans and sinners, the philanthropist, the open friend of the poor and unfortunate! If religion consists in conveying, by acts, God's life into the life of society; if it consist in enlarging and spiritualizing the streams of public morals; in ministering to the necessities of the sick, the outcast, and in alleviating the conditions of the struggling millions of poor men and women; in improving the structure of society, which, by its present selfishness and shameless injustice, generates one hundred criminals to one saving angel; if it consist in practical efforts to prevent the insane, rash, and reckless struggle for wealth; in overcoming the heartless extravagance about the persons and in the homes of the so-called higher classes—if true religion consist in these works of righteousness, and in loving your neighbor as you love yourself—then, then—why, the plain truth must be acknowledged, there is no true religion in the established churches of the nineteenth century.

CHAPTER XV.

A GEOGRAPHICAL GOD IMPOSSIBLE.

ANY metaphysical revelation that violates the positive requirements of the intellect, is no aid to human progress; yet, there is in man's mind a power—call it the INTUITION of all his thinking and feeling faculties—which transcends the perceptions, capacities, and attainments of his Intellect; a faculty of PURE REASON, to which the knowledge-acquiring faculties are constitutionally subservient, while they protect and guard the whole mental nature from myths and sentimental delusions.

The chief error of the religious world consists in heeding the mysterious intimations of the higher and intuitional, to the exclusion of the legitimate offices and truly friendly guardianship of the intellectual part. Hence the discrepancies and vagaries of supernaturalism, so repugnant to every philosophical mind, because they are impossibilities in the very nature of things. The intellect has a self-ruling and self-governing power, which, while it brings to its possessor a sure and perfect knowledge of its own limitations, acts beneficially and conservatively in protecting the higher faculties from error and extravagance.

It was an error in my interpretation of the "Arabula" to suppose that it was a person who addressed me. And yet it said, or, rather, I made it say, "I am come a LIGHT into the world, that whosoever believeth on me should not abide in *darkness*." In the presence of that illumination I *realized* the existence of a fundamental, unchangeable, and impersonal PRINCIPLE—which also seemed like an invisible personage—which could, would, and did *judge* me not only, but all mankind, and also possessed the power of *saving* me and all who would love him (or it) and follow his (or its) commandments. Without Intellect I should hereafter be superstitious, and a believer in the supernatural; with it, guided by the more profound love of eternal truth, I am *saved* and reconciled.

To say that the Light, which lighteth every man that cometh into the world, emanates from a person, is to annihilate all relation and proportion between cause and effect. Give God geographical limitations and you destroy his infinite existence; in other words, Intellect detects your absurdity, and proclaims your atheism. A special history, limited to time and space, with local associations and worldly events, are compatible to finite beings. The shocking absurdity of Christendom consists in affirming the philosophical and scientific impossibility that the Infinite once had a local, special, finite expression. Until that stumbling-block is removed, there will be, in the religious and theological world, *no* progression. Intellect, without trying to enter the saving light-realm of Arabula, will advance the Arts and Sciences; and, adhering resolutely to its positive requirements for experimental knowledge, will end in atheism, selfishness, and disgust.

CHAPTER XVI.

IMPERSONALITY OF ARABULA.

Like the "desire of the night for the morning" was my persevering prayer for one prolonged communion with the white golden Light, which had burst through the selfishness of Intellect and enfranchised my being.

One afternoon far spent, when the sun was gathering in its evening urn the ashes of its day of golden burnings, I walked to a sequestered seat beneath the dark maples, and resigned my soul to the voice of Eternal Light.

The dawn's rays, awakening the depths of intuitive life and love, entered my being and blessed me. Father Eternal! Thy universe is loaded and flooded with love, light, hope, and harmony. The dismal darkness of selfishness has departed. All is charity, faith, unfathomable goodness, infinite perfection. Moments, days, years, ages! They appear and disappear like the lights and shadows among flowers and trees. Persons, families, races, empires! They come and go like the rise and fall of waves upon the ocean's bosom. Heavenly Voice of Light! O, let me ask—

Intellect.—"How can I comprehend thee?"

Arabula.—"By studying my manifestations."

Int.—"How am I to commence?"

Ara.—"With the history of mankind."

INT.—"Does the history of mankind contain evidences of your presence?"

ARA.—"I am inseparable from human life; for I am *the* LIGHT, which lighteth every man that cometh into the world."

INT.—"How can I comprehend this mystery?"

ARA.—"It is no mystery. My life is your life; my light is your light; my existence is your existence."

INT.—"Do you mean that heaven lies about man in his infancy; or, that we are nearer God when innocent and youthful?"

ARA.—"Not that alone. I am born into man's intellectual consciousness only through the virgin mother—*the love of the soul for truth.*"

INT.—"Is the soul's *love* for Truth an evidence of its virginity?"

ARA.—"When the soul loves Truth for *selfish* purposes, it is lustful and corrupted. A virgin soul is single-eyed for Truth, and in the love of such a soul the Saviour is born."

INT.—"What Saviour?"

ARA.—"The Light."

INT.—"From what does the Light save man?"

ARA.—"It judges his actions, approves his virtues, condemns his evils, rewards his obedience, punishes his transgressions, shines into his darkness, rebukes his selfishness, overthrows his skepticism, lifts him above the animals, and makes him immortal."

INT.—"What are the circumstances under which this virgin mother brings man's Saviour into the world?"

ARA.—"In the utmost simplicity—a manger of natural relationships is the cradle, wherein the holy mother reposes her babe, to the surprise of worldly shepherds, beneath the wandering stars of power, compelling the admiration of proud magi in Science, and rejoicing the hearts of watching angels."

INT.—"Why do you speak after the manner of a received history of the birth of a personage?"

ARA.—"Because that history is the familiar drapery worn by an Eternal Verity."

INT.—"What Eternal Verity?"

ARA.—"This! That that Light, 'which is the light of the world,' the living Emmanuel in the minds and hearts of men, is born of a virgin, is cradled in simplicity, preaches to the world, works wonders among the selfish, is too certainly crucified, dies into temporary darkness, is most loved by women, is guarded by angels, is resurrected, is revealed in greater glory on the mountain of experience, and in clouds of light returns to continue the work of salvation among men."

INT.—"Is Christ the name of an historical personage?"

ARA.—"Christ is an ancient title for the present word, 'Arabula'—an idea, the mystery of Judean religionists, the sacred Shekinah of the Oriental secret sects, the holy name for the Pure Presence, the Word, the Logos, the Symbol, the Holy Ghost, THE LIGHT OF THE WORLD."

INT.—"What is meant by the other title, *Jesus?*"

ARA.—"Jesus is the name of a personage, in whose half-mythical history is mixed the mysteries of the secret Christ. The error of sacred history, is this mixture of personalities and events with ideas and principles."

INT.—"Did not Jesus manifest all that is attributed to Christ?"

ARA.—"It is impossible for any *one* person to display the full glory of Eternal Light, but every one according to his love and capacity for Truth."

INT.—"Then all men, of all countries, and in all conditions, may manifest more or less of Christ, if they will?"

ARA.—"It is Life, and is seen in all life; it is Love, and is manifested in all love; it is Truth, and is present in all truth; it is Light, and is visible in all wisdom; it is God, and is embodied in whatsoever is good, beautiful, and everlasting."

INT.—"Is this feeling, this holy yearning of the spirit for the Light, common to all men?"

ARA.—"There is a feeling, there always was a feeling, that the Infinite had its place in the soul; that God, however much He may have been elsewhere, was most truly in the breast of His child; that however magnificent His temples of stone and gold might be, the temple He best loved to be worshiped in was the heart. There was, and is, a vague, dim belief that the human somewhere melted into the Divine, and that the Divine somewhere melted into the human. The inward being of man was always reaching out after God, and always returned from its reaching to find out that no reaching out was necessary, that God was nestling close to the heart. In all times, under all skies, men have had fleeting intimations of the presence of Deity, sitting vailed, shadowy, shrouded in the dark corners of their souls. One side of their being touched the Infinite—*was* the Infinite. *Conscience* was the eye, the voice of God."

INT. "In studying history, is it best to look at the items and the specialties in the biographies of distinguished personages, or at the quality and amount of Life and Light (love and wisdom) they manifested?"

ARA.—"Great souls require no history. It is of no consequence where they were born, where they lived, what dress they wore, what fortune they met. Of some of them it may be said that they had no history whatever; hardly a cord of trustworthy tradition holds them to the earth. We have them nevertheless; they lived, they are ours, they are we;—the scantiness of their clothing permits us to see the majestic grace of their walk. The muse of history never introduced anybody to a Son of God."*

INT.—"The Eternal Light, as I now understand it, lifts a person out of and above *self*. And furthermore, I understand that *conscious* individuality is based in selfishness, which is incompatible with the true birth and growth of *Arabula* in the soul?"

ARA.—"The Spirit (Christ) must be born a living Emmanuel; man must know, by the heart's interior witness, of the Divine in his own nature. The Christ is revealed in the human through these three elements, these three principles, viz.: (1) the vital connection of man with the Eternal through the affections of his heart and the laws of his conscience; (2) the vital connection of man with man by force of a common origin, a common nature, a common discipline, and a common

* See Sermon on "The Birth of Christ," by Rev. O. B. Frothingham, 1861.

destiny; (3) the vital connection of man with himself by virtue of that sacred individuality which invests his personal character with supreme and inviolable worth, and makes his personal dignity and development the end of all his experience."

CHAPTER XVII.

FROM HEAVEN TO HADES.

WHILE in the superior condition I had no difficulty in comprehending the underlying principles of ancient mysteries and modern myths in religion. Immersed in the waters of everlasting truth, I did not marvel at the emblematic ordinance called "baptism." Neither did I marvel because the Arabula had said, and was always saying, to man's materialistic intellect: "You must be born again." Indeed, intuitively realizing with my impersonal consciousness, as I reverently did, the existence of the grand cardinal ideas and the inherent omniscience of the unchangeable principles of infinity, I should have marveled if the Light had *not* said to human ignorance and selfishness, "Ye must be born again." The universal allegorization of physical events, and changes in the sun, moon, stars, and other heavenly signs—the early custom of clothing, with oriental material splendors, the undefinable religious mysteries of birth, life, death, immortality, rewards, punishments, God, Paradise, pandemonium, and spiritual communications—all was made plain to my exalted understanding, even down to the very *origin* of all religion among the earliest of earth's inhabitants.

O, the ineffable harmony of that Superior Condition! in which the faculties of the human spirit immortal are awakened to their native conscious relationship with the heavenly love and omniscient goodness of the INFINITE WHOLE!

The Eternal Arabula—divine goddess of the spirit—lifts the thoughts to heaven's highest orbs. From her golden lips flow silvery sermons, like flowery balm from the life-trees of Elysian; and in her *voice* is heard the murmuring, mellow, deathless music of immortal love. The illimitable expanse of sublime Summer Lands—the choral birds, the whispering breezes, the melodious streams, the gentle groves, and ever-fragrant flowers of the heavenly clime—with the poet's deathless strain, the tender reciprocations of angels, once earthly men and women, and the ravishing love-laughter of sweet, rosy-lipped, ever-beautiful childhood—all, all, and unutterably more, is brought into the spirit's essential consciousness by the presence and voice of Arabula. Yea, all is harmony, and enchantment, and sunlit love to him who, from the transfiguring mount of awakened Intuition, sees the fundamental, impersonal, infinite principles of the universe. The dark night of ignorance and the wily imps of selfishness are vanquished by the full-orbed heavenly daylight of undying Truth. O, that the spirit could at once enter unerringly upon its true association with God's fatherly, motherly life!

The next day I began to review the answers of Arabula.

The perpetually appearing and disappearing of the divine light in persons and events, I could not comprehend. I am not a principle, but a person; how, then, am I to understand a principle? I am in space, bounded and educated by its limitations; how then am I to comprehend infinity, which is the annihilation of space?

Dreaming does not satisfy my intellect. You tell me that a principle is eternally at work in the human heart, yearning to make itself manifest in the flesh, dividing itself up unceasingly without divisibility, touching and impressing and departing, like day into night; and, knowing that I possess no faculties akin to such a principle, you tell me that I must perceive it, and preach it, and live it!

Let us not be deluded by chimeras. Matter I am; therefore, matter I can comprehend. I can be extended, solidified, liquidated, divided; therefore I cannot understand matter, which has extent, solidity, levitation, gravitation, and divisibility. But of an infinite being, what can I *know?* Shall I say, with Spinoza, that men are modes of the manifestation of the infinite intelligence? Therefore, I must conclude that the absolutely indivisible essence is divided and organized into men, which is admitting that the mathematically impossible is possible. Will, design, power! Are they qualities of the absolute essence? or, are they evolutions of the dynamics of that substance men call Matter?

No answer! No answer! Where is the Light now? Darkness, thick blackness, covers the face of the deep. O, why do I not remember the lessons of Arabula? Vagueness profound presses the eyes of my intellectual powers. It is the old-time demon, an incubus—the return of selfishness—the enemy of the goddess of Light.

O, the night-life of this under world! Who can paint

the scenes of this horrible hadean world? Faintly come weeping memories of joys once tasted in the beautiful garden. Baldur, the beloved son of Odin, never descended to this low estate. Here live Loki and Ahriman, the arch-enemies of Ormuzd, the prince of goodness, and the Light of the world. Here prowl and howl the selfish men whom the dread Anubis has consigned to judgment and the terrors of justice. The Thammuz of Chaldea sent all his evil genii to this nameless place of passion and despair. Here, in grandest misery, in a style of elegant wretchedness most magnificent, resides the opponent of Arabula—the devil of Selfishness, who fought and fled the presence of "the Light of the world."

Hades is the habitation of the passions. The spirits here are "spirits in prison." The heavenly Arabula, the Adonis of the inner life—"the Light which lighteth every man that cometh into the world"—descendeth here, clothed in the effulgent splendor of myriad-sided Truth, Love, and Wisdom, and, addressing the imprisoned spirits, says,—"Repent ye! repent ye! Marvel not that I say unto you, *ye must be born again.*"

CHAPTER XVIII.

HOPEFUL SIGNS.

INTELLECT, without the lifting light and holy loving eyes of Intuition, is a poor player; he "frets and struts his hour upon the stage, and then is heard no more." He is limited in power; proud as limited; jealous as proud; selfish as jealous; and demoniac as selfish; and thus, Othello-like, he atheistically says, first, "Put out the light, and then—put out *the* Light."

The selfishness of the inferior conditioned Intellect is the original sin. Its possessor thinks only for himself. To compass sea and land, to trample on the rights and liberties of others, to triumph over the downfall of compeers, to erect fortunes on the hopeless ruins of opponents; these are a few of the countless crimes of this part of man's nature. It eats and drinks and sleeps to gratify the selfish instinct. Marriage, habitation, pictures, furniture, children—all sought and secured for selfish gratification. Nothing is sacred—not husband, not wife, not children, not love (for of love it can know nothing), and not even human life is sacred; for it will spoliate, burn, and assassinate, to accomplish its special selfish ends. It is cunning, tricky, stealthy, insinuating, treacherous. It is the enemy of the beautiful spirituality and unapproachable purity of Arabula. It ridicules the intangible; it condemns poetry as useless; it appreciates music as a voluptuous sensation; it values mirth as the antidote for the still small voice of Arabula; it prizes the duration of bodily life beyond the wealth of Crœsus; it sees in sexuality no meaning but a means of varying the instinct of pleasure; it lives in the present, with no hope, no heaven, no God, and is crazed at the thought of death.

I have described no one civilized man's character; only painted *the selfishness of Intellect*, when it is not "born again;" when it is a proud, overbearing stranger to the superior condition; when it persistently resists the influx of that holy Light, which floods with eternal beauty and harmony the infinite universe.

In myself I found hopeful signs. Although I could still intellectualize, and pick flaws in the logic of Arabula, and philosophize disparagingly on the undefinable affirmations of Intuition; yet, somewhat to my surprise, my negative theories and materialistic criticisms, after imparting a momentary feeling of triumph, because I had perplexed and silenced the inner angel, reacted upon my soul like the alarm-chill of a sudden cold. I no longer took pleasure in combating the angel of Light! "Why persecutest thou me?"—sounded in the sanctuary of my spirit.

Was not this a foregleam of the possible resurrection of my Intellect? I was subdued, thoughtful, prayerful, hopeful.

CHAPTER XIX.

GLIMMERINGS OF LIGHT IN MYSTERY.

MYSTERY! O, thou bountiful mother of blessings, evils, faiths, skepticisms, piety, cruelty, hope, wretchedness, progress! Mystery! the vehicle of all ancient systems of religion; the material clothing, the seamless garment, worn by the Angel of Immortality on her first visit to earth. Spurn mystery; refuse to entertain its most extravagant tales; shut from patient observation its philosophically impossible feats of miracles; repel its large-eyed and loquacious stories of the gods, of the phenomena in nature, of the marvels of the four seasons, of the meanings and movements of the celestial bodies, of the signs, and secrets, and solemn ceremonials, vestments, enchantments, imposing tableaux, pomp, anthems, mechanism, lighted candles, cymbals, ringing bells, incantations, prayers, pilgrimages—spurn these, repel these, turn away scornfully from these, proudly trample over these up to the summit of mount Science—and you forsake *the mother of all religion*, you leave to perish miserable the gorgeous goddess of unnumbered spiritual benefits, you turn, like an intellectual ignoramus, like a pedantic inductionist of the Baconian school (which is perfect in its place), and, in that one act of treachery and stupidity, you shut out the Light of God, and take down the spiral stairway which leads through the thorny experimentally-paved avenues of knowledge to the royal road, the straight and beautiful way of eternal principles within and without your existence.

Mystery! Are you not a miracle? If you are not, then there never was a miracle. Is it not marvelous that you should be so ignorant of the universe? Here you are! born but yesterday, on the high table-land of the infinite past, at whose base lie the skeletons of countless hosts, a hecatomb of human ashes, once animated, like your own chemical bodies, with feelings, instincts, passions, thought, activity, grief, pleasure—and yet, with all this opulent repository of history and learning at your very feet, you are ignorant of the latent meaning in religious mystery!

It is to-day a mystery to me how, yesterday, I could so drop below the superior condition as to irreverently question the positive declarations of the world-enlightening Arabula. O, the blood-sweat agony — O, the darkness over the face of Nature—O, the fiendish power of the spirit of selfishness! Why did a little worldly care, some external anxiety in business, an act of injustice by a neighbor, so rapidly drive me out of the peaceful, musical, flowery garden of harmony?

Why did I not say yesterday, as my light-lifted soul now says, to the unspiritualizing propensity of groveling, unredeemed Intellect—"Cursed art thou; upon thy belly shalt thou go, and dust shalt thou eat all the days of thy life." Is it not a religious mystery? And is it not a miracle that *you*, refined and noble-natured as you are, do not at once accept the Light and "be born again?" Verily, it is more marvelous that you do not, than that you should. O, you do not want to "change your base" of operations in religion! Yes, you self-aggrandizing and consistency-worshiping foe of progress! *You are seen as you are!* You have married a society-wife, and therefore cannot march in Truth's army. And, moreover, it is so agonizingly "hard" to be born again; it is, likewise, "inconvenient;" it is, also, exhaustingly "expensive;" and, here's the rub, it is painful to your fashionably-religious "relatives;" for are you not bone of their bone and flesh of their flesh?

O, ye typifiers of the mimicking quadrupeds of the tropical forests! Do you not ape the monkeys of fashion? Are you not living on the "lost sheep" side of eternal Light?—That is sinless, the pure, the spotless, the unselfish; it is good in the sight of God; it bears our burdens; it carries our infirmities; it is the angel-presence in the devilhood of our unprogressive mental states; it is the infinite inherent perfection, ever-preaching, "Be ye perfect;" by it we absolutely see that "there is no man good—no, not one;" it unceasingly says, "Come unto me, all ye that are heavy laden, and *I will* give *you rest;*" it does not give us stones when we ask for bread, but, opening its life-larder, says, "Here is my body, and here is my blood—take, eat;" this is the dispensation of "holy spirit;" it descendeth from the heaven of "many mansions;" it taketh manifold forms, variable historical incarnations, but is immutably one and the same Light; it bringeth a harmonious gospel through antagonistic systems of religion; and, as the Light has before written, it is the same to the Indian as to the Judean; it is not given to one and withheld from another; but it descends upon the devil as well as upon the angel in us, and upon every intermediate condition of life; it moveth upon dark waters, and upon bright and shining oceans; it rideth upon the storm and flieth upon the whirlwind, and it broodeth over the placid lake of the soul; it is not here nor there, but everywhere; it melteth the stony heart that it may become a heart of flesh; and poureth oil and wine into the wound of the earthly traveler; it is the good Samaritan, who will pay two pence for the healing of his brother's sores, and it will come again to see if more can be done for the sufferers of earth; it is the star of the East guiding wise men to the young child, Arabula, who will hold out His hands to them, laden with the spiritual blessings the Light alone can bestow. This is the Holy Spirit of truth that shall guide you into all happiness. This is the Comforter; this is the "baptism of fire" with which every one shall be baptized.

CHAPTER XX.

THE PAINS OF MEMORY.

INTELLECT is an imbecile without Memory, as it is an evil genius without the uplifting spirit of Arabula.

Too well do I recall the warnings—the sympathetic shadow-winged prophecies—of the stern saint of Light. It told me day by day to wash away my sins of selfishness. Day by day it imprinted the Cain-mark of shame upon my brow, because I wanted to substitute for a cross-bearing life of public usefulness a flower-crowned life of private idleness and luxury.

Like you, my reader, I wanted a thousand things I did not *need;* in truth, my wants, besides being expensive and unnecessary, were taxing the time, talents, labor, and patience of others. I wanted to have a servant at my call, who would brush my clothes, black my boots, comb my hair, spread the table with rich viands, and fan away the flies while I ate. I wanted a living without working for it! I wanted to be rich, and did not care if it was made by profits sheared, by the legitimate scissors of trade, from commodities sold as necessities to the poor. Of society I wanted nothing but what was conducive to personal gratification. Do you see yourself in this mirror?

Do not say that I must first *merit* the Good, the Fine, and the Beautiful; no, no, I am impatient for happiness; therefore, first supply my greedy *wants*, and if "I like it I'll take some more." O, bright Angel of the Spirit! how selfishly did I "want" to live, while thou wert suffering "on the cross." Forgive! forgive! Ravines, rocks, forests, birds, with setting suns and summer skies, and the

> "Beautiful flowers round Wisdom's secret well,"

with the affections of earth and the final beatitudes of heaven—all, I was willing, yea, *anxious* to appropriate, without so much as once thinking that "I ought to be thankful" for the possession of the senses by which the appropriation was possible.

Like my penitent reader, who, by this time, should be serenely living in good works, I recall all selfish impulses with miserable distinctness. To-day I sit meditatively "dreaming over the past," and all too easily remember the "wholesome smart" and the "remorseful stings" of hours wasted in life's spring-time, vainly looking for happiness in self-will, self-seeking, self-gratification. But, glory be to God! the night is past, the storm clouds dispersed, a boundless blue sky enfolds the world, the feet of angels press once more the celestial pathway, my chastened spirit is obedient to its laws, and my affections, with my redeemed Intellect, are hospitably open to the influx of the Infinite.

CHAPTER XXI.

HISTORY OF CHRISTIAN RELIGION.

THE constant, and yet inconstant, glimmerings of the divine Light, in the materialism of religious history, can be seen by those only who "have eyes to see." Voltaire, who was steady in his devotion to the Light (?) of the Intellect, set forth, in his Philosophical Dictionary, the obvious beginnings of the Christian religion, as follows:—

In the years which immediately followed Jesus Christ, who was at once God and man, there existed among the Hebrews nine religious schools or societies,—Pharisees, Sadducees, Essenians, Judaites, Therapeutæ, Recabites, Herodians, the disciples of John, and the disciples of Jesus, named the "brethren,"—the "Galileans,"—the "believers," who did not assume the name of Christians till about the sixtieth year of our era, at Antioch; being directed to its adoption by God himself, in ways unknown to men.

The Pharisees believed in the metempsychosis. The Sadducees denied the immortality of the soul, and the existence of spirits, yet believed in the Pentateuch.

Pliny, the naturalist (relying, evidently, on the authority of Flavius Josephus), calls the Essenians "gens æterna in qua nemo nascitur;"—"a perpetual family, in which no one is ever born;" because the Essenians very rarely married. The description has been since applied to our monks, and to the "Shakers" of our day.

It is difficult to decide whether the Essenians or the Judaites are spoken of by Josephus in the following passage :—"They despise the evils of the world; their constancy enables them to triumph over torments; in an honorable cause they prefer death to life. They have undergone fire and sword, and submitted to having their very bones crushed, rather than utter a syllable against their legislator, or eat forbidden food."

It would seem, from the words of Josephus, that the above portrait applies to the Judaites, and not to the Essenians. "Judas was the author of a new sect, completely different from the other three," that is, the Sadducees, the Pharisees, and the Essenians. "They are," he goes on to say, "Jews by nation, they live in harmony with each other, and consider pleasure to be a vice." The natural meaning of this language would induce us to think that he is speaking of the Judaites.

However that may be, these Judaites were known before the disciples of Christ began to possess consideration and consequence in the world. Some weak people have supposed them to be heretics, who adored Judas Iscariot.

The Therapeutæ were a society different from the Essenians and the Judaites. They resembled the Gymnosophists and Brahmins of India. "They possess," says Philo, "a principle of divine love, which excites in them an enthusiasm like that of the Bacchantes and the Corybantes, and which forms them to that state of contemplation to which they aspire. This sect originated in Alexandria, which was entirely filled with Jews, and prevailed greatly throughout all Egypt."

The Recabites still continued as a sect. They vowed never to drink wine; and it is, possibly, from their example, that Mahomet forbade that liquor to his followers.

The Herodians regarded Herod, the first of that name, as a Messiah, a messenger from God, who had rebuilt the temple. It is clear that the Jews at Rome celebrated a festival in honor of him, in the reign of Nero, as appears from the lines of Persius—"Herodis venere dies," &c. (Sat. v. 180.)

> "King Herod's feast, when each Judean vile
> Trims up his lamp with tallow or with oil."

The disciples of John the Baptist had spread themselves a little in Egypt, but principally in Syria, Arabia, and towards the Persian Gulf. They are recognized, at the present day, under the name of the Christians of St. John. There were some also in Asia Minor. It is mentioned in the Acts of the Apostles (chap. xix.) that Paul met with many of them at Ephesus. "Have you received," he asked them, "the holy spirit?" They answered him, "We have not heard even that there is a holy spirit."—"What baptism, then," says he, "have you received?" They answered him, "The baptism of John."

In the mean time, the true Christians, as is well known, were laying the foundation of the only true religion.

He who contributed most to strengthen this rising society was Paul, who had himself persecuted it with the greatest violence. He was born at Tarsus in Cilicia,* and was educated under one of the most celebrated professors among the Pharisees, Gamaliel, a disciple of Hillel. The Jews pretend that he quarreled with Gamaliel, who refused to let him have his daughter in marriage. Some traces of this anecdote are to be found in the sequel to the Acts of St. Thecla. These Acts relate that he had a large forehead, a bald head, united eyebrows, an aquiline nose, a short and clumsy figure, and crooked legs. Lucian, in his dialogue "Philopatres," seems to give a very similar portrait of him. It has been doubted whether he was a Roman citizen, for at that time the title was not given to any Jew; they had been expelled from Rome by Tiberius; and Tarsus did not become a Roman colony till nearly a hundred years afterwards, under Caracalla; as Cellarius remarks in his Geography (book iii.), and Grotius in his Commentary on the Acts, to whom alone we need refer. * * * All the first believers were obscure persons. They all labored with their hands. The apostle St. Paul himself acknowledges that he gained his livelihood by making tents. St. Peter raised from the dead Dorcas, a seamstress, who made clothes for the "brethren." The assembly of believers met at Joppa, at the house of a tanner called Simon, as appears from the ninth chapter of the Acts of the Apostles.

The believers spread themselves secretly in Greece; and some of them went from Greece to Rome, among the Jews, who were permitted by the Romans to have a

---

* St. Jerome says that he was from Giscala in Galilee.

synagogue. They did not, at first, separate themselves from the Jews. They practiced circumcision; and, as we have elsewhere remarked, the first fifteen obscure bishops of Jerusalem were all circumcised, or at least were all of the Jewish nation.

When the apostle Paul took with him Timothy, who was the son of a heathen father, he circumcised him himself, in the small city of Lystra. But Titus, his other disciple, could not be induced to submit to circumcision. The brethren, or the disciples of Jesus, continued united with the Jews until the time when St. Paul experienced a persecution at Jerusalem on account of his having introduced strangers into the temple. He was accused by the Jews of endeavoring to destroy the law of Moses by that of Jesus Christ. It was with a view to his clearing himself from this accusation that the apostle St. James proposed to the apostle Paul that he should shave his head, and go and purify himself in the temple, with four Jews, who had made a vow of being shaved. "Take them with you," says James to him (chap. xxi. Acts of the Apostles), "purify yourself with them, and let the whole world know that what has been reported concerning you is false, and that you continue to obey the law of Moses." Thus, then, Paul, who had been at first the most summary persecutor of the holy society established by Jesus,—Paul, who afterwards endeavored to govern that rising society,—Paul the Christian, Judaizes, "that the world may know that he is calumniated when he is charged with no longer following the law of Moses."

St. Paul was equally charged with impiety and heresy, and the prosecution against him lasted a long time; but it is perfectly clear, from the nature of the charges, that he had traveled to Jerusalem in order to fulfil the rites of Judaism.

He addressed to Faustus these words (Acts xxv.): "I have neither offended against the Jewish law, nor against the temple."

The apostles announced Jesus Christ as a just man wickedly persecuted, a prophet of God, a son of God, sent to the Jews for the reformation of manners.

"Circumcision," says the apostle Paul, "is good, if you observe the law; but if you violate the law, your circumcision becomes uncircumcision. If an uncircumcised person keep the law, he will be as if circumcised. The true Jew is one that is so inwardly."

When this apostle speaks of Jesus Christ in his epistles, he does not reveal the ineffable mystery of his consubstantiality with God. "We are delivered by him," says he (Romans, chap. v.), "from the wrath of God. The gift of God hath been shed upon us by the grace bestowed on one man, who is Jesus Christ. * * * * Death reigned through the sin of one man; the just shall reign in life by one man, who is Jesus Christ."

And, in the eighth chapter—"We are heirs of God, and joint-heirs of Christ;" and in the sixteenth chapter—"To God, who is the only wise, be honor and glory, through Jesus Christ. * * * * You are Jesus Christ's, and Jesus Christ is God's" (1 Cor. chap. iii.).

And in 1 Cor. xv. 27—"Every thing is made subject to him, undoubtedly excepting God, who made all things subject to him."

Some difficulty has been found in explaining the following part of the epistle of the Philippians:—"Do nothing through vainglory. Let each humbly think others better than himself. Be of the same mind with Jesus Christ, *who, being in the likeness of God, assumed not to equal himself to God*."* This passage appears exceedingly well investigated and elucidated in a letter, still extant, of the churches of Vienna and Lyons, written in the year 117, and which is a valuable monument of antiquity. In this letter the modesty of some believers is praised. "They did not wish," says the letter, "to assume the lofty title of martyrs, in consequence of certain tribulations; after the example of Jesus Christ, who, being in the likeness of God, did not assume the quality of being equal to God." Origen, also, in his commentary on John, says: "The greatness of Jesus shines out more splendidly, in consequence of his self-humiliation, than if he had assumed equality with God." In fact, the opposite interpretation would be a solecism. What sense would there be in this exhortation: "Think others superior to yourselves; imitate Jesus, who did not think it an *assumption* to be equal to God?" It would be an obvious contradiction; it would be putting an example of full pretension for an example of modesty; it would be an offense against logic.

Thus did the wisdom of the apostles establish the

---

* Our English version gives the foregoing passage—"Who being in the form of God, thought it no *robbery* to be equal with God."—See Epistle to Philippians, c. ii. to 6th verse—a directly contrary translation. Voltaire, the context, the Fathers, and the ancient letter, *versus* the English translation.

rising church. That wisdom did not change its character in consequence of the dispute which took place between the apostles Peter, James, and John, on one side, and Paul on the other. This contest occurred at Antioch. The apostle Peter, formerly Cephas, or Simon Barjonas, ate with the converted Gentiles, and among them did not observe the ceremonies of the law, and the distinction of meats. He and Barnabas, and the other disciples, ate indifferently of pork, of animals which had been strangled, or which had cloven feet, or which did not chew the cud; but many Jewish Christians having arrived, St. Peter joined with them in abstinence from forbidden meats, and in the ceremonies of the Mosaic law.

This conduct appeared very prudent: he wished to avoid giving offense to the Jewish Christians, his companions; but St. Paul attacked him on the subject with considerable severity. "I withstood him," says he, "to his face, because he was blamable." (Gal. chap. ii.)

This quarrel appears the most extraordinary on the part of St. Paul. Having been at first a persecutor, he might have been expected to have acted with moderation; especially as he had himself gone to Jerusalem to sacrifice in the temple, had circumcised his disciple Timothy, and strictly complied with the Jewish rites, for which very compliance he now reproached Cephas. St. Jerome imagines that this quarrel between Paul and Cephas was a pretended one. He says, in his first homily (vol. iii.), that they acted like two advocates who work themselves up to an appearance of great zeal and exasperation against each other, to gain credit with their respective clients. He says that Peter (Cephas) being appointed to preach to the Jews, and Paul to the Gentiles, they assumed the appearance of quarreling, Paul to gain the Gentiles, and Peter to gain the Jews. But St. Augustin is by no means of the same opinion. "I grieve," says he, in his epistle to Jerome, "that so great a man should be the patron of a lie" (*patronum mendacii*).

This dispute between St. Jerome and St. Augustin ought not to diminish our veneration for them, and still less for St. Paul and St. Peter.

As to what remains, if Peter was destined for the Jews, who were after their conversion likely to Judaize, and Paul for strangers, it appears probable that Peter never went to Rome. The Acts of the Apostles make no mention of Peter's journey to Italy.

However that may be, it was about the sixtieth year of our era that Christians began to separate from the Jewish communion; and it was this which drew upon them so many quarrels and persecutions from the various synagogues of Rome, Greece, Egypt, and Asia. They were accused of impiety and atheism by their Jewish brethren, who excommunicated them in their synagogues three times every Sabbath day. But in the midst of their persecutions God always supported them.

By degrees, many churches were formed, and the separation between Jews and Christians was complete before the close of the first century. This separation was unknown by the Roman government. Neither the senate nor the emperors of Rome interested them selves in those quarrels of a small flock of mankind, which God had hitherto guided in obscurity, and which he exalted by insensible gradations.

Christianity became established in Greece and at Alexandria. The Christians had there to contend with a new set of Jews, who, in consequence of intercourse with the Greeks, were become philosophers. This was the sect of *gnosis*, or *Gnostics*. Among them were some of the new converts to Christianity. All these sects, at that time, enjoyed complete liberty to dogmatize, discourse, and write, whenever the Jewish courtiers, settled at Rome and Alexandria, did not bring any charge against them before the magistrates. But, under Domitian, Christianity began to give some umbrage to the government.

The zeal of some Christians, which was not according to knowledge, did not prevent the church from making that progress which God destined from the beginning. The Christians, at first, celebrated their mysteries in sequestered houses, and in caves, and during night. Hence, according to Minutius Felix, the title given them of *lucifugaces*. Philo calls them gesséens. The names most frequently applied to them by the heathens, during the first four centuries, were "Galileans" and "Nazarenes;" but that of "Christians" has prevailed above all the others.

Neither the hierarchy, nor the services of the church, were established all at once; the apostolic times were different from those which followed.

The mass now celebrated at matins, was the suppen performed in the evening: these usages changed in proportion as the church strengthened. A more numerous society required more regulations, and the prudence of the pastors accommodated itself to times and places.

St. Jerome and Eusebius relate, that when the churches received a regular form, five different orders might be soon perceived to exist in them—superintendents, *episcopoi*; whence originate the bishops—elders of the society, *presbyteroi*, priests—*diaconoi*, servants or deacons—*pistoi*, believers, the initiated; that is, the baptized, who participated in the suppers of the agapæ, or love-feasts—the *catechumens*, who were awaiting baptism—and the *energumens*, who awaited their being exorcised of demons. In these five orders no one had garments different from the others, no one was bound to celibacy: witness Tertullian's book, dedicated to his wife, and witness also the example of the apostles. No paintings or sculptures were to be found in their assemblies, during the first two centuries; no altars; and, most certainly, no tapers, incense, and lustral water. The Christians carefully concealed their books from the Gentiles: they intrusted them only to the initiated. Even the catechumens were not permitted to recite the Lord's Prayer.

CHAPTER XXII.

RELIGIOUS SIGNS AND MYSTERIES.

It is the office of enlightened reason to investigate all mysteries, to search their meanings, to strip off all the tales and trappings of superstition; and, finally, to discern the under-current of Truth, the spirit of Light and Deity, in the contradictory and apparently irreconcilable events and personages of history. There is in the world (says a writer) a distinct class of books, written "within and without," Ezek. ii. 10; or, "within and on the back side," Rev. v. 1; that is, they are symbolic books, having a double sense; and they have proceeded from the members of esoteric societies in different ages of the world, who have written under the restraint of an oath of secrecy. What is the true key to these books? It is a state of the soul, and is not a transferable possession. "In thy light shall we see light," Psalm xxxvi. 9.

We shall never make any real progress in understanding the Scriptures until we advance so far as to recognize *principles* in the *persons* represented. The seeming historical persons must be regarded as shadows passing before us, to draw our attention to the spiritual truths or principles by which they were, or rather, by which they are perpetually cast: for if there is any thing in the Scriptures which is not true to us, and to our time, it can have no importance to us. The value of the Scriptures lies in their application to life; but no application is possible, except a perverted one, when the truth is not recognized; and to recognize the truth, the Scriptures require to be interpreted; yet not as history, but as parables.*

M. Renan, with philosophic calmness, and a truly majestic and pure style of criticism, conducts his readers to the same conclusion. He is not lost in the limitations and killing associations of the letter, but, perceiving *the interior light* sought to be conveyed by the gospels, does much to rescue the Testaments from the utter oblivion to which, long since, the fact-loving intellect had consigned them.

Sir Philip Sidney said there were no writings in the world so well calculated to make a man wise as those of Plato: and yet this is not because Plato has anywhere defined GOD, or wisdom, or virtue, or justice, or love, or beauty, or goodness, or truth; for this was not the purpose of his writings; but he has nevertheless written so about all these things, that an attentive student may find something to satisfy his reasonable longings, even though they should reach out after immortality; while the unapt or careless reader may wonder why so wise a man as Plato has advocated a system in the Republic, which, taken literally, would destroy any society in the world. We ought to see that for this very reason the Republic is a piece of ancient esoteric writing, needing interpretation. If we call the intellectual qualities masculine, and the affectional feminine, we may finally discover in what sense they may live in

* This is the opinion of M. Hitchcock, a careful thinker and writer.

a blessed *community*, in which, in Scripture language, the lion and the lamb shall lie down together.*

Socrates called his art of teaching the art of the midwife; because, according to his philosophy, no man could learn any thing who had not a seed of the knowledge in himself: and the art of Socrates consisted in bringing the seed into life and action. A soul, therefore, acquiring great truths, was compared to a woman in labor; and Socrates compared himself to his mother, who, he tells us, was a midwife.

Mysteries in religion will continue until man's Intellect is lifted and sanctified, so to speak, by the unselfish impersonal Light of God. Goethe remarks: "There is something magical at all times in perspectives. Were we not accustomed from youth to look through them, we should shudder and tremble every time we put them to our eyes. It is we who are looking, and it is not we; a being it is whose organs are raised to a higher pitch, whose limitations are done away, who has become entitled to stretch forth into the infinite." Now it is every man's privilege to look in "perspectives" in the fields of spirituality. But whether he see an infinity of absurdity, or an infinity of truth, will ever be determined by the amount of intuition he lets into his eyes.

The Arabula began at the beginning of human history to incarnate itself, and to utter itself in all human relations, feelings, and interests. It comes forth in the incarnations of Brahm, in Kreeshna, Budha, in Osiris,

* For further thoughts on this subject, see a chapter on "Christ the Spirit," by the author referred to.

in Ormuzd, in Adonis, in Apollo, in Bacchus, in Jupiter, in Pythagoras, in Socrates, in Plato, in Confucius, in Jesus. Says an author: "The most important of these mysteries were those of Mithras, celebrated in Persia; of Osiris and Isis, celebrated in Egypt; of Eleusis, instituted in Greece; and the Scandinavian and Druidical rites, which were confined to the Gothic and Celtic tribes. In all these various mysteries we find *a singular unity* of design, clearly indicating a common origin, and a purity of doctrine as evidently proving that this common origin was not to be sought for in the popular theology of the Pagan world. The ceremonies of initiation were all funereal in their character. They celebrated the death and the resurrection of some cherished being, either the object of esteem as a hero, or of devotion as a god. Subordination of degrees was instituted, and the candidate was subjected to probations varying in their character and severity; the rites were practiced in the darkness of night, and often amid the gloom of impenetrable forests, or subterranean caverns; and the full fruition of knowledge, for which so much labor was endured, and so much danger incurred, was not attained until the aspirant, well tried and thoroughly purified, had reached the place of wisdom and of light."

The secret doctrines of the Egyptian rites (according to the Lexicon) related to the gods, the creation and government of the world, and the nature and condition of the human soul. They called the perfectly-initiated candidate *Al-om-jah*, from the name of the Deity. *Secrecy was principally inculcated, and all their lessons were taught by symbols.* Many of these have been preserved. With them, *a point within a circle* was the symbol of the

Deity surrounded by eternity; the *globe* was a symbol of the supreme and eternal God; a serpent with a tail in his mouth was emblematic of eternity; a child sitting on the lotos was a symbol of the sun; a palm-tree, of victory; a staff, of authority; an ant, of knowledge; a goat, of fecundity; a wolf, of aversion; the right hand, with the fingers open, of plenty; and the left hand closed, of protection.

In Dr. Oliver's account of the Mysteries of Bacchus, we read: "The first actual ceremony among the Greeks was to purify the aspirant with water, and to crown him with myrtle, because the myrtle-tree was sacred to Proserpine; after which he was free from arrest during the celebrations. He was then introduced into a small cave or vestibule, to be invested with the sacred habiliments; after which his conductor delivered him over to the mystagogue, who then commenced the initiation with the prescribed formula, *Εκας, Εκας, εστε βεβηλοι, Depart hence, all ye profane;* and the guide addressed the aspirant by exhorting him to call forth all his courage and fortitude, as the process on which he was now about to enter was of the most appalling nature. And being led forward through a series of dark passages and dismal caverns, to represent the erratic state of the Ark while floating on the troubled surface of the diluvian waters, the machinery opens upon him. He first hears the distant thunder pealing through the vault of heaven, accompanied by the howling of dogs and wild beasts. * * * * These terrific noises rapidly approach, and the din becomes tremendous, reverberated, as it doubtless was, in endless repetitions, from the echoing vaults and lofty caverns within whose inextricable mazes he was now immured. Flashes of vivid light now broke in upon him, and rendered the prevailing darkness more visible; and by the momentary illumination he beheld the appearances by which he was surrounded. Monstrous shapes and apparitions, demoniacal figures, grinning defiance at the intruder; mystical visions and flitting shadows, unreal phantoms of a dog-like form, overwhelm him with terror. In this state of horrible apprehension and darkness he was kept three days and nights."

From the Lexicon may be gleaned other details, showing the strugglings of the Divine Light in man's nature for utterance; and how, when its pure promptings are not comprehended by minds in darkness, it ultimates in painful superstitions and mysterious ceremonies. "The Grecian rites were only a modification of the mysteries of Bacchus or Dionysus, and were thus called, because it was said that Orpheus first introduced the worship of Bacchus into Greece from Egypt. They differed, however, from the other pagan rites in not being confined to the priesthood, but in being practiced by a fraternity who did not possess the sacerdotal functions. The initiated commemorated in their ceremonies, which were performed at night, the murder of Bacchus by the Titans, and his final restoration to the supreme government of the universe, under the name of Phanes." * * * * "In the day, the initiates were crowned with fennel and poplar, and carried serpents in their hands, or twined them around their heads, crying with a loud voice, *enos*, *sabos*, and danced to the sound of the mystic words, *hyes*, *attes*, *attes*, *hyes*. At night the mystes were bathed in the lustral water, and having been rubbed over with clay and bran, he was clothed in the skin of a fawn, and, having risen from the bath, he exclaimed, '*I have departed from evil and have found the good.*'"

As to the use of the term *Jehovah*, the same authority remarks, that "an allusion to the unutterable name of GOD is to be found in the doctrines and ceremonies of other nations, as well as the Jews. It is said to have been used as the pass-word in the Egyptian mysteries. In the rites of Hindostan it was bestowed upon the aspirant, under the triliteral form AUM, at the completion of his initiation, and then only by whispering it in his ear. The Cabalists reckoned seventy-two names of God, the knowledge of which imparted to the possessor magical powers. The Druids invoked the omnipotent and all-preserving power, under the symbol I. O. W.

"In fact, the name of God must be taken as symbolical of truth; and then, the search for it will be nothing else but the search after truth. The subordinate names are the subordinate modifications of truth, but the ineffable tetragrammaton will be the sublimity and perfection of Divine Truth.

"The doctrines of the Druids were the same as those entertained by Pythagoras. They taught the existence of one Supreme Being; a future state of rewards and punishments; the immortality of the soul, and a metempsychosis; and the object of their mystic rites was to communicate the doctrines in symbolic language."

CHAPTER XXIII.

LIGHT IN THE WINDOW.

MAN'S intellectual powers, led by the hand of Arabulà, naturally solve the mysteries of religion. The mystery is revived, however, the moment the individual's higher consciousness is suspended, or descends to the hades of selfishness, to live on a plane with the intellect's atheism and utter disbelief in things spiritual.

But however dark and thorny man's mind may be at times, there is ever a Light burning in the window of his inner existence, saying, "I am the way, the truth, and the life; follow me!" By giving a tongue to this inherent celestial guest, and then listening with heart and intellect to what it says, the message would substantially be, "Hearken to me, I speak not from myself; I speak only the words of my Father. If you love me, you will keep my commandments, and then you shall know whether what I teach be of the intellect, or of the Father that is in me. Then you shall know that I am in the Father, and the Father in me. If ye continue in my word (the light), then are ye my disciples indeed; and ye shall know the Truth, and the Truth shall make you free. To this end came I into the world (into your externals), that I should bear witness unto the Truth. Every one that is of the Truth (in the Light of God) heareth my voice. Obey my *voice*, and then we shall all be one; as the Father is in me, and I in the Father, that you may also be one in us; for the essence of all spirit is the same. The words that I speak are spirit and are life. Fear not them which kill the body (the forms and doctrines), but are not able to kill the soul; but rather fear him which is able to put both soul and body in hell, by the logical tricks of the selfish intellect. Take my interpretation of life, and ye shall find rest for your souls. For my yoke is easy, and my burden light. This yoke is easy usefulness when the spirit acts instinctively from within outward; but it is a burden when the duty is imposed by priestcraft or fashion, from without."

That the whole Light should be manifested in one person, is conceived to be impossible. To affirm this of Jesus, as modern theologians do, is to say (in the language of Robert Collyer, a true preacher) "that he knew infinitely more of every thing than all the great masters knew of any thing; that his sense of what befitted the Messiah alone held him back from announcing the most important facts that have come in the opening ages; and from doing, by a single act of the will, greater things than have been done by the loftiest souls that came after him. And I mean by this, that the compass, the printing-press, the locomotive, the steamboat, vaccination, Peruvian bark, chloroform, ether, iodine, subsoil plows, photography, anthracite coal, air-tight stoves, horseshoes, infirmaries, sanitary commissions, cheap window-glass, the art of engraving, tea, coffee, and savings banks, were just as clearly present in the mind of the Saviour then, as they are present in the world now.

"Now, I think you will not accuse me of trying to push

my statement unfairly, when I say, that if this theory —that Christ on the earth knew all things, his mind a perfect encyclopedia of the universe and of time—be true, then the greatest of all the mysteries in his life, greater than miracle and prophecy, is this mystery, that he should be here, with that heart so full of pity, that hand so ready in the labor, and that tongue so wise in the wisdom of the divinest love; should foresee all the sorrow, and agony, and death resulting from ignorance, through long ranges of centuries; should see all the steam escaping, all the poor barks creeping along the shore for want of a compass; in a word, the whole difference between that world and this—yet should maintain a resolute silence! I know it will be said that these things could not take root until the true time; and, if this was not the true time, it were useless to reveal them. But I answer, that the possession of a secret that will benefit the world is the obligation to reveal it. We judge that man criminal who has found a sovereign remedy for cholera, and yet buries it in his grave. We say he did not love his fellow-men; and so, in defending his silence, if he knew of a preventive for the small pox, and did not tell it; or of chloroform, to assuage extreme human agonies, and did not tell it—we assume the ground, that, being in the likeness of a man, he was less than a man. And if you say, 'But God the Spirit did not reveal these things until our time, and so why should you expect that God manifest in the flesh would do it?' I answer, God the spirit is surrounded by mystery, his ways are past finding out. I accept the mystery just as it is, and hold on by my faith until I can do better. But the ultimatum here is, that there is no mystery at all about it. The mystery was, how shall these things flash across the brain, and be revealed by the tongue, and done by the hand of a man? Now, here is a brain in which these unutterable philanthropies are a quenchless fire, you say; and an eye seeing into the eighteenth century, how to prevent the small-pox, how to save human life, human beauty, human every thing; a tongue crying, 'I am come not to destroy life, but to save it.' And in that mind a secret how to save life, beside which the cures that he did (apart from their spiritual influence) were as nothing—yet he refused to tell it! So that the mystery is not in the possession of divinity, but in the want of humanity, if this claim be true. And so I do not really sorrow because he did not build a railroad or a steamboat, or the dome of St. Peter's, or anticipate the Riverside Press in printing, or the Waltham chronometer. There may be questioning about those things: there can be no question about these other things. By all the holiest institutions and inspirations of the human soul; by the loftiest teachings of our own, and, so far as I know, of all other Bibles; by the greatest utterances of his own holy, loving, and divine nature—if he knew every thing, he was bound at least to tell this, because he had the face and touch and pity and love of a man, or his divinity was not so good a thing as a decent humanity."

CHAPTER XXIV.

STORIES OF EARLY PERIODS.

The infancy of the race, like the period of infancy in the individual, is excessively productive of grotesque fancies in the supernatural, which is the philosophically impossible. But this term "supernatural," under the interpretations of the wisdom-light, is a perfectly harmless word, meaning the unpositive, the speculative, the metaphysical, the realm of unformed ideas and semi-poetical sentiments; in which boundless realm, before the era of the inductive and exact sciences, the human spirit freely roamed, regardless of the limitations of sense or the remonstrances of intellect. And, strange to say, these mythical fancies were invariably connected with religion. St. Hippolytus relates, for example, that St. John the Divine is asleep at Ephesus, awaiting the great trumpet's twang; and Sir John Mandeville, in his "Travels," gives the circumstance as follows:—

"From Patmos men go unto Ephesim, a fair citee and nyghe to the see. And there dyede Seynte Johne, and was buryed behynde the high Awtiere, in a toumbe. And there is a fair chirche. For Christene mene weren wont to holden that place alweyes. And in the toumbe of Seynt Johne is noughte but manna, that is clept Aungeles mete. For his body was translated into Paradys. And Turkes holden now alle that place and the citee and the Chirche. And all aise the lesse is yclept Turkye. And ye shalle undrestond, that Seynte Johne did make his grave there in his Lyf, and leyed himself there inne all daryk. And therefore somme men seyn, that he dyed noughte, but that he resteth there till the Day of Doom. And forsoothe there is a great marveule. For men may see there the earthe of the toumbe apertly many tymes steren and moen, as there weren quykke thinges under."

The wandering Jew and the circumstances connected with his doom, vary in every account; but all coincide in the point that such a person exists in an undying condition, wandering over the face of the earth, seeking rest and finding none. Though S. Baring-Gould, the author of a curious manual on "Curious Myths" (from which the following extracts are made), thinks the Jewish cobbler, who would not let Jesus sit on his door-step, may have been kept alive to fulfill the words, "There be some standing here who shall not taste of death till they see the Son of Man coming in his kingdom," yet there is no mention of the Wandering Jew, either historical or mythical, till the year 1228. In the sixteenth century he was an assistant weaver in Bohemia. Next he appeared in Western Asia, as Elijah. The Bishop of Schleswig examined him carefully, and believed in his story of having seen Jesus and all the centuries. In the days of Cromwell he was in Leipzig. In the next century he appeared in England, traveled into Jutland, and vanished in Sweden. He has been explained as a personification of the Jewish race. Some have identified him with the Gypsies. In Swabia he is a wild hunter.

Prester John was a Priest-King reigning in unimaginable pomp somewhere in Asia, over a country whose bourne widened and contracted according to the geographical knowledge of the age. He was a conceited pope, rather condescending and gracious to the one on the Tiber; but the latter rebuked him, and quoted, "Not every one that saith unto me Lord, Lord," &c. Orthodox Alexander, Vicar of God, believed in the mythical sovereign of the emerald palace, and sent him a letter; but the messenger never returned, and who can imagine the loss to enthusiastic antiquaries! The myth may have grown out of Nestorianism; and may have foundation in fact.

The divining-rod is full of wonders; and all the facts cannot be treated with levity. That Aaron's rod budded and brought forth almonds is rather doubtful, but the evidence is not easily set aside that Jacques Aymar's rod helped him to find criminals. Tacitus speaks of a queer sort of German divination by the rod. The Greeks had their rhabdomancy. Even Jacob cheated his dames of the sheep-pastures with them. The Frisons had a law that murderers should be discovered by the rod. A great many doubters who sought to expose impostors of well-finding have converted themselves to the contrary view; and, on the other hand, a large number of the wonder-makers have failed when taken before the curious and the great in large cities. The power is said to languish under excitement; the faculties are to be in repose, and the attention concentrated. Bleton went into convulsions when standing over running water. Angelique Cottin, a poor girl, was so highly charged with electricity, that any one who touched her received a violent shock. Mdlle. Olivet had conscientious scruples against her own power. A priest and prayer got her out of the faith, and her power was gone.

The story of the seven sleepers is very beautiful. They remained unconscious in a cave of Mount Celion during three hundred and sixty years. Being persecuted Christians, imagine their surprise when one of their number returned, after what he thought a night's rest, to find the gates of his native Ephesus decorated with the cross and the name of Jesus honored. The charming story is fruitful of poems and dramas; and Mahomet has put it in the Koran, with the improvement that the sleepers prophesy his coming, just as Dr. Cumming and others patch up prophecy after the event. In the Museum at Rome is a curious and ancient representation of them in a cement of sulphur and plaster.

But the myths of this kind are without number. St. George rose from his grave three times, and was thrice slain. Charlemagne sleeps in Mount Odenberg in Hess, seated on his throne, with his crown on his head, and his sword at his side, waiting till the times of Antichrist, when he will wake and burst forth to avenge the blood of the saints. Frederick Barbarossa is in the great Kyffhausenberg in Thuringia. A shepherd crept to the heart of the mountain by a cave, and discovered therein a hall where sat the emperor at a table, through whose stone slab his red beard had grown and wound itself back toward his face. Rip Van Winkle slept twenty years in the Katskill Mountains. Napoleon Bonaparte is asleep somewhere. Mandeville says St. John yet sleeps at Ephesus, and the earth kindly swells and sinks to the rhythm of his breathing.

It is remarkable that through all these tales the number *seven* has such prominence. Barbarossa changes his seat every seven years. Charlemagne stretches himself at similar intervals. Olger Dansk stamps his iron mace on the floor once every seven years. Olaf Redbeard of Sweden opens his eyes at precisely the same distance of time. The curious coincidence has been thought to have some relation to the winter months of the north. But this does not explain the Hebrew sevens.

There is a myth that Moses drove the man to the moon who gathered sticks on the Sabbath. In Swabia a wood-chopper cast brambles in the way of church-goers, and an old woman made butter on Sunday. For their heinous crimes both were banished to the moon, and there they are to this day, bramble-bundle and butter-tub on backs. The man in the moon, the woman and her tub, the dog, the pole, the crime, the whole myth is of very ancient origin, probably reaching back to the worship of the heavenly bodies.

The terrestrial paradise has been located in China, Japan, some continent east of Asia, within three days' journey of Prester John's empire, an island in Australia, Ceylon, an unapproachable fastness in Tartary, the top of a very high mountain in the East, Armenia, trans-Gangic India, all toward the rising sun; while the ancient classics put the deathless land to the west. In his travels Sir John Mandeville comes to paradise and tastes of the waters of life; indeed he tells Englishmen he had "dronken three or four sithes" from the fountain. The Mediæval preacher Meffreth, who denies the immaculate conception, refuses also to accept the

Euphrates paradise, and hoists it above the possibility of Noah's flood. Its four rivers rush down to earth with such roar as to make coasters deaf. Eirek went to Constantinople and learnt of the emperor that the earth is a million of miles in circuit, and a hundred thousand and forty-five miles from heaven. But Eirek found the goal of his journeyings, and after bravely meeting the dragon that guarded the bridge, he marched, sword in hand, into the open maw of the beast, and in the transformation of a moment found himself in the world of beauty and everlasting life.

CHAPTER XXV.

THE OLD AND THE NEW.

STREAMING through all these curious religious fancies, is the *light* of the immortal destiny of spirit. Thus spirit perpetually declares its attractions, and prophetically announces its affiliations. It belongs to the eternal world of individualized, unselfish life; and its crudest intuitions and most infantile revelations point thitherward as unerringly as does "the needle to the pole." The grand old Hindoo poem, *The Bhagvat-Geeta*, according to Mr. Ripley of the *Tribune*, has been reprinted for Mr. G. P. PHILES, in the beautiful typography of the Bradstreet Press. It was originally translated from the Sanscrit, toward the close of the last century, at the instance of Warren Hastings, while Governor-General of India, and the present issue is a fac-simile of the English volume. The "Bhagvat-Geeta," forms an episode of a much larger work, which has been supposed to date from more than two thousand years before the Christian era, and containing an epic history of an ancient Hindoo dynasty. Oriental scholars have always found a favorite study in this poem, as illustrating the theological and ethical system of the Brahmins,—a form of religious mysticism congenial to the intellect of the East, and which has also been often known to captivate the imagination of more sturdy thinkers in European civilization. The work is in the form of a dialogue between Kreeshna, an incarnation of the Deity, and a favorite pupil, whom he instructs in the mysteries of creation, life, virtue, and immortality. In its ethical spirit it approaches the sublime stoicism of Marcus Antoninus and Epictetus, while its theology is founded on the conception of an Infinite Power and Godhead, that is the ground of all finite existence and consciousness, with which it becomes identified in act. "I am the sacrifice," says Kreeshna; "I am the worship; I am the spices; I am the invocation; I am the ceremony to the manes of the ancestors; I am the provisions; I am the fire, and I am the victim; I am the father and mother of this world; the grandsire, and the preserver. I am the holy one worthy to be known; I am the journey of the good; the comforter; the witness; the resting-place; the asylum, and the friend. I am generation and dissolution, the place where all things are reposited, and the inexhaustible seed of all nature. I am sunshine and I am rain; I now draw in, and I now let forth. I am death and immortality; I am entity and non-entity." The problem of human destiny, in its moral aspects, is solved in a similar manner. "A man being endued with a purified understanding, having humbled his spirit by resolution, and abandoned the objects of the organs; who hath freed himself from passion and dislike; who worshipeth with discrimination, eateth with moderation, and is humble of speech, of body, and of mind; who preferreth the devotion of meditation, and who constantly placeth his confidence and dispassion; who is freed from ostentation, tyrannic strength, vain glory, lust, anger, and avarice; and who is exempt from selfishness, and in all things temperate, is formed for being 'Brahm.' And thus being as 'Brahm,' his mind is at ease, and he neither longeth nor lamenteth. He is the same in all things, and obtaineth my (Kreeshna) supreme assistance; and by my divine aid he knoweth, fundamentally, who I am, and what is the extent of my existence; and having thus discovered who I am, he at length is absorbed in my nature." The principles of the "Bhagvat-Geeta" have become familiar to students of the history of philosophy by the admirable illustrations of M. Cousin, and readers of Emerson and Theodore Parker can trace both its ideas and its phraseology in some of the most characteristic writings of those authors.

Thus the Arabula shines, with a blaze of oriental conceptions of divine ideas, in the propositions and teachings of the Shaster and Vedas; manifesting the eternal glory of its presence as *perfectly* in the Indian as in the European consciousness. But new thoughts and new inspirations have penetrated the land of "The Bhagvat-Geeta," and the Light is appearing in new forms and higher human expressions.

Alphonse Esquiros, a French writer (to use the editor's preface), has written an admirable work on *Religious Life in England*, which contains a striking passage or two on the state of things in India. English ideas respecting liberty of conscience have loosened the bolts and bars of the old faith; the Indian temple tumbles into ruins in the sun, and ancient gods lie moldering in their wooden representatives, at the bottom of the wells, and nobody cares for them. But the new Hindoo is a "free inquirer;" and the English missionary who thinks he has only to fight with the

Buddha in that Hindoo finds that Voltaire, Colenso, Michelet, and Renan are as well known to the Hindoo as they are to freely inquiring Europeans. As a consequence, this is how we stand, religiously, abroad, after claiming a certain amount of triumph:—

"But Christians must not be too precipitate in rejoicing at this triumph; for the breaking up of the colossal edifice of Hindoo superstition seems but little likely to result in much profit to their own faith. Under various names, such as Brahmo-sijah, Brahmo-somaj, and Veda-somajam, a new sect has lately arisen, which stands aloof from all relations, true or false. The members of these Indian fraternities agree with each other in one point only—the belief in a Supreme Being. Opposed as they are both to Christianity and to the religion of the Hindoos, and finding, or thinking that they find, in the Bible, as well as in the Vedas, passages which are inconsistent with science, they determined, as they themselves say, to cut the cable which connects the minds of other men with supernatural authority. These disciples of rationalism are also distinguished by a liberal spirit of toleration, and they mutually engage to respect every opinion. They sometimes have to observe various customary ceremonies, as, for instance, in marriages and burials; but they only do this to avoid wounding the feelings of the community in which they live. With the exception of these trifling sacrifices to existing prejudices, their course of action indicates the greatest freedom of thought; they openly declare, that in all forms of religion which go beyond pure Deism, they can recognize nothing but the lifeless relics of worn-out superstitions. Associations such as these, surrounded by all the *éclat* which intellect and wealth can give, cannot fail to exercise a powerful influence over the educated youth of Bombay, Madras, and Calcutta. Thus a generation of thinkers is being formed, who astonish the English missionaries by the boldness and comprehensiveness of their philosophical opinions. When they speak at public meetings, the high moral tone which they assume defies the censure of the very Christians themselves; without making any distinction of race or country, they quote, in support of their ideas, all those authors, travelers, and *savants* who have, as it were, brought together the uttermost parts of the earth, and smoothed the way for the unity of the human race."

As some men are learned and sagacious without attending a university, so some men are religious and spiritual without attending a church. And tho timo will come when all men shall see and *know* the Light, "from the least to the greatest;" and unto it every knee "shall bow and every tongue confess," saying: "Behold, the height, length, breadth, and depth of True Religion are revealed and fulfilled in the union of man with the love, justice, power, and beauty of Omniscient goodness."

CHAPTER XXVI.

LAMPLIGHT AND SUNLIGHT.

INTELLECTUAL light, whose oil is sensuous observation and external experience, is lamplight; but the light of Wisdom is the light of the sun. By intellectual light we perceive and value the "things of sense;" while by the light of Wisdom, whose oil is derived from the immortal essential principles of all life, we perceive and accept the "truths of eternity."

Contemplate yourself! Do you not find "life" in your affections, and "death" in your sensuous interests? By the exercise of your intellectual faculties and perceptions, do you not achieve all your terrestrial and temporal success? When you use them exclusively, in conjunction with your selfish instincts, or ordinary affections and interests, do you not realize, at times, that the higher powers of your spirit are covered with a blinding skepticism concerning invisible things? Dark indeed is that temple when the "lights in the upper chamber" have gone out!

Now the instincts, which are the roots of the affections—the latter, when in full-orbed development, becoming INTUITION—are derived from the fountain of all life and light. But they are first radicals or roots—the same principles in animals as in men—and receive very properly the title of "instincts." Next, by a process of progressive development, they become refined and less selfish—looking after the interests and guarding the welfare of their own offspring and chosen darlings—and, still the same in animals as in mankind, they are known by the higher and more appropriate term "affections." Next, by a continuation of the progressively developing process, when they have rounded out into ultimations, magnanimous and beautiful—having "grown large, and public," and unselfish, but, above all things, loving whatsoever is Good, and Beautiful, and True, divine and eternal, with universal LOVE in their hearts, and everlasting LIGHT in their eyes, occupying the highest chambers in the temple, holding open converse with the very soul of Poetry, Music, Painting, and Mathematics — then they receive the lofty and significant title of "INTUITIONS." But the charmed and most holy name for them—which is above all other names for human endowments, signifying at once the possession, the exercise, and the fruition of the intuitive seers of the spirit—is WISDOM.

The opponent, the sworn antagonist of Wisdom, is Intellect. The instincts, in themselves the very quintessence of selfishness, are the natural allies of the intellectual faculties. Wisdom is a strange, supernatural faculty when viewed and measured by the earth-looking eyes of the Instincts. Even the "affections," properly so called, do not understand the royal nature and heavenly characteristics of Wisdom. The Affections rise like fruit-bearing branches out of the solid trunk of the tree of instinctive life. Therefore they sustain the same relation to Wisdom that is in nature established by the body of a tree, which is the sustaining and grand transmitting column of strength and growth, midway between the roots (or instincts) in the earth beneath and the fruit-boughs (or intuitions) in the heavens above. As it is impossible for the greater to be comprehended by the less, so is it impossible for the instincts to sympathetically fellowship with the Intuitions. And inasmuch as the instincts and the Intellect are natural allies, as the affections naturally take sides with Intuition, so is there a controversy, a struggle, perpetually going on in man's nature, as between the powers of darkness and the powers of light.

Why this antagonism should exist, in an organism elaborated by Omniscient goodness, I do not now halt to consider. Let us first *discover the fact;* then, under greater light, let us *utilize* the fact; thus, lastly, the *origin* and the *wherefore* of the fact will be revealed.

The theologians and religionists, and, indeed, the world's profoundest philosophers, seem not to have made this discovery. In classifying the human mind, the religionists and philosophers alike adopt the short definition—Sense, Will, and Understanding. Then churchmen bring in an indictment from the Grand Jury of old theology, to the effect that man's soul has offended God, by breaking one of his eternal laws. Wherefore a new definition is published: "Man's heart is desperately wicked, depraved totally, and his thinking powers are twisted and blighted by the curse of God." On this finding man is arrested, and brought for trial before the tribunal of Old Theology; whose throne is oriental mystery, whose history is the history of human tyranny and wretchedness, whose policy is opposed to all progress in science and knowledge, whose lever works on the fulcrum of human ignorance, whose power is almighty among the cowardly and superstitious, and whose government on earth will endure as long as there shall exist a million minds not touched by the spirit-lifting light of Wisdom.

The church's definition, therefore, is the church's explanation of this antagonism in man's spiritual constitution. Under their definition, what can they do, if they are logical, but trim their lamps and fill them with oil from the rock-fountains of St. Peter? The wondrous "light of other days" is their sun and their salvation. "The soul's return," not the soul's progress, is the burden of their evening prayer. They believe it was *a person* who said, "I am the light of the world." On this belief they all rush in "where angels fear to tread," and attempt to light their "humble tapers" by the lamp carried almost two thousand years ago by a Nazarene! With such belief the Christians cannot improve themselves, nor allow of improvement in others. They neither enter heaven, nor let others enter, but swing their Peter-oil lamps, and shout: "The curse of God is on thee! Haste ye! Haste ye! Bow down at the foot of the cross! Lay all your sins at the feet of Him who died to save the world!"

But the millions do not hear, and thousands of millions, they think, will never behold the "Light of God." They think heaven's blight and curse (O, beautiful consistency!) have passed over this hapless age; that the Eternal God has sent a strong delusion among men, that they might believe it and be damned; that the shipwrecking monsoon of Jehovah's Omnipotent wrath has swept through the world of human hearts; that, in a word, the whole family of man is at enmity with the spirit and purposes of God, and that this, and *this only*, will account for the antagonism, the darkness, the evil and misery in man's intellectual and spiritual constitution.

CHAPTER XXVII.

GOD IS MY LIGHT.

"God is my Light," the motto of the University of Oxford, "Deus illuminatio mea," originally slipped from the beautiful tongue of Arabula. Only the white light of Wisdom could have uttered the motto, which eternally shines with the golden rays of innumerable suns on the banners of all alumni now dwelling in Summer Lands.

"Ignorance is the curse of God," said the great dramatist, "but knowledge the light whereby we reach to heaven." Substitute the term "Wisdom" for knowledge, and how distinctly do you hear the voice of Arabula! What is that which is "without father, without mother, without descent, having neither beginning of days nor end of life?" Who was, who is, this mysterious impersonation called "Melchisedek," without beginning, reft of age and place, wandering all through the earth, yet above the world, independent, self-poised, gentle as an angel, with a universal heart, never sick, performing cures instantly, with a word and a breath, binding up the broken-hearted—this high-born noble impersonality, this friend of humanity, this sacred presence in the soul—Who? What? Whence? Whither?

No man's intellectual lamplight can bring this mysterious presence into photographic visibility. Wisdom, with her impersonal intuitions, is the only artist who can throw the image of the Angel-Arabula upon the burnished plate of the enlightened reason. Only that inextinguishable Light, which "lighteth every man that cometh into the world," can paint the formless personality of Melchisedek. Without this lifting light, "my soul is among lions;" without it, "I lie even among the children of men, that are set on fire, whose teeth are spears and arrows, and their tongue a sharp sword;" without this light "my days are full of darkness," the sweet life of "my God has forsaken me," and I "walk in a vain shadow" from day to day in my lonely journey down, down to the "land of the silent."

CHAPTER XXVIII.

FROM DEATH TO LIFE.

THAT the grave can open and the "dead arise," I *know;* for my Intellect, although impelled and flattered by the primal selfish instincts, "heard the Master's voice;" and I came forth clad in garments of purest white light; and then, O, how my whole heart prayed that I might be spared another journey back to dismal hades! There is no deeper, damning death—to the great powers of man's immortal mind—than that death which stills and kills every emotion and impulse, save the instinct of self-preservation and self-gratification—an instinct that works for Self—cost what it may to others.

My grave was dug not so deep as are the graves of some, for my death was only that of Intellect *versus* Wisdom; in the materialisms of which, the light of the angel of Intuition was well-nigh extinguished. But, Oh, joy! I saw the living light, and heard the love-laden voice of Arabula. It was a burning and "a shining light," and its voice was the voice of infinite and eternal Truth. "Marvel not at this," it said, "for the hour is coming in the which *all* that are in their graves shall hear my voice." Oh, glorious hour! when all the dead intellects and selfish animals in the shape of men shall hear the voice of the Light of God. I was fully prepared to believe that they who had tried *sincerely* to do good would come forth, as I did, to "the resurrection of life"—beautiful, free, progressive, loving life! While they who had employed their intelligence and selfish instincts to do evil would experience "the resurrection of damnation," — shameful, tyrannical, stultifying, shriveling, hateful death. Even this moment I shudder at the remembrance that, once, merely as my own selfish private luxury, I was "willing for a season to rejoice in the light" of the pure and holy Arabula.

But I had a positive evidence that my resurrection was true and perfect, and, I hoped, everlasting. My evidence was this: I had unfolded in my affections a powerful, sweet, *pure love for every thing human.* And I remembered that Arabula had said long, long ago: "We know that we have passed from death unto life, *because we love the brethren.*" Oh, how beautiful is Truth! It is death—dark, chilling, diabolizing, damning death—to hate a human being. Arabula is the perfect, the eternal love-light and light-love of the universe; and when it dwelleth in our superior consciousness, we not only love *it* without fear, but also love tenderly all humanity, and even the least and lowest things of the earth, and the earth itself; and likewise all things in the starry heavens, with a love that is unutterable, mysterious, sublime, and blossoming with happiness.

CHAPTER XXIX.

LOVE WORKING FOR OTHERS.

It is no part of my testimony that the Intellect, *per se*, is the source of all the follies and wickedness that have been perpetrated in the world. I would not weaken man's confidence in the natural excellence and inwrought integrity of his powers and endowments. It is against the fruits of the unresurrected intellect, which is based in selfish instincts and fed by experience solely derived through the five senses, that I protest with all my might.

Soon after my glorious intellectual resurrection,—when, hearing the awakening voice, I passed from "death unto life,"—I entered upon the work of serving and saving others. My pen and speech said: "Oh, brother man! fold to thy heart thy brother." The holy fire began to burn on the altar of my heart. When the Omnipotent power of fraternal love shall be *felt* by every one—

"Then shall all shackles fail; the stormy clangor
Of wild war music o'er the earth shall cease;
Love shall tread out the baleful fire of anger
And in its ashes plant the tree of peace."

No love seemed to me at that time so all-embracing and so heart-purifying as the *love fraternal*. Like the glory of the morning light, and yet more like the fertilizing warmth of the noontide sun, seemed that love which bound heart to heart, raised to the angel-state of unselfishness. Sounding in my soul were the familiar words—

> "How blest the sacred tie that binds,
> In union sweet, accordant minds."

In all moments, and in all places, I could feel the very life of the injunction, "Love ye one another." It has been truly said that one of the most beautiful words which our language has borrowed from the Greek is *Philanthropia;* or, as we have it, *Philanthropy,* signifying the "Love of Man." It has a musical sound; and the very utterance of it begets pleasant thoughts, and inspires prophecies of good. The truth it unfolds, and the lesson it teaches to the thoughtful, when we come to look into its meaning, make, as it were, a golden link in the chain which binds us to the good and the great of the past. They had their inspirations, those old men; they saw more or less clearly, at times, what ought to be among the nations, and caught sight of that sublime truth which recognizes the unity of our race. This word *Philanthropy* shows so much as this: A vision, however far off, of the relation existing between all men, as members of one great family; the duty and pleasure of loving and helping one the other; the dwelling together of the nations in peace, as being of the same flesh and blood and bone, and bound together by the ties of a common brotherhood and a common interest—these are the thoughts and feelings which must have lived somewhere, in some hearts, in the olden time; and which, struggling for utterance, gave birth to this beautiful and musical speech. Plain is it that to some true souls in the far-off ages of the Past these great truths were partially visible—at least a glimpse of them had been caught—else we had not known that noble and brave word *Philanthropy*. Let us rejoice in its existence, and seek to give a divine second birth in action.

Under the *plenum* of this holy power of love—the eternal tie, unselfish, which is the happiness of angels, and the principle which conjoins men and angels to God—under the blaze of this holy fire, with which my entire intellect accorded, I issued a call to all who would, if they knew how, "overcome evil with good." Policy, self-guarding cautiousness, I did not consult.

"Grown wiser for the lesson given,
  I fear no longer, for I know
That where the share is deepest driven,
  The best fruits grow."

The fact cannot be disguised, I said, that modern theories of sin, evil, crime, and misery are numerous and extremely conflicting. Not less antagonistic are existing laws, systems, and institutions respecting the rearing of children, and the treatment of criminals. The vindictive and coercive code has been for centuries administered to the workers of iniquity; yet vice and crime seem to be increasing in proportion to the spread of civilization. The progressive and benevolent everywhere begin to believe that this prevalence of crime and suffering is mainly traceable to *erroneous doctrines* respecting man and his acts, out of which have been evolved equally erroneous systems of education, tyrannical institutions, and depraving plans of punishment. Therefore it is believed that a true philosophy of human existence will ultimate in more ennobling institutions and philanthropic systems of education.

All thoughtful and humane persons, of every profession or form of faith, were invited to a convention, with a platform perfectly free to all who could throw what they believed to be true light upon THE CAUSE AND CURE OF EVIL.

It was urged that the question should be presented in all its aspects. And it was recommended that persons should come *prepared* to treat this subject with dignity and wisdom, from every stand-point of observation and discovery—the physical, social, political, intellectual, theological, and spiritual. The presence and influence of all true friends of Humanity were invoked, to speak and to hear dispassionately upon the causes of evil and misery; so that the best principles and truest remedies might be discovered and applied.

CHAPTER XXX.

THE SPIRIT OF BROTHERHOOD.

THE voice of Fraternal Love was heard by many, for *the Light* had reached and resurrected hosts of women and men not only, but a multitude of little children also, and the assemblage was large and influential. We gathered in the spirit of the "Progressive Friends," who said:—Mingling with the chime of church bells, and with the tones of the preacher's voice, or breaking upon the stillness of our religious assemblies, we heard the clank of the slave's chain, the groans of the wounded and dying on the field of bloody strife, the noise of drunken revelry, the sad cry of the widow and the fatherless, and the wail of homeless, despairing, poverty-driven

"By foul Oppression's ruffian gluttony
Forth from life's plenteous feast;"

and when, in obedience to the voice of God, speaking through the holiest sympathies and purest impulses of our Godlike humanity, we sought to arouse our countrymen to united efforts for the relief of human suffering, the removal of giant wrongs, the suppression of foul iniquities, we found the Church, in spite of her solemn professions, arrayed against us, blocking up the path of reform with her serried ranks, prostituting her mighty influence to the support of wickedness in high places, smiling complacently upon the haughty oppressor, "justifying the wicked for a reward," maligning the faithful Abdiels who dared to stand up for the truth, and to testify against popular crimes,—thus traitorously upsetting the very foundations of the religion she was sacredly bound to support and exemplify, and doing in the name of Christ deeds at which humanity shuddered, obliterating her indignant blushes only with the tears that welled up from the deeps of her great, loving heart.

In the plenitude of omniscient truth, and aided by the insight of intuition, I *felt*, although, intellectually, I did not fully concur with Byron, that—

"They never fail who die
In a great cause. The block may soak their gore;
Their heads may sodden in the sun; their limbs
Be strung to city gates and castle walls—
But still their spirit walks abroad. Though years
Elapse, and others share as dark a doom,
They but augment the deep and sweeping thoughts
Which overpower all others, and conduct
The world at last to freedom."

It was a sad, foreboding thought that my intellect did not, even after all my interior trials, quite come up in perception to the lofty standard revealed by Arabula. Oh, must I ever again go down into hades? Am I, intellectually, yet unborn? No, no; keep me from the hollow cave of doubt! Help, help, O ye angels of the sacred Summer Land! help me to stand on the solid rock of Wisdom, which gardenizes the earth, enlighteneth the intellect, pours light through all the ties and affections, and leadeth to God.

But the *fear* was born of the alarmed instinct of

caution. "I am not in darkness," said I; and "I will not borrow trouble."

At that very moment the love fraternal was beautifully burning and shining in my heart. Filled with its bounty, as the ocean is formed by uncounted rivers from mountain streams, I realized that the world-redeeming spirit of Brotherhood had descended from higher spheres.

Practical works of benevolence, deeds of fraternal love, efforts to overcome evil with good, labors for the uplifting of down-trodden millions, combinations for deepening justice and diffusing liberty throughout the land, mark the present day, and this, too, notwithstanding the mighty wars which now distract and threaten to disintegrate the nations, and in spite of the demon of sectarianism, that would overthrow the temples of brotherly love in every land. Truly said the poet—

"We are living, we are dwelling
In a grand, eventful time,
In an age on ages telling—
To be living is sublime."

Brotherhood, the sun of universal unity, beams with gladness over land and sea. A mighty spirit stands in the heavens before humanity, calling nations to repentance and urging individuals to action. Fraternity comes with the new morning, kindling a golden love-fire in every gentle heart, inspiring with new life and joy thousands who dwell far away beyond gilded hills and mountain summits, and strengthening mighty hosts with truths at once beautiful, heaven-revealing, heart-uplifting, and harmonious. The angelic song of "Brotherhood" comes from surrounding Summer-

Lands, and streams like a holy river through desert souls and humble homes—causing the very earth to rejoice, and the people to sing the hymns of gratitude.

Heaven's kingdom comes to mankind through man. It comes through manifestations of brotherly affection, through unselfish love, and through the saving deeds of unfolded wisdom. Chance and change, and the decay of ages, cannot efface from the soul the impress of fraternal love. Its changeless goodness is steadily poured into the open heart—causing it to swell like a fountain brimming over with the living waters of the Father's wisdom and the Mother's love. Such love brightens the spirit's sky, and lightens all life's burdens. In *misfortune* it enters at the open door, and saves your failing and falling soul. In *sickness* its gentle hand is outstretched to soothe and heal you. In *loneliness* it traces out your silent steps, and extends to you the hand of faithful friendship.

Believe me, the human heart is full of kindness, and is ever ready to overflow with angelic affection. Only in moments of blindness and impatience do men spurn one another, and violently trample down the fragrant flowers of fraternal love. Hand in hand, heart to heart, soul clinging to soul,—all equal children of God and Nature,—travelers in the path of one destiny,—all facing the same way,—all progressing together toward higher realms of life; thus, thus fraternally working and onward marching are mankind,—governed by the laws of necessity,—regulated by similar interests—and influenced to better growth by unchangeable principle. Let the world become better acquainted with itself, for you will find that

"There is no dearth of kindness
  In this world of ours;
Only in our blindness
  Take we thorns for flowers!
Cherish God's best giving,
  Falling from above;
Life were not worth living
  Were it not for LOVE."

Thus was born "THE MORAL POLICE FRATERNITY." Fraternal men and women enrolled themselves beneath its broad banner, bearing the motto: "LET NO ONE CALL GOD, FATHER, WHO CALLS NOT MAN, BROTHER." The members, while receiving and enjoying the co-operation of minds who inhabit higher spheres, held that natural, persistent, progressive agencies were required to bring the heavenly state on earth. The effect of the fraternity was to harmonize the ideas and sentiments of its members, and to direct their benevolence and labors upon individuals in discord, in misfortune, in sickness, in prison, in poverty, in crime, in ignorance, and in misery.

A humanitarian movement so natural and fraternal, or something akin to it, I thought, would build its altars throughout civilization. Its plan of operation was broad, comprehensive, philanthropic, and practical. The ends of charity and justice to individuals can be surely and quickly accomplished through the instrumentality of a self-moving body so simply and effectively organized. I thought that every person would wish to become a "member" of an organization in which no one member could "suffer" without attracting the attention and securing the *sympathy* of "the whole body." Unlike many self-protective and beneficial societies, this plan did not exclude Woman from any of its departments, privileges, or benefits. A solemn covenant was thus made between man's spirit-inmost, the universe of Angels, and the Most High.

It was urged that a lost and "a shipwrecked Brother" could not be reached and saved unless the Body had "living members" in every part of the land. Fraternities, with few signs and secrets, should multiply, and they *will*. Darkness and despair will roll away from human hearts on the approach of these redeemed Brothers and Sisters. The lamps of Hope will once more shine o'er man's bewildered lot; in the secret chambers of long-suffering hearts a new life will come forth; and homeless women, young and old, under equal care, and blest by faithful justice, will stand resurrected by the side of their noblest brothers.

A mighty lever for accomplishing good among the millions was thus born,—a Christ in the manger, over whom the angels sang "glad tidings of great joy—peace on earth, good-will to all men." Who can do more for the individual than a loving-hearted woman or man? "Though wandering in a stranger-land," the truly fraternal is the sure medium of loving-kindness to a Brother or a Sister in affliction. The morning stars did not more harmoniously chant the songs of truth. Just think of overcoming evil, and shedding, whenever you can, light and love in desert hearts! To prevent crimes, to lessen evils, to remove ignorance, to lift the fallen, to brighten the weapons of truth, to oppose intemperance, to resist sectarianism, to overcome passion, to strengthen virtue, to dethrone tyranny, to promote progress, to do all the good you can to whomsoever and wheresoever. What mission more full of human sympathy and love, or more grateful to grief-stricken, time-tossed, joy-bereft, suffering, saddened humanity? Your spirit will grow under the warmth of heavenly blessings. With wide-extended arms it will impartially embrace the acquaintance and the stranger, and freely shower fertilizing influences upon kindred, neighbors, foes, and friends.

CHAPTER XXXI.

A CHILLING WIND.

A FEW kindred ones residing in the metropolis, into whose inner life the light of Arabula had penetrated, engaged actively in the work; and seven of the number were, by the people interested, elected trustees and managers of the institution for the first year. They procured the legal certificate of incorporation, under and by virtue of an Act passed by the Legislature of the State of New York, in the year 1848, entitled, "An Act for the Incorporation of Benevolent, Charitable, Scientific, and Missionary Societies," and Acts subsequently passed. And it was declared in the application, that "the business and objects of said Association are to furnish aid to the destitute, instruction to the ignorant and degraded, and employment and homes to the poor and friendless, and thus take away incentives to crime."

The few workers hoped much and accomplished much. There was a beautifulness in the righteousness of their free offerings. It was felt to be a glorious privilege, and not a hardship and a dry duty, to work for those in poverty and disease.

But the imp of Selfishness arose like Apolyon in our path; not in the associated workers, but in those for whom they worked. Impostors, simulating abject poverty, attempted to avail themselves of our bounty; ten of this class would apply for assistance, to one *real* case of sorrow and despair. We found these real cases, and exposed the impostors, by a careful system of visitation. The name and residence of every applicant were entered upon a journal. Then letters bearing such name and address were immediately sent to two members of the association, requesting the recipient to forthwith investigate the case recorded. Care was specially taken that neither had knowledge of the other's intended visit. The object was to get from two investigators (one a man and the other a woman) of the same case, testimony which could be compared and made a basis of work in the applicant's behalf. The facts and the fictions developed by the visitors were elicited by asking the applicant's occupation? Age? Place of birth? Whether married, widowed, or single? How long in country, or city? Number of persons for whom relief is asked? Whether relief is received from any relative or acquaintance? Whether assisted by any charitable institution, and how much? Any means of support, and what are they? Member of any Church or religious society? If any sick; how many, and how long? These questions were put by each visitor.

The cupidity and rapacity of the instinct of Selfishness came out in bold relief. It being ascertained that ten-elevenths of all applicants were self-seeking, dirty, idle, aimless social impostors, the members changed their labors somewhat, so as to search out and help the really suffering. I need not dwell upon the amount of holy work performed by this quiet method. We did not let our right hands know what our left hands accomplished; and although the good done was not large, the *quality* was like the love of angels.

Our usefulness was limited by the lack of money in

our treasury. One day, while walking through the street, "filled with an ever-shifting train," I met a wealthy merchant acquaintance, who kindly asked, "What are you doing now days?"

"Many things," I replied: "Editing and publishing, lecturing twice on the first day of the week (usually called Sunday), superintending a Progressive Lyceum full of children, acting as president and treasurer of the Moral Police Fraternity, and constantly and courageously searching for truth."

"Well" (with a cold, practical, hardened, selfish, sarcastical expression spreading over his honest countenance), "you've got a damn big job on hand."

"Yes," said I, just a little thrown back upon myself; "yes, but before me lies all eternity, and you know I do not like idleness."

"What are you trying to do with that Fraternity?"

"We are trying to help those in trouble, and to prevent crime, by helping the poor (specially poor women) to remunerative employment."

"That *sounds* very well, very well, very well indeed; but, my dear sir, it won't amount to a row of pins." And he sent the atmosphere of his cold eyes upon me, with an arrogant, self-conceited positiveness which produced an effect analogous to a northwest wind suddenly blowing upon one's warm flesh in the middle of August.

But I replied: "We have already done many charitable things, helping and saving more than one homeless girl and boy, and aiding many wounded soldiers on their weary way to anxious friends at home."

"I'll tell why you won't succeed," he rejoined. "You are not doing your work in the name of Jesus Christ."

"True, neither do we work in the name of Lincoln, President; nor in the name of Napoleon, emperor; nor in the name of Confucius, philosopher; nor in the name of Socrates, psychologist—but, instead, we work in the presence of God and angels, and in *the name of Humanity.*"

"You don't understand me," resumed the merchant. "What I mean is, it matters not how pretty your language is, your charitable plans, and all that. If you don't work under the wings of some established religious denomination, your institution will be bankrupt in six months."

"We propose," I answered, "to work independent of any sectarian body, and do good where we can to a Hindoo the same as a Christian, making no difference on account of country, sex, color, or belief. And yet the Fraternity affiliates and co-operates, as far as practicable, with the municipal police, all charitable institutions, school systems, and industrial associations, in accordance with objects set forth in the 'Letter of Instructions,' for the detection and overthrow of ignorance, poverty, injustice, corruption, and tyranny—for the overcoming of evil with good, and the development of the Kingdom of Heaven on earth."

"All that's well enough, well enough, but you can't succeed."

"Our treasury is rather low," said I. "Cannot you do something?"

"No, I have as much as I want to do to take care of my own family. They must go to meeting somewhere, and I am now paying all I can afford for that purpose." And the feathery fumes of his first-class cigar covered my face, and so besmoked the air I could scarcely breathe. I said:—

"Allow me to ask you a question?"

"Certainly, certainly, my dear sir—go on."

"Do you smoke cigars every day?"

"Yes; every day for the past ten years; my cigars, and a glass of lager now and then, is about all the damn comfort I have during business hours."

"Well, be kind enough to tell me exactly how much your cigars *cost* you per annum?"

"Well, let me see. Oh, I don't smoke all I buy, you understand. A gentleman must always look out for the comfort of his friends, you know. Well, let me think. Excuse me, your question is rather impertinent, ain't it?"

"Oh, no; not at all. Not being a smoker myself, I am naturally a little curious to know."

"Well, well; all right. Three times ten are thirty, add five; multiply thirty-five by twelve, makes four hundred and twenty. Yes, that's about it. Four hundred and twenty dollars a year I pay for cigars."

"Now," said I, kindly, "I shall not say one word about the filthiness, the uselessness, the unwholesomeness of tobacco; but this proposition I make to you:— That you pay into the treasury of the Fraternity every year just *half* the money you spend for cigars, and you, having an expensive and fashionable family, need not increase expenditures, if you will smoke just half the amount of the narcotic weed."

The merchant smiled scornfully, not to say bitterly and revengeful, looked at his watch, stiffly bowed, blushed with a momentary sense of unworthiness, and rapidly walked away. But I felt a chilling wind whistling and shrieking around my heart.

CHAPTER XXXII.

STRENGTH OUT OF WEAKNESS.

The merchant was a true prophet. He was, he is, a positive, selfish, intelligent, go-a-head man of the world. All matters of public financial interest engage his best powers. He spends twelve thousand dollars a year for a fashionable family life and household conveniences. He is a decided *force* in the great city of America, and *he* knows it. He is majestically self-conceited, arrogant, dogmatic, and yet blest with a large nature, and, being full of warm animal, social, convivial instincts, he is a first-rate club man, a successful merchant, influential in political circles, always gets elected to a high office under the City Government, attends a rich up-town church once every Sunday; and yet, in secret, is four-fifths an atheist; but, in the reserved fifth part of his nature, longs for the celestial light of Arabula, and takes every opportunity to investigate the scientific relations between mankind and the inhabitants of the Summer Land.

But he sent a thrill of horrible doubt into my warm heart. The dreary darkness of hades once more opened before me, but I did not enter there. The Arabula had beautifully spoken to my soul through Emerson: "Our strength grows out of our weakness. The indignation which arms itself with secret forces does not awaken until we are pricked and stung, and sorely assailed. A great man is always willing to be little. Whilst he sits on the cushion of advantages, he goes to sleep. When he is pushed, tormented, defeated, he has a chance to learn something; he has been put on his wits, on his manhood; he has gained facts; learns his ignorance; is cured of the insanity of conceit; has got moderation and real skill. The wise man throws himself on the side of his assailants. It is more his interest than it is theirs to find his weak point. The wound cicatrizes and falls off from him like a dead skin, and when he would triumph, lo! he has passed on invulnerable. Blame is safer than praise. I hate to be defended in a newspaper. As long as all that is said is said against me, I feel a certain assurance of success. But as soon as honeyed words of praise are spoken for me, I feel as one that lies unprotected before his enemies. In general, every evil to which we do not succumb is a benefactor. As the Sandwich Islander believes that the strength and valor of the enemy he kills passes into himself, so we gain the strength of the temptation we resist. * * * * Let a stoic open the resources of man, and tell men they are not leaning willows, but can and must detach themselves; that with the exercise of self-trust, new powers shall appear; that a man is the word made flesh, born to shed healing to the nations; that he should be ashamed of our compassion, and that the moment he acts from himself, tossing the laws, the books, idolatries, and customs out of the window, we pity him no more, but thank and revere him,—and that teacher shall restore the life of man to splendor, and make his name dear to all history."

CHAPTER XXXIII.

THE FACE OF HUMAN LIFE.

THE face of human life is more wondrous and beautiful than imagination can paint, when seen in the tender and holy "light" which cometh from above. Though sundered far, yet, as by an ineffable tie of imitation, all men come very near together, and consociate kindly as members of one family.

One morning, not long after the last conversation, the tranquil deep and quickening "light" filled the world with golden grandeur. It seemed to illuminate, with a sweet expression of unusual gladness, "the melancholy face of human life." Streams of golden beauty flooded the lowest caves of poverty and wretchedness. In that beauty I saw descending a spirit of mercifulness, a magnetic rain of holy tenderness, dripping through the Stygian darkness that hung over our rudimental sphere. It changed the hideous night of human evil into a bright, happy day. The rivers of life swelled with the fullness of gladness, and the oceans of love ebbed and flowed musically, with the reciprocal rhythmical tides of infinite wisdom.

In that light I contemplated society in different parts of the world. And there and then was born in my bosom, with a grander power for work, an infinite hope and trust; yea, a higher *knowledge* of the possibilities and achievements in the future history of human nature And I saw that:—

"No radiant pearl, which crested fortune wears—
No gem that twinkling hangs from beauty's ear;
Nor the bright stars, which night's blue arch adorn,
Nor rising suns, that gild the vernal morn,
Shine with such luster, as the tear that breaks
For others' woe, down virtue's manly cheeks."

But knowing that some of my fellow-workers did not perceive the "face of human life," either in its "better or worse" aspects, I went to my desk and painted the picture, and mapped-out the field of work for philanthropists, thus:—

1. Vagrant Children.—Thousands are born and cradled amid scenes of drunkenness, beggary, sensuality, and crime. They are early taught the low vices of the rum-hole, dance-house, and brothel. Talk with them in the spirit of an angel's love. Find out where they sleep, what they do day by day, and by what means they obtain their subsistence. Many of them beg, others peddle, some pilfer, and too many *sell* themselves to secure a living.

2. Orphans.—Many, having ignorant and vile parents, are orphaned from their earliest moments. Their tenderest and most spiritual impulses are crushed; their tongues are trained to the language of ignorance, cruelty, and vice; houseless, forsaken, hungry, dirty, and immoral, they are *orphans*, and, like those who have no parents, need your solicitude, loving-kindness, and protection. All such want good homes in the country. The warmth of spiritual hearts will elevate their affections and purify their lives.

3. Diseased.—Give to such a few words of instruction concerning the laws and conditions of Life and

Health. Caution them against the evils arising from the use of alcohol and tobacco. Encourage them to abandon all habits which tend to prostration, sensuality, and disease. A few words may, in after years, take root and save the little sufferer. Bestow healing from your magnetic hands. Let no opportunity of doing good escape you.

4. Street Quarrels.—Children whose birthplace was in the midst of dissipation and crime, are quarrelsome and profane in the streets. Never fail to speak to either boys or girls when you see them disputing, or hear them using vulgar and profane language. Step in between them at once, but invariably with great gentleness. Ascertain, if possible, the cause of their quarrel and fighting. Explain the better way. Instruct them to walk in the paths of wisdom. They will feel and acknowledge that you love them; and that, though a stranger, you are a true *friend* to them.

5. Destitute Women.—There are multitudes of this class—young girls, and women of all ages—who need timely counsel and wise assistance. They want faithful friends, and opportunities to gain their living by honest toil. Superintendents of the Poor, the Commissioners of Emigration, and the Governors of the Almshouse have great duties and responsibilities in behalf of this class of women. You should know what can be done with and through these Institutions. You can point out to many a lone heart the way to industry, purity, and happiness. Be a true guide to the stranger, and a source of strength to the poor and fallen.

6. Unfortunates.—Many have gone into misfortune and crime. They wait your healing friendship. They

have had no society but that of vice-incrusted men—swearers, drunkards, thieves, profligates, and criminals. They want you to speak to their souls the words of fraternal welcome to a higher life. Give them knowledge of the angels. Unfold to their minds the Father's wisdom and the Mother's love. Find a kind home for the honest-hearted girl, and procure profitable labor for the impoverished and broken-spirited woman.* She is your unfortunate Sister. She is pure and beautiful within. You will meet her after death in the Summer Land. Fail not to do her much good.

7. Imprisoned.—Hundreds of women have abandoned themselves to low vices—petit larcenies, pauperism, and other misdemeanors from which you can arrest and wholly redeem them. By the sentence of the Court, under the laws of the State, such Sisters are imprisoned like masculine criminals of deeper depravity. Thus they fall beneath self-respect, into a moral condition *below* the state from which they offended the interests of society. They need your timely aid. If possible, keep them from prison. Stand between them and the requisitions of the law. Shield them from the impertinent questionings of lawyers. Let your fraternal love warm the heart of the criminal woman. Let the light of your better faith shine upon her pathway. No part of your work can be more successful.

8. Intemperate Men.—The rum-shop is the death-gate of society. It is the fountain of want, wretched-

* Recently a movement has been inaugurated for "Working Women" in New York, which, if it can be kept non-sectarian, will accomplish desirable results. What is now most needed is a "Temporary Home" for girls and young-women who seek aid to rise from evil.

ness, beggary, vice, cruelty, crime, and sensuality. Sore-eyed, dirty, filthy, houseless, forsaken, hungry children are born and cradled in the hovels, garrets, damp cellars, and loathsome alleys which are sought by the victims of intemperance. In this city the youthful population—the offspring of intemperate parents—consists of "newsboys," "street-sweepers," "dock-boys," "beggars of cold victuals," "cinder-snipes," "peddlers of stolen articles," "boot-blacks," and "dead-rabbits." There are fifty thousand children in New York who never enter any place of instruction. The cause of this over-population of unfortunates is intemperance. Thousands of children originate in sensuality. Of 32,172 men sent to prison in one year, 30,200 were victims of alcohol. These men want your fraternal arms to arrest them in their career. They can be saved through love and truth. Instruct them in the laws of life and immortality. Impress them with the "consequences" of their bodily and mental habits. Teach them concerning the life after death—of the realities of the Summer Land—where the results of the practices in this life are revealed as parts of the individual's character.

9. Criminals.—This class is large and increasing. They are for the most part men who emanate from foreign penitentiaries and foreign poor-houses. Such characters are shipped to this country, and our jails, State-prisons, almshouses, and asylums become filled with them. Yet they are children of Father God,—the offspring of good Mother nature,—and are destined to live and bloom in the gardens of eternity. They are Irish, Germans, Italians, English, French, Polanders,

Welsh, Portuguese, Hungarians, Scotch, and Africans. The cost to the people of the United States, of arresting, convicting, and punishing these criminals, is enormous—being not less than $19,000,000 (nineteen million dollars) every year. The combined salaries of the lawyers amount to $35,000,000 per annum. Tobacco and rum—the active agents of vulgarity and crime—cost *one hundred and forty millions* ($140,000,000) every year. Of course criminals are being rapidly multiplied. Intemperance is at the bottom of it all. The condition of these criminals calls for *your* fraternal love and good works. From their imprisonments they beseech you to visit them. Eternity alone can reveal the good your ministrations may do for them. Some of them are weary and broken-hearted; others are bitter toward their enemies, and vindictive; the first need strength, and the latter demand the lessons of wisdom. You can convey glad tidings to their grateful hearts. Lead them out of darkness, and obtain their pardon. There will be joy in heaven when *one* such is redeemed from his discords and evil.

10. Disabled Animals.—Always be ready to assist the fallen, whether animal or human. The lower kingdoms should feel the gentle, healing love of your justice and harmony. The harmonial age should descend, like a universal blessing, to the fishes, birds, and animals. They live for us, and serve us day by day, and are susceptible to the law of kindness.

11. The Abused.—Cruelty and injustice should not be meted out to dependent creatures. Whipping, stoning, maiming, teasing, or otherwise abusing creatures beneath man, should not be permitted. It is

your duty to arrest the attention of men or boys whenever they transgress the law of kindness.

12. FIGHTING.—It is especially your mission to separate animals, as well as men or boys, who may be engaged in fighting. Street fights and neighborhood quarrels come within your sphere of operations. Always be peacemakers.*

"All history shows," says a magazine writer, "that familiarity with the sufferings of inferior animals infallibly leads to cruelty toward one's own species. Tastes are vitiated, hearts hardened, minds brutalized by such acts, till they acquire an *appetite* and thirst for blood. Thus the barbarities of the Coliseum, where polished Romans sought their sport and pastime in the savage rending and dying agonies of brute animals, led in due time to the demand for hecatombs of human sacrifices; and who can tell how often from such scenes as these veterinary amphitheaters of France, reeking with the warm blood of writhing victims, may have gone forth a Nemesis to mete out the same measure to the sons and daughters of the land?

"In the hideous catalogue of cruelties which have marked each successive revolution in that country, human creatures have, in numberless instances, been mangled, mutilated, and tortured to death with equally ruthless indifference. 'Murders were committed wholesale,' as one of their own writers has observed, 'not from any lust or revenge, or avarice, but merely from the luxury to the perpetrators of seeing their victims die, to feast

* Since the suspension of the Moral Police, "A Society for the Prevention of Cruelty to Animals" has been duly organized in New York, and is doing great good.

the ear with their groans, and to delight the eye with their contortions,' till these fiends in human form attained to such a refinement of cruelty, that witnesses of their deeds are known to have died with horror.

"Time was, as Pope tells us, when our huntsmen passed upon the ladies of quality who were present at the death of a stag, the savage compliment of putting the knife into their hands, to cut the throat of a helpless, trembling, and weeping creature; but times and manners have changed. Our women are now cast in softer mold, and loathe the infliction *and the inflictor* of cruelty. The bare recital of these atrocities moves them to tears. Surely in the land where Rosa Bonheur has shown upon the glowing canvas—in touches of nature which make us feel 'the whole world kin'—how like ourselves horses may be in their affections and their joys, there are not wanting noble women who can feel that, like us, these poor dumb fellow-creatures of ours have their sufferings, too—miseries enough from the injustice and ingratitude of man, without any aggravation of them from his wanton barbarity. Surely in a country which sends forth her Sisters of Charity in thousands, to minister, with unwearied self-devotion, to suffering humanity, some good angels will be found to set about this work of mercy—a task which will win for them the honor of the good and the brave, and be not unremembered of Him whose 'tender mercies are over *all* His works.'"

Of criminals much might be written. The history of Windsor Prison (Vt.) was investigated, and the following testimony on the religious question is submitted: "It has been very often said that the convicts of State prisons are either Atheists, Deists, or Universalists, than which, however, nothing can be further from the truth. I have known as many as five hundred while they were in confinement, and I have always made it a practice to learn the religious opinions of all with whom I have conversed, and what I am going to write may be depended on as the actual result of my personal inquiries.

"Those whom I have known have been educated in the doctrines of the endless punishment school, and but few have departed from these doctrines. I have found only two Atheists, not one Deist, and but one Universalist. *The doctrine of endless punishment is*—strongly and broadly speaking—*the orthodoxy of State prisoners.* I am confident of the truth of this statement, and I make it not by way of slur, or insinuation against any sect of Christians, but as a fact which all denominations may use as they may have occasion. Very many of the convicts have been members of churches, and a few of them have been preachers. This is a subject of painful reflection; it shows how extremely liable the best of men are to be overcome temptation, and says to those who glory in their strength, 'Let him that thinketh he standeth tak lest he fall.'"

CHAPTER XXXIV.

THE GREATEST WONDER OF ALL.

THE bells of Time tolled solemnly one evening, and I heard a voice, which made me tremble through and through—a voice which poured out of the sky like the mellow-throated nightingale, yet sad with the holy depth of an angel-mother's love—the same voice that I had heard years and years ago, when first journeying up and down the mountains with the Magic Staff, saying: "*Gather-in-the-Children; they-will-bring-to-earth-the-Kingdom-of-Heaven.*"

"Thanks! thanks!" I exclaimed. "Your voice, mother, never before sounded so sweetly; never did it impart a message more welcome."

And from that hour my work was specially directed to the discovery of the laws and needs of the spirit of Childhood. The brightest blossoms in the land, I saw, were children. The greatest angels were planet-born and reared by terrestrial parents. Little children die, but they at once ascend in the arms of their celestial friends, and by them are led into heavenly paths, where love and wisdom bloom with an immortal beauty. The sky-schools must be discovered, revealed, and instituted. The starry ways of wisdom are ways of pleasantness. Let us look clairvoyantly into "those mighty spheres that gem infinity;" let our eyes convey inwardly the high meanings of the mountains, the leaves, and the streams of the Summer Land.

Panoplied by this consecration and positive resolve, the rough squalls and chilling winds of adult selfishness could no longer visit me. The haughtiness and limitations of the questioning intellect could not now return. Pure white clouds began to float in the clear blue of my spirit's sky. They were filled with the dewy blessings of skies infinitely more lofty and superpernal.

The work was before me, extending into the future like an unlimited landscape, and I accepted it.* All my friends wondered, and many objected to the misappropriation of time and powers susceptible of a wider range. It seemed to them that I had deserted the army of great progressive labors, and gone over to the trifling occupation of "keeping a Sunday-school." But the "light" shone around me unceasingly; the Magic Staff was firmly in my grasp; and so, whether understood or misunderstood, my path was straight, my work was beautiful, and the yoke easy to bear.

Very soon I discovered that *the greatest wonder in the world is a baby.* It is a little world of miracles, a little separate sphere of infinite possibilities, incognizant of the world around it; with wondrous eyes wide open; its screaming, laughing, sighing mouth; its fair, sweet, round form; the autocratic impatience of its tiny hands; its flower-like unfoldings from day to day; the future-feeling hand of its whole instinctive nature; yea,

---

* What was discovered and practically put forth, the reader can find in the author's Manual for "Children's Progressive Lyceums."

the greatest wonder is a little, a very little child—lying trustingly, sleeping, waking, crying, crowing, on the ever-welcoming bosom of its mother.

How expressive the words of an English writer, Mr. James Martineau:—"There is no sentiment more natural to thoughtful minds than that of reverence for childhood. Many sources both of mystery and love meet in the infant life. A being so fresh from non-existence seems to promise us some tidings of the origin of souls: a being so visibly pressing forward into the future, makes us think of their tendency. While we look on the 'child as father of the man,' yet cannot tell of *what kind* of man—all the possible varieties of character and fate appear for the moment to be collected into that diminutive consciousness; that which may be the germ of any, is felt as though it were the germ of all; the thread of life, which, from our hand that holds it, runs forward into instant darkness, untwines itself there into a thousand filaments, and leads us over every track and scene of human things;—here through the passages where poverty crawls; there, to the fields where glory has its race;—here, to the midnight lake where meditation floats between two heavens; there to the arid sands where passion pants and dies. Infancy is so naturally suggestive, it is the representative of such various possibilities, that it would be strange did we not regard it with a feeling of wonder.

"There was a theory in ancient times, and somewhat revived in these days, that the souls of all men come hither from a pre-existent state, where they dwelt within the shelter and near the light of God; where truth and love were as affluently poured on perception, as light and sound upon the senses here; and the sublimest thoughts of beauty, of virtue, of science, of Deity, streamed amid the spirits of that purer air, like sunbeams amid the clouds, bathing them in glory. Birth into this world was the transference of the mind from a celestial to an earthly life; its benumbing contact with material things; its retirement from the boundless and brilliant freedom of a spiritual life, to the dark and narrow cave of a corporeal being. The further it advanced into the interior of its mortal existence, and the more skilled it became in groping along the ways of experience, the more faint grew the impression of the immortal region it had left, and the more dim were the rays of reminiscence that yet painted a divine vision on its path. Education was a process of forgetfulness; the gradual extrusion of the godlike by the human; the drowning of abstract truth in experimental knowledge; the tapering-off of sublime perceptions of the universal into mean individual sensations. When, under the influence of this doctrine, Plato looked upon a child, he saw through that shell of life an intelligence fresh from God; it was a star dropped from its sphere. Still filled with dreams and memories of the invisible, half present still in its divine abode, it was a thing of sanctity to behold; for its orb of existence floated yet on the margin of the unknown world, and, though creeping on to be eclipsed by the shadows of mortality, had its edge yet illumined by the past.

"But childhood presents not the wreck, but the elements, of a heavenly existence; not the ruin, but the design, of a temple not made with hands. Its glory is not of the past, but of the future; its experience is to be not a loss, but a gain, of truth and goodness; its education here, not a vain struggle to preserve memories that inevitably vanish, but an aspiration, which can never disappoint the willing heart, after mental and moral excellence, rising always to more godlike forms. It were a task of sadness to take up the infant life, as if it were the fallen petals of a celestial flower, borne to our feet by the stream of things, and every moment fading more; but it is a task of gladness to accept it as the seed and germ of an everlasting growth, which, planted in the rock, and strengthened by the storms of earth, shall bloom at length in the eternal fields.

"To educate a child is an office of which no one can think lightly. To administer perceptions, and unfold the faculties in their season and proportion; to give power to the affections, without impairing their symmetry; to develop, in their right order, and to their full intensity, the great ideas of duty and of God; to exhibit human virtues and relations in so beautiful an aspect, that the soul may pass from them with ease to the venerating love of the Infinite Mind, is a task of responsibility so solemn, as to invest every parent's life with the sanctity of a divine mission.

"If the philosopher's doctrine had been the true one, and the soul had been like a bird fallen from the skies, —its plumage soiled in the dust, and its forces drooping in our heavier air—it would seem a cruel office to stimulate it to ascend again, by convulsive efforts, to an element native, but natural no more. But as the truth really stands, we have not to provoke a strength jaded and expiring, but to aid and develop one that is half formed; ourselves to bear it awhile into the heights 'as upon eagles' wings;' and then launch it from the precipice alone, to sweep down the gale, and soar into the light it loves.

"Many, however, have but a feeble impression of the delicacy and responsibility of this task—of training the early mind to aspire, by the power of the noblest ideas. There is no department of education in which wrong methods are so fatal;—in which the conveyance of a thought into the mind at an unhappy moment, or by an unhappy process, may leave a more indelible and prejudicial effect; in which the penetrative and considerate spirit of sympathy—which is the true secret of educational as of all other moral power—is more absolutely demanded; in which different minds more require to have their individuality consulted; yet is there none to which a more hard, technical, and wholesome system is applied."

CHAPTER XXXIV.

MOODS AND TIDES.

THE new work prospered and expanded over the land, because its spirit-foundations, holy aims, and attractive methods harmonized with the rational sense and the primal instincts of every non-sectarian father and mother. But infinitely more will it prosper and bear the fruits of righteousness in the great future of humanity.

Oh, the happy, happy faces of the thronging children! Oh, their songs of gladness! Oh, the warm kisses of spontaneous, innocent, unselfish affection! Oh, the free, tender touch of their open hands! Oh, the tuneful tread of their marching feet! I do not wonder that Pythagoras, and Plato, and Jesus, and John, all true men, and that all true mothers, love, welcome, worship children. There can be no "kingdom of heaven" without these little angels of immortality!

Who can, who will, paint the picture of an outcast, vagrant, lost child? "We reformers," writes a friend of children, "who are mindful of what we seek, find none that are *entirely* bad. There is always to be found, by those who diligently search for good, a ray of moral light, or truth, or beauty, even in the most depraved, revealing that link in the chain of being which connects the Divine Mind with the lowest, the most unfortunate of His children. And these poor creatures are not to be blamed because they are vulgar, and licentious, and profane—no more than because they are hungry, and their clothes are ragged, and their skins dirty; for good moral example and teaching could no more be found in their miserable attics and cellars, than wholesome food, and tidy garments, and pure water. And now, as I look at them more closely, I can see an expression of discontent—of strange and vacant wonder, as if at the present distribution of things; and their large wild eyes look out from the tangled meshes of their shadowing hair with a longing earnestness, as if, in the face of all experience, they had faith, yet, that some good—a little good—would come—even to them. The expression was infinitely touching; and as I continued gazing on the poor little creatures, my whole soul dissolved within me.

"How quickly they were sensible of the interest I felt; for the perceptions of these wretched itinerants are necessarily, educated; and while they were again clamorous for charity, or their sweeping fees—for they had been, for a moment, hushed—one of them looked up, with the largest, bluest, saddest eyes I ever saw, holding out her little hand with a silent gesture of entreaty. There was something so beautiful in the act, so gentle, so imploring, and at the same time so sweetly confident of help, that my heart was filled with a strange and pleasing wonder, and I forgot to reply to her demand, but stood gazing earnestly into the depths of those uplifted eyes. There was nothing wrong there. They were clear, and deep, as the living wells of Truth—but, oh, how sorrowful! She returned my gaze by a look that seemed struggling to utter, in a single moment, all the brokenness of that little suffering heart; and then the lids fell with a sweet and modest expression, and the long fringes rested upon a cheek which I could see through the spatters of mud was pale as marble. I whispered to her, as I placed in her hand a shilling, asking: 'Where is your home, my little girl?'—'Home' she repeated, in a voice that seemed the concentrated melody of sorrow, 'indeed I don't know!' It was the saddest voice of a child I ever heard; and the saddest sight I ever saw, was the poor little desolate creature weeping—the tears carrying the mud in stripes down her pale face—and unfeeling boys, and ladies, too, laughing jocosely at her appearance, as they went by. But I knew there was a sad story behind those beautiful eyes."

Another child-lover says:—"When little three-year-old sister lays her fair cheek against mine, and, with dimpled arms clasped around my neck, prattles in her innocent way, don't I think of the path her little feet must tread? Are there any thorns to pierce them—any pits into which she may fall? Now I think of it, I must tell you of her little speeches. I think she is so cunning—though perhaps I am partial; if so, pardon. One night last week she crept into my lap, and, ere I was aware of it, fell asleep. I took her up to her little bed, but before putting her in, I said—'Nellie must not forget her little prayer.' She commenced—

'Now I lay me down to sleep.'

"'Dod knows the rest,' she murmured; and the white lids closed over the bright eyes, and she was asleep again."

Wondrously picturesque is the harmonious grouping of children! The scene is suggestive of the tented fields of the Summer Land, where all things prove Plato's saying, "Poetry comes nearer to vital truth than history."

But, externally, the work slowly wore its way into flesh and blood; especially when combined with the care and toil inseparable from the issuance of the *Herald of Progress.** The object of that publication was plainly expressed in its motto: "*The Discovery and Application of Truth.*" The editors and conductors of that paper proposed, in general terms, an object not much unlike that announced by Pope in his introduction to the inimitable Essay on Man:—

> "Let us (since life can little more supply
> Than just to look about us, and to die)
> Expatiate free o'er all this scene of man;
> A mighty maze; but not without a plan;
> A wild, where weeds and flowers promiscuous shoot,
> Or garden, tempting with forbidden fruit.
> Together let us beat this ample field,
> Try what the open, what the coverts yield;
> The latent tracts, the giddy heights explore,
> Of all who blindly creep, or sightless soar;
> Eye Nature's walks, shoot folly as it flies,
> And catch the manners living as they rise;
> Laugh where we must, be candid where we can,
> But vindicate the ways of God to man."

The central principle was PROGRESS. This principle is the "Philosopher's Stone," which converts all metals into pure gold, and explains all the "ways of God to

---

* The title of a weekly journal in New York, edited by the author three years, now suspended.

Man." If, however, the reasonings and illustrations advanced by them seem to others inconclusive and illogical, they invited a candid examination and expression of opinion from readers and correspondents, no matter how widely and painfully their convictions might differ from and antagonize with each other.

They felt no fear of public opinion, and cherished no love for the fleeting applause of the multitude; therefore, their eyes were at all times open to every department of human concern, and were ready to portray any evil in high as in low places, and to prescribe the remedy, as far as it was comprehended. Being actuated by the principle of Progress, their faculties unfolded more and more by the industrious and fraternal uses they put them to. To help on the world's advancement toward peace and unity, and thereby promote all spiritual progress, was their paramount aspiration.

CHAPTER XXXVI.

THE GREAT REBELLION.

The great rebellion had to come, because there is matter, and in man an infinite Perfection. The natural modes of the operation of that infinite Perfection are called "The laws of Nature." These laws operate perfectly in the world of Politics, as they operate perfectly in the empire of Principles. The statutes and creeds of men are but the surface manifestations of the surface motives, operating through surface materials, for the accomplishment of surface ends; the root of all being the selfish instincts, acting, with more or less glimmerings of wisdom and benevolence, through the exercise of the intellects of prominent men pre-eminently gifted with the selfish propensities and perceptions of *meum et tuum*.

Associated and mingling with all selfish instincts, is what men term "Religion"—the voice of the ever-coming, never-come, omnipresent, indistinct, ever-visible, never-fully-incarnated Arabula—the Spirit inmost to all "natural laws;" the watchful Providence behind and within all events; the omniscient Cause at the heart of all effects; the holy virgin Mother of infinite Love in the maternal affections of all propagating and prolificating powers; the supreme Father of Wisdom in the paternal forces of all centrifugating and executive organs and functions—called "God" by some; by others,

"Nature;" by yet others, "Providence;" but, under each and every name, it is unchangeably in human nature that ever-pressing consciousness of a yet *higher* consciousness, —the irrepressible intuition of a yet *higher* destiny than to live and die an everlasting death—which is generally termed "Religion."

I think the wings of Arabula hovered and brooded upon the spirit of Theodore Parker, when he wrote: "In its primitive form, Religion is a mere Emotion; it is nothing but a feeling; an instinctive feeling; at first vague, shadowy, dim. In its secondary stage it is also a Thought; the emotion has traveled from the heart upward to the head. It is an Idea, an abstract idea, the Object whereof transcends both time and space, and is not cognizable by any sense. But finally, in its ultimate form, it becomes likewise an Act. Thus it spreads over all a man's life, inward and outward, too; it goes up to the tallest heights of the philosopher's speculation, down to the lowest deeps of human consciousness; it reaches to the minute details of our daily practice. Thus Religion wraps all our life in its own wide mantle. So the sun, ninety-six million miles away, comes every morning and folds in its warm embrace each great and every little thing on the round world. Religion takes note of the private conduct of the individual man, and the vast public concerns of the greatest nation and the whole race of mankind."

And so, as the infinite Light taketh knowledge of "the concerns of a great nation," even as it does of "the private conduct of the individual,"—because, simply, *it is never separate* from the inmost of an individual's or a nation's life—so, the Great Rebellion had to come! It came as agonizing pains come to a man surcharged with disease; and it *died*, too, as inexorable death comes to close the eyes and draw the breath of the man who will not turn from his consuming sins.*

But let us look a little more closely into detail, and see, by a brief survey of under-lying fundamental causes, the effects of a nation's transgressions. A true and genuine Democracy, which is the *dream* of the great Western world, is founded on JUSTICE. Justice regards and rewards all men equally and impartially. There is, in the eyes of Justice, a perfect harmony between endowments bestowed and individual responsibilities. Obligations are equal to powers conferred. All men are born alike; not equal. All men are alike independent; but not to the same extent. A full measure of "independence" is given and guaranteed to each; but each does not go to the fountain with the *same* measure to be filled. True Democracy, therefore, is as natural to a just man as health is natural to a harmonious man.

But American Democracy, so far, is a sham, is based, nevertheless, on the beautiful dream of the idea of Justice. The dream recognized the right of each to "life, liberty, and the pursuit of happiness." In political dream-life, "all men are born free and equal." The true future government is to derive its just powers "from the consent of the governed." No taxation without representation is another dream; so very beautiful and dreamy is the democratic theory of American government and administration.

---

* In a volume by the author, entitled, "Answers to Questions," the subject here mentioned is familiarly elucidated.

Therefore, for generations upon generations, how has America violated humanity, and crushed the best hopes of enslaved millions! What injustice, what aristocracy, what tyranny, what oppressions, have marked her course!

Democracy, when genuine, recognizes the social individuality of each, and the political *equality* of each also; if he can reason intelligently, is not imbecile, and act with a conscience. False Democracy, or that which really exists in the administration of either party, denies the manhood of a black man, rejects the political individuality of woman, however refined and intelligent, and exalts the ignorant, the brutal, the swindler, and the drunkard, to the commanding position of "American citizens," entitled to vote at elections, and to have a voice in the enactment of laws for the government of sober, docile, intelligent Africans, and also our white mothers and daughters, who are equal, often superior, to the white fathers, sons, and brothers of the world.

This crime, this inherent inconsistency, which has been continued from the first day of American independence (?) to this hour, had grown into mighty proportions, and merited a punishment of equal magnitude, and this punishment offended *Justice* was rapidly concentrating upon the Government and the people.

Rebellion is a disease incidental to an evil social condition, brought about by political inequality and oppressive forms of injustice. The obscene, the fiendish, the burning and murdering riots which, in 1863, disgraced American civilization in New York, were natural outbursts of wrongs and oppressions long pent up. Idleness, intemperance, false democracies, political chicaneries—all selfish imps, broke loose with the first excuse and opportunity. The Government, notwithstanding its beautiful professions and published dreams, had long *degraded* the honest, industrious, modest, docile *black* men—had denied to them the "right" of being represented—had, instead, given prominence to selfish, ignorant, and dishonest characters (because *their skins were white*), and, as a sequence, what more natural than the development of a murderous Rebellion?

Wise people, who carry the light of Arabula in their hearts, do not generate discords. Injustice does not, because it cannot, flow from equilibriums. Anarchy is the opposite of order. Rebellion, which is *not* revolution, is the antagonism of Justice. If, therefore, there be discords, injustice, discontent, and rowdyisms in society, the causes may be traced to unwise (or selfish) statesmanship—to loss of equilibriums, a consequent persecuting fight, between labor and capital—and, in a word, to injustice in the workings of the political mechanism, however beautiful the dream of its original inventor, and however high-minded his immediate heirs and administrators.

When a Government is intrusted with an *unjust power*, another selfish party is immediately organized to get hold of it, and, as a counteracting movement, an *opposition* party is engendered, which, without designing it, acts conservatively and beneficially by preventing the exclusive use of the power. Thus, happily, there can be no perpetual monopoly in politics on this Continent.

The *unjust power* in American government was, and still is, exhibited in the enslavement of the innocent, in the political rejection of woman's individuality, in the establishment of bad institutions, and in the enactment of unjust laws, by which the best are kept practically *beneath* the selfish masculines who swarm and wallow about the grog-holes of great cities.

Party strifes, guided by the selfish intellects of public men, result in elections by which the *unjust power* changes hands. Now one sect in politics is in power, and now another—the so-called "Democrats" for a term of years, next the so-called "Republicans;" still the "unjust power" remains, and the imps of Selfishness continue to get offices. So long as there remains a single "unjust power" in government, so long will there be party strifes, corruption, injustice, and rebellious developments in the social body.

Self-government in the individual is possible only in that state of mind which rests upon Justice—upon the unselfish Light of eternal Love and Wisdom. The same is true of a nation. All is arbitrary and discord, until the absolute requirements of Justice are fulfilled. "Careless seems the great avenger;" but history's pages show, that

> "Ever the truth comes uppermost
> And ever is *Justice* done."

Selfish developments will not cease till government is based upon Justice—to black as well as to white—to woman and to man alike—*providing for the largest growth of freedom in the individual.* Property questions, and the inseparable relations of Capital to Labor, will all be gradually answered by, and adjusted to "the laws of Nature"—after the Government is established upon the largest Liberty, which is the only true Democracy. Local injustice, special corruptions, isolated evils, social inequalities, party antagonisms, will vanish under the rays of a Government founded on righteousness. O that the American Continent might unfold the sublime realities of its glorious dream! The resistance of the State to injustice, to the Rebellion, must be carried forward to the destruction of selfish conditions—the worst form of which is the slaveholding power—for it works to establish a terrible despotism *upon the ruins of human liberty!*

CHAPTER XXXVII.

A MEMORABLE VISION.

THERE was, in the early stages of the Great Rebellion, a strange, prophetic, fearful, mystical, memorable day, never to be effaced from the history of my inner-life; but, rather, always to be remembered, and hallowed, and reverenced, as marking the period of a vast movement among higher powers in behalf of the earth's inhabitants.

In the morning of that day (the first Tuesday in November, 1861), I felt peculiarly unfit for either thinking or writing, notwithstanding the large packages of letters, and the numerous contributions for our Journal, which demanded immediate attention and editorial labor. There was a complete solstice in my mental machinery. Not a thought-wheel would turn that morning. Being thus disqualified for study and labor at the desk, and just then having "nothing to do" about the house or in the garden, I went motivelessly, listlessly, forth for a ramble—"anywhere, anywhere," on the solid earth beneath the autumnal sky.

My favorite resort was, and is, away among the hilly slopes and mountain-paths of Llewellyn Park,* one

* This Park was conceived by a public-spirited gentleman of Orange, N. J., Llewellyn S. Haskell, Esq., who has by industry, and by faithful love to forest, flower, and mountain, opened up nine miles of shaded paths and carriage-ways, attracted New Yorkers to build mansions therein, and influenced the whole township to become a beautiful rural city.

mile west of our home in the beautiful village. From the sheer force of attraction and habit, one would naturally think, my steps would have involuntarily turned thither; but, unthinking and objectless still, and contrary to the routine of custom in rambling, I went through the village eastward, in the direction of Newark, following the railroad as far as the Bloomfield Station, and there took the side-path leading toward a grove of almost leafless trees.

At length observing a beautiful rock near the corner of an open field, I hastened to its side, and rested tranquilly for many minutes. Those moments were filled to the brim with a peculiar happiness. Strains of distant bands of music seemed to touch the very fibers of the brain, thrilling each organ with thoughts and sensations of melody—more delicate and enchanting than any emotions ever awakened by the music of earth.

The reader will not require me to apologize for the length and particularity of these prefatory remarks, inasmuch as, without them, no one could conceive why the day to which I have alluded made an impression so memorable and prophetic. If I had been long laboring in mind to solve the problem of the war with the Great Rebellion then going on, or if I had been considerably anxious to get at the ultimates of the recent naval expeditions, the following vision might be in part accounted for on common causes, like dreams and visions of the night, after a day of intense mental activity, anxiety, or suspense. The case with me was exactly the reverse. I had had no great anxiety or curiosity about the operations of the army, nor any sleepless hours over the results likely to flow from the bosom of Destiny, during the terrific struggles and exceedingly sorrowful experiences of the people, in their patriotic efforts to preserve the present form of government.

Naturally enough, when the music reached the outer ear, stirring the waters of my inner life to wavelets of corresponding harmony, I turned my eyes in all directions, looking over the adjoining fields, to discover the authors of such exquisite strains. Language will not convey any just conception of that music, which was wafted over the earth like the melodious breathings of celestial seas. No earthly compositions exactly resemble any of the combinations of sounds that floated dreamily, musically, sacredly, through the upper air; and yet there was, now and then, a strain that reminded me of certain national hymns, and of choice fragments of operas, which I have had the happiness to hear from human lips and instruments. There was a wonderful blending of vocal with instrumental sounds. I thought of earthly minstrels whom I had heard; of anthemnal music from the sweet singers of cathedrals and church choirs; of bands of music in the street, concerting with the sustaining voices of a singing multitude; but all such thoughts were soon swallowed by the incomparable melody which pulsated and waved through the heavens. The delicious sensations that bridge over from physical consciousness to spirit life, crept stealthily, dreamily, musically, over my individuality; and, as thousands of times before, the curtains of the interior world were rolled up, disclosing a scene of beauty and grandeur far beyond the power of words to picture. It would require the pen of a "ready writer," and the descriptive powers of a Shakspeare, to convey to mankind the realities of that Vision.

Facing the east, and looking with spirit eyes into the upper immensity, I beheld an ocean filled with islands. They arose one above another, and between each other, as far as clairvoyant sight could reach, apparently beyond the path of the planet Saturn, millions upon billions of leagues away into space, until lost in the mystical and unexplored depths of infinitude. The islands were barren of vegetation—dark, rough, rocky, desolate—with not so much as one bird of night to redeem the dreary solitude. The waves of the ocean gently kissed their craggy lips, and gave forth a musical sound as of many waters laving the rocky sides of a distant shore. But the music before heard was heard no more. A sad sound of low, wailing, mournful melody went up from the feet of those desolate isles, and died away with innumerable echoes, or was lost amid the dreary distances and empty spaces of the immensity. "Alps on Alps" arose before my vision, and I began very earnestly to ask for interpretation, or else a change of scene. * * * *

Months seemed to depart—oh, how long I waited—ere the scene was changed. During all those weary weeks I suffered intensely, in body and in soul, dying daily, and being resurrected again with the sound of mournful music vibrating through ear and brain, until the clouds, and isles, and oceans melted away into chaos, and the heavenly music first heard again filled the air and world.

The heavens opened all the way across from the

north to the south, in the form of a vast rainbow, spanning the entire eastern section of the sky, the clouds sailing rapidly behind each other, and floating off in mountainous masses toward the northwest and the southwest, until the open *buena-vista* to the east, beneath the over-arching rainbow, was renovated and gorgeously arranged for the exhibition of some new scene. Meanwhile the whole heavens were filled with the sounds of that first most marvelous music, emanating from performers and vocalists not yet visible to the eyes of the spirit, and every preparation was made for a stupendous development.

Behold! In the dim distance, beneath the many-colored archway, emerging from the remote infinity, was visible what seemed to be the shining vanguard of a mighty army, with all the precision of military order, keeping step to the sound of the indescribable music: onward came the resplendent host. The golden light of an unseen sun shone on their armor, and upon their beautiful faces and symmetrical forms, producing an effect the most inexpressibly enchanting and bewildering to the beholder. As the celestial army drew nearer, it was easy to discern all the system and discipline of an army—generals, colonels, captains, lieutenants, and subordinate officers—at the head of brigades, battalions, regiments, companies — away, far away, as remote as the eye could trace the divisions and persons. And as the hosts marched nearer still, the features of many faces became distinct enough to recognize, and lo! *I beheld many whom I knew well in private life*, and renowned characters also, with celestial mold and military manners—Ellsworth, Winthrop, Lyon, Baker, and others, who were yet in this world,* all at the head of immense battalions, obedient to the sublimity of a divine impulse, marching above the world of men to encounter foes yet unseen in the wilds of mind and matter.

It seemed to me that hours were consumed in marching from the encampments of an unexplored infinity to the front, beneath the gorgeous archway of many colors. Arrived at the foreground, the advance guard separated in equal numbers, and marched harmoniously to the right and left of the rainbow, halting at each extreme of the arch. The central column continued its march, in time with the music, and as they approached, the faces of other acquaintances shone with the radiance of enthusiasm.

All this seemed to occur in the upper heavens, centrally over the Atlantic Ocean. As the army drew near the base line of the grand arch, the white-clad soldiers, with armor unspotted, and their two-edged swords unnotched by crime, divided into four separate and independent columns or armies, and stepped out into the atmosphere over the continent of America. One of these armies slowly marched over a portion of Connecticut, over a part of the State of New York, and as it wended its way toward the extreme Northwest, it seemed to take in only a part of Ohio and Indiana, all of Michigan, and a part of Illinois, Wisconsin, and Iowa, and reached all the way to the Pacific shore. The second of the four armies marched directly west,

* It is remarkable that all distinguished Generals and prominent military men seen in this vision, though living at the time, either died or were killed in battle during the war.

until it reached Illinois River; it then turned southwest, crossed Missouri and Kansas, and disappeared far over the mountains of California. The third army marched directly north, separated New England from New York and New Jersey, and disappeared in the clouds over Canada. The fourth division of the mighty host, obedient to its commanders, who were then recognized generals in the Southern army, marched to the South, separated Pennsylvania, Maryland, Delaware, Virginia, Kentucky, and Tennessee from more Southern States, and disappeared in the clouds over the land of Mexico.

Still the invisible bands and choristers continued to pour music upon the scene. When the different armies had disappeared, there suddenly formed beneath the arch a regiment of white-clad soldiers, each with a deep blue sash about his waist, and each in his left hand carrying a book, and in his right hand a small gold hammer of exquisite workmanship. These were venerable men, beautiful in their faces, exceedingly intelligent and refined—their uncovered heads and snow-white brows radiant with light. The music sounded grander than before, and new strains of inexpressible sweetness filled the whole temple of the heavens as these venerable soldiers commenced their march toward Washington.

They reached the capital of the country while Congress was in session, and halted in the air just above the palatial edifice. At a word of command, each man raised his strong right arm, hammer in hand, and with the quickness of lightning each hammer fell upon the vast structure, which, as if rent by an earthquake, trembled, reeled, crumbled, and was scattered into countless fragments over the soil! A cloud of dust filled the air, and there were some faint sounds of suffering and shouts for help. But rapidly the dust departed on the winds, and the place where the capitol stood was grassy, and looked like the land of the Silent.

It was suddenly changed into a burial-place, or cemetery, of great solitude and quiet beauty. Amid the trees and flowering shrubs which ornamented the grassy slopes, I beheld the tombs of all the Senators and Representatives who had assembled in the capitol.

Their names were distinctly carved on the little marble tombs that covered the sacred dust beneath.

Meanwhile, above, in the air, calmly stood the venerable soldiers who had wrought all these wonderful changes. They seemed to bend down over the grave of each Congressman with beaming countenances. While stooping thus, each, at a word of command, lifted his book and dropped it upon a grave. Each buried politician was thus provided with a book from the sky. Again the hammer of each soldier was uplifted high in air, and simultaneously each gravestone was struck as by lightning, when lo! the grass opened in wide folds, and each Senator and Representative, dressed in white, with pale face and uncovered head, walked forth from his tomb, armed with a book in his left hand and a golden hammer in his right.

The whole heavens were again filled with music, and a sound of rejoicing came up from the surrounding country; while distant people seemed to express great consternation, and trembled with fear. A great thunder-storm now arose in the east. It rolled violently through the rainbowed archway, which was thus effaced from the sky. The storm-cloud seemed to be filled with armed soldiers from other countries. They sped onward, amid peals of thunder, over New York, and rolled toward Washington. Instantly, in the West, the Capitol became visible. The seats were all filled with the newly-arisen men, each with a book and a hammer, and the storm passed over the land like a whirlwind, terrifying the people, destroying their crops and cattle, but without injuring the New Capitol, or disturbing the Resurrected Men.

Suddenly all the music ceased, and there was nothing more exhibited. And the Vision was thus terminated, even before one question could be asked as to interpretation, and immediately I returned to the ordinary state. The first impression was, that I had been from home several months, lost in a journey of observation and enchantment; but, on reaching my study, I found that *only three hours* of life had passed in this manner.

That there is a world of prophetic meaning in the foregoing I cannot doubt; and that something more will be yet given, by way of interpretation, I fully believe.

CHAPTER XXXVIII.

A NAME IN THE SKY.

For many years I had been urged to secure the establishment and publication of a weekly journal or magazine, devoted to the exposition and advocacy of the Facts, Ideas, and Principles of Harmonial Philosophy. There seemed to be a *need* of, if there was not a want for, a popular form of disseminating knowledge concerning the new facts and inspirations. Speculation of Sensation and Logic had apparently reached its highest triumphs in Hegel, Kant, Fichte, Schelling, Spinosa, Feuerbach, and Schiller, in Germany; and the profoundest penetration to the *interior essence* of history, ideas, and things, with the largest magnitudes of scientific and philanthropic Thought, had been achieved by Comte, Cousin, Renan, Colenso, Hugo, and Emerson; so that, unless the limitations of sense and the semi-intuitive speculations of high-cultured intellects could be surpassed and assisted by the telescopic powers of independent clairvoyants, and by the microscopes of spirit-mediums, it seemed that the acme of all divine knowledge had been reached, and man could attain to nothing positive in the realm of Spirit.

With this view many friends urged me "to start a paper." I agreed with them in the main. But steadily did I *decline* taking the "editorial chair," and yet more *dreaded* assuming any "business responsibility." All my feelings and undefined impressions were opposed to the proposition, and for honest personal reasons which I need not mention. Readers of the "Magic Staff"* will recall "the shadows" visible to my mother's eyes whenever "something was going to happen." Although, whenever the plan of publishing a paper was broached, the way was always light, yet a dark shadow hovered in my front whenever it was urged that I should take the chief position.

> "Whence the strange inborn sense of coming ill,
> That of times whispers to the haunted breast,
> In a low tone that naught can drown or still,
> Midst feast and melodies a secret guest?
> Whence doth that murmur wake, that shadow fall?
> Why shakes the spirit thus? 'tis mystery all!"

Let the reader for a moment step into the "Confessional." I ask, Did you never, guided by the plausible cogitations and logical conclusions of your intellect, go counter to the admonitions of the "low, sweet voice" of *a light more interior?* And were you not, in every such case, beset with difficulties, crippled, and ultimately defeated? Your reply, I know, will be in accordance with your ideas of *what* constitutes "success." But, with an idea that there is no success in any thing that does not promote the highest ends of spiritual development in yourself and in others, you will answer—"I was *never* successful, either in business or in any other interest, when, following my intellect, I went *counter* to the inward monitor."

Again and again I invoked the suggestive hints of angel friends. "O, help me to understand the signifi

* The title of the Author's Autobiography.

cance of 'the shadow.' Why cannot I see my way clearly? O, aid me to discern the right; for, seeing, ye know that I will pursue it."

Instead of voices from the Summer Land, there rushed into my mind the reply of Carlyle, when asked by a student what course of reading he thought best to make him a man:—"It is not by books chiefly that a man becomes in all points a man. Study to *do* whatsoever thing in your actual situation, then and now, you find either expressly or tacitly laid down to your charge—that is, stand to your post; stand to it like a true soldier."

On this principle I resolved to act in the work proposed, and thus I accepted all that followed. But first, what *name?* Of all funny things, the funniest, as well as the most perplexing, is hunting up a suitable title for a new paper, or magazine! There were at least six "beautiful, blue-eyed, laughing babies" in the neighborhood beautifully named before we could begin to feel satisfied with captions suggested for the journal. One suggested "The Plain Truth." The other objected, because there was somewhere published a paper called "*The Plain Dealer*," which did not always tell the "plain truth." "We want something *new*—something *taking*," said a worldward-looking speaker. Call it the "Spirit's Advocate"—or, the "Messenger of Light"—or, the "Standard Bearer"—or, the "Spiritual Reformer"—or, but I need not multiply suggestions. The name that was finally accepted appeared to the writer, in all the colors of the rainbow arching the sky, revealing far more of beauty than promise. Title fixed, an announcement of the forthcoming "*Her-*

ald of Progress" was made public by suitable advertisements. All the time, interiorly, feeling a painful reluctance. Mentioning this feeling to a gentleman of education and experience, he remarked: "Doubtless, you feel embarrassed because the position is novel to you. Go ahead; you are to have, you know, talented editorial associates." And now, added to Carlyle's wholesome advice, I remembered a maxim of the old Levitical Law: "*That which is gone out of the lips, thou shalt keep and perform.*" Yes, the advertisements had gone forth, subscriptions were rapidly coming in from beloved friends, and I said (yet all the time irresolute), "It's too late to back out now; I am the last man to keep the word of promise to their ear, but break it to their hope." And so, with not a dollar of stock paid in, out of thousands that were supposed unfailingly pledged to the enterprise, when it should start, the little ship was prematurely launched upon the troubled waters, in 1860, while the business of the country was still struggling to overcome "the Panic of '57," and just when the Government and popular politics were afflicted with the approaching shadows of the Great Rebellion.

CHAPTER XXXIX.

AIMS AND EFFORTS.

THE birth and objective appearance of the paper had been postponed from time to time, because of the existence, or probable development, of certain well-conducted periodicals; each dedicated, more or less distinctly and positively, to the elucidation and inculcation of those all-comprehensive truths which we cherish and profoundly reverence.

But we thought "the time" had now come for the establishment of a journal wherein the facts and principles of "PROGRESS" might be justly presented, irrespective of the social, political, or religious prejudices that everywhere exist in and sway society. To meet the present needs (not to say "wants") of the world, a reform publication should not only be cosmopolitan in character, but it should be absolutely loyal to the demands of progressive Truth, and not afraid to attack whatever is proved to be evil in time-honored systems and institutions. It should aim at a position of equal altitude to that exalted standard of social, philosophical, and spiritual progress, which advanced and enlightened minds have everywhere erected. Instead of *pandering* to, or *reflecting* the popular sentiment merely, and seeking, from selfish desires for success, to harmonize with prevailing modes of thought and feeling—instead, it should strive to *educate* the world out of its multiform errors and unrighteousness. Any magazine or journal which is pledged to advocate the interests of particular sects or parties, or which, because lacking something, either in purse or in principle, attempts to maintain positions of amiable *neutrality* on questions of great moment to all mankind, is a publication which travels and performs its labors far *behind* the inherent needs and aspirations of the world.

On the other hand, a periodical which perpetually harps upon and exaggerates, beyond its intrinsic importance, any *one* particular branch of progress and reform, while other branches of equal magnitude and moment (called by such persons "side issues") are either wholly overlooked or greatly underrated, fails in a just perception of the unity and sacredness of all truth; and hence the eternal Truth cannot impress her heavenly image and likeness on the world's great heart through the columns of such a periodical. It seems to us that there is demanded of the Press—that mighty agent of influence upon the bosom of the "tide in the affairs of men"—a mission which is as yet barely prefigured—a work impartially grand, world-wide, and universally redemptive.

To such a mission, we undertook to promise, the new journal would be sacredly and earnestly devoted.

But all work of this kind, like the principle of electricity, presents a negative and a positive side. To detect and expose error and superstition; to proclaim against the existence of moral wrongs and wretchedness; to paint and portray in vivid colors the miseries of the ignorant, degraded, and down-trodden—is only the *negative* pole of the true reformer's mission; his *positive* and self-rewarding work is seen in the discovery and application, and strenuous inculcation, of those gracious Truths and essential Reforms which strike at *the minutest rootlets of evil* within the soil of sects, systems, institutions, and individual life.

Behold, O, ye men of the world! The holy, harmonious "light" of another sphere has descended and diffused its immortal radiance upon this! Oh, how true it is that only those who "have eyes" singled to Truth can discern it; and none comprehend save those attentive ones who have "the heart to understand." Yet thousands of human minds, in consequence of that heavenly "light," have arisen, as it were, from the dark-age sepulcher of ignorance and despair. Inspired with a divine courage, and appreciating, to some extent, the intrinsic dignity of individual existence, they have thrown off every clog and chain with which theological superstition had fettered them. Such emancipated intellects freely and fearlessly think and propound questions upon almost all thinkable subjects. In the spontaneous freedom of their newly-awakened aspirations, and in the yet unsystematized exercises of their so recently unshackled reason, not a little extravagance and extremism are manifested. These intellects, however atheistic they may seem, are nevertheless the *real friends of humanity*. They ask important religious questions — sometimes without much reverence for either the problem or the solver of its mysteries; but, notwithstanding, they are stout and stubborn in their determination to have all sides investigated. "Give the facts to the world!" they exclaim; "Let each man's reason first see the facts, and then he may candidly render the verdict."

This unpopular, unsectarian, important, and impartial task of discovering and justly reporting Truths in all possible directions, I had thoughtfully, reluctantly, yet deliberately assumed. The many and weighty responsibilities incident to such a position I also assumed, and resolved to deserve the possession of both light and strength to promote the objects at which all persons co-operating would aim their efforts.

And it was furthermore declared that the conductors of the journal had at heart greater aims than the foregoing—in harmony, as they fully believed, with the desires and aspirations and labors of all the good and true of every age and denomination—first, *the harmonization of the Individual;* secondly, *the harmonization of human Society.* For the *unfolding* of these blessings they would unceasingly pray and untiringly labor. But they frankly differed widely from the convictions of sectarians and politicians, regarding *the means* of obtaining these sublime results. If it were not so—if our convictions and inspirations had flowed into the popular form—the journal would not have been proposed. But we held, and still hold, that the development and establishment of the kingdom or government of heaven, all over the globe on which we live, is possible only by and through man's spiritual interior—*the elevation and harmonization of* ALL THE FACULTIES AND AFFECTIONS OF THE INDIVIDUAL.

Realizing that mankind's physical and spiritual needs (*not* their "wants," remember) are identical with the ample supplies in Nature's bosom, and appreciating that the beautiful laws of the universe are the unchangeable *thoughts* of the Eternal Intelligence, and believing that "true religion" consists in reverencing and *harmonizing with the Divine Will*—which is perpetually flowing forth through all spheres, revealing itself to human reason only in, and by means of impersonal Ideas and the fixed laws of Nature—so perceiving, and so believing, we promised to endeavor to live and to work out the true life on earth, and from week to week to instruct and encourage our fellow-men to believe, think, and do likewise.

CHAPTER XL.

THE PICTURE IN OTHER EYES.

It is always beneficial to take lessons in war from candid, intelligent opponents; for such, in most cases, are better helps to progress than hosts of indifferent soldiers in the rear of your army. "It seems a very easy thing," says a writer, "to look at both sides of any question, and yet, practically, nothing has been found to be more difficult, in respect to all matters of importance; and even when you get over this difficulty, it is no easy matter to acknowledge what you really see on both sides. In the case of the lawyer pleading a cause, it is his duty, or at least his business, to conceal what he sees on one side. He is like the moon with the earth—he always shows one side to the Bench; the other side he keeps out of sight. And the lawyer is merely like the rest of the world in this respect, only with him it is more professional. He acknowledges it; and allows that he cannot afford to be candid; he must plead for his client. If you belong to a party, or a sect, you must do the same; you are witness of it, not judges of it; and if in a mere mood of indifference you fall into controversy at a dinner-table, it seems so natural to take one side or other, that you do it as a matter of course, and plead as if you were a professional lawyer pleading before a bench of judges, hiding what you think will weaken your argument, and adducing what you think will gain the case."

One day I chanced to meet in the street an acquaintance, a kind-hearted, sensible, thorough-going New York business man, who, at the same time, had a decided taste for liberal ideas and progressive literature. I ventured to ask his opinion of our publication (the paper), for I knew that he read it; or, rather, "looked it over," every week, while the Choir was singing at Dodworth's Hall.

"Oh, pretty well," he replied, looking at the moment perfectly lukewarm, and yawning, too, as much as to say—"It's a great bore, though." But he knew that I was a friend of "free-thought and free-expression," and so added:

"I have, however, one criticism to make on it. There is not enough Spiritualism in it. The people want facts, facts, facts—well-authenticated *facts.*"

"Yes," I replied. "We have a department in our columns containing every week some account of 'spiritual manifestations.'"

"True, very true; but those prosy reformatory articles by correspondents, remind me of the description I once read of a Fourth of July celebration: 'The procession was very fine, and nearly two miles in length, as was also the prayer of Rev. Dr. Perry, the chaplain.'"

"But," I responded, "we promised *free* columns to all well-written articles on any important question or progressive subject."

"Well, what of *that?* My judgment is, you can't publish such a paper much longer. You can't afford to keep your columns open to political controversies, and to other topics not connected with Spiritualism. Why, your paper is scarcely any better than a reform paper, a woman's rights paper, an infidel paper, giving very few well-authenticated facts in Spiritualism. You must show more of your *own* side. Print more facts, more facts—that's what the people want, facts."

CHAPTER XLI.

AN ANGEL IN THE HOUSE.

THOMAS FULLER said, "God sends His servants to bed when they have done their work." The shadows thickened over my head and all around me. No man ever spoke truer than the criticising merchant: "You can't publish such a paper much longer." Health failed, and I prayed, "Oh, Mother, Oh, Father, take my weary and wounded feet from this weed-tangled and stony field. The world's winds shiver and chill; the waters are bitter, and my thirst is not quenched."

No prayer was ever more promptly or thoroughly answered. True thought is devotion, and true devotion is thought. "Is not prayer also a study of truth," asks Emerson; "a sally of the soul into the unfound Infinite? No man ever prayed heartily without learning something. But when a faithful thinker, resolute to detach every object from personal relations, and see it in the light of thought, shall, at the same time, kindle science with the fire of the holiest affections, then will God go forth anew into the creation."

Through all these years, and through all the toils and trials and joys of these years, there walked by my side, with patient, self-poised, and faithful step, *the companion of my heart!* Fed by the crystal fountains of supernal affection; true as the stars that in heaven shine; gentle in feeling as the breath of song; with divine sympathy in her eyes for needful child, or woman, or man; a truthful thinker, with a holy love for truth—she steadily performed her part, cheerfully, bravely, buoyantly, as angels labor in the immortal Lands of Love.

Happy the man, and happy the woman, who is blessed with a spirit Mate! To every loving one, uncompanionated, life is cold and dark. Sadly roams and moans the unloved soul. But like an angel of beauty seen through the gloaming, into which the soul is roaming, cometh the true adorer and savior of the longing heart. Whether waking, whether sleeping, sacredly the heart is keeping its boundless love for its deathless lover; and with earliest thought, with latest prayer, the resting spirit blesses, and presses to its bosom, the holy fellow-angel of its immortal life.

The shadows of evening came damply upon my weary form. Disease invaded the citadel of life. The sun of eternal light did not shine; only the white moon silvered my path down the valley. "Thou shalt rest and slumber in thy home," said Mary; "a bed is prepared for thee more soft than clouds." And thenceforth, in the morning as at evening, in our room, for many months, the healing hands of the "Angel of the House" were magnetically bringing back to my form the breath of life. Whether quietly resting at home, whether guiding the steps of grouped children in the great city,

---

NOTE.—The readers of the "Magic Staff" will be rejoiced to learn that Time, who heals all wounds, brought to Mary her beloved children, Fannie and Charlie; they came two years ago, and came to stay; they have grown up healthy, well-educated, industrious, harmonious, and full believers in the gospel of Progression.

whether writing or laboring, in poverty as in abundance, the same sweet soul, like the atmosphere of many flowers, filled all parts of the house with affection.

During this period, which embraces the varied experiences set forth in these chapters, she wrote many beautiful things; one of them, "The Mountain Path," which is biography as well as poetry, I must bequeath to the reader:—

Shadows crept along the valley, sunshine played upon the green,
On the boughs the leaflets parted, showing flecks of cloud between;
Dimpling brooklets floated onward where the wandering breezes sigh,
Flowerets breathed their sweet-toned welcome to the children passing by.

In that valley, shadow-haunted, listening to the water's chime,
Listening to the many whispers, telling of a fadeless clime,
Suddenly my soul was lifted as on amber-tinted wings,
And my heart was filled with sunlight, such as joy supernal brings.

For a voice broke on the stillness, full of tenderness and truth,
Breathing words my spirit pined for in the years of blighted youth,
Calling me to leave the valley and the mists that roll below—
Leave the dim, sequestered arbors, and the water's plaintive flow.

Eyes there were that beamed upon me, through the pale and pensive light,
Earnest, loveful, calm, and holy, like the stars upon the night;
And a voice of sweeter music than the song of bird or tree,
Whispered: "Darling, leave the valley, climb the mountain-top with me."

Silently we sought the pathway Nature's loving hand had wrought;
Sweetly fond the gentle tokens by her forest-minstrels brought;
Glad and gay and hushed and tender were the notes she chanted there.
And the mountain path was sacred as a holy shrine of prayer.

Hand in hand we hasted onward, where the eagle led the way,
Scaled the grand and glorious summit, resting in the lap of day,
Stood upon the moss-grown carpet, stood where man has seldom trod,
And, with reverent brows uncovered, in that hour we worshiped God.

CHAPTER XLII.

SPECIAL PROVIDENCES AND OBITUARIES.

COMMUNION of Spirit with Spirit, or deep answering unto deep, is the ultimate fact of consciousness. By the senses, man comes in contact with the things of sense; by the reasoning processes, man comes in contact with the reasonable processes of Nature; and by Intuition, man's whole nature comes in contact with the Absolute and Essential, where he rests tranquilly on the bosom of Love and Wisdom.

The special providences and facts of guardianship, which occur in the realm of sense, flow from intelligent causes which the senses cannot detect. It is my experience that, while faithfully engaged in life's serious labors and difficulties, there are invisible hands ever stretched forth to aid one's will in ordering and subduing outer circumstances, and in tempering one's petty annoyances; so that harmony may stream, as music flows from an Æolian lyre, through the ten thousand cords of present terrestrial life. Prayer and its fulfillment, desire and its gratification, want and its supply, interior aspiration and beautiful communion, like the interlaced relations and fixed equilibriums of cause and effect, go hand in hand throughout the life and government of the Infinite Reason. Blessed is that spirit, whether in earth or in heaven, who can interchange emotions and exchange thoughts and benefits with the SPIRIT OF ALL ideas, principles, essences, laws, persons.

To come to personal relations—to sense, leaving the realm of communion—my testimony, based on numerous experiences, is: That, by some agency, not always cognizable by the senses, when one is doing, or is trying to do, his *best*, friends or strangers will be influenced to come with open hands to help lift the load. Many times, when weary waiting in the valley for the coming light, or when, through the heavily shrouded morning, we were trying to reach the hills of Beulah, a letter would come, or an almost-forgotten acquaintance of former years would ring the door-bell, when lo! the aid which we that very day pressingly needed had arrived! A shower of plenteous blessings falls just in time to save the soul from the death-stings of petty cares, loss of credit, empty larder, broken health, and killing despair. Oh, the entrancing goodness of hearts beating in the music-bosom of the Summer Land!

But, believe me, I do not attribute all manifestations of human kindness to interior spiritual causes. Only *some* instances, which are not coincidences, occurring under circumstances which admit of no explanation by the usual laws of sensuous contact, are properly attributable to our kindly watching guardian angels.

Human goodness must be recognized and appreciated in justice to human nature. But how shall it be done? How say, while a person is still "above ground," just the grateful and glorious words that are his or her due? Is it not an absurd and a barbarous custom, often a source of wretchedness to the living, which prohibits or discountenances the utterance of just and appreciative sentiments; until, perhaps, through lack of the encouragement which the expression would have afforded, the heart breaks, and the victim is buried by a weeping multitude with "pomp and circumstance!" Neglect and abuse him, or her, until death suddenly slams the door in your face; then, Oh, then, how *black* your dress, how *tearful* your eyes! You recall the friendly smile, the tender words, the noble bearing, the sweet scenes, the hallowed associations; and—Oh! Oh! Oh! your grief is great to behold! During the deceased's lifetime you seldom spoke a comforting word. You would croak over little failings and exaggerate common faults, never whispering an approving word for fear of "flattering" or "injuriously complimenting" the familiar one; but now that the beloved form lies stretched and cold before you, your heart is breaking with grief! Alas! Alas! And you desperately *want* the minister to hold the cross before you, to breathe the prayer of consolation; and you also want him to loan you, at least for a few days, his holy anchor of hope in this hour of sorrow! Rather quaintly it has been said, that "death is the consoler of the lowly, the Nemesis of the mighty, the avenger of all wrongs. Death robs the wicked of their prosperity, and delivers the good from all evil. Death takes away the sting of poverty and the need of wealth. In the grave the poor shall possess what they desire, and the rich shall lose what they possess; the portion of both shall be rottenness and nothingness. The grave is a garment for the ragged Lazarus, and nakedness for the purpled Dives. Death is the heir of all earthly sovereignty, and, in this world, the king that never dies."

Under the embarrassments of custom, I am forbidden to render in plain English an expression of the gratitude we feel toward certain individuals in this world. Suppose, for example, it should be related that a gentleman (who, of course, must be nameless), knowing that our hearts and labors were consecrated and devoted to the Lyceum for children, and knowing also that we then had not a dollar of income from any source—and mark! plenty of wealthier men knew all this just as well as he—went, with tender humility and true modesty, to an intimate acquaintance of ours, ascertained from him how many dollars per week would cover our home expenses, then deposited in the bank the amount required for almost a whole year, and thus put us above temporal anxieties, so that we could give free lectures, write letters, compile the Lyceum Manual, organize Lyceums, and, in a word, give our whole time and energies to the work for children, which was, and is, so all-important in our feelings and understanding.

If that gentleman's physical form was now quietly reposing in the cemetery, and if his superior soul-form had entered upon its mission of being forever the temple of the spirit, then it would be most becoming and appropriate for me to write his obituary; in which I could freely set forth his "kindness," his "intelligence," his "virtues," &c., &c.; but now, because he is living among men, in good health, and trying to become very wealthy, just like all the other selfish sinners, I will only say: "Sir, we are very much obliged to you. We think you did just right, and nothing more. You were a friend of children (there are to-day fifteen thousand in the Lyceums), whom you may meet for the first time in the bright Summer Land. We think, on the whole, that you are no better than you should be. We hope that you will 'keep your health' and be fruitful in all laudable undertakings."

While on this subject, *post-mortem* praise, perhaps it may be instructive to observe, in the language of a cotemporary, "that some of the most affecting episodes in the lives of literary men have been connected with domestic bereavements." These accounts demonstrate that human conjugal affections, when not raised to the superior condition by an unfolded intelligence, guided by true spiritual insight, are first surcharged with grief, and subsequently inconstant; yet how beautifully tender and touching and true when writing obituary reminiscences or *post-mortem* eulogies! The tribute of Sir James Mackintosh to his wife (says the compiler of cases) is among the most remarkable in the language.

"I was guided in my choice," he says, "only by the blind affection of my youth. I found an intelligent companion and a tender friend, a prudent monitress, the most faithful of wives, and a mother as tender as children ever had the misfortune to lose. I met a woman who, by the tender management of my weaknesses, gradually corrected the most pernicious of them. She became prudent from affection; and, though of the most generous nature, she was taught economy and frugality by her love for me. During the most critical period of my life, she preserved order in my affairs, from the care of which she relieved me. She gently reclaimed me from dissipation; she propped my weak and irresolute nature; she urged my indolence to all the exertions that have been useful or creditable to me, and she was perpetually at hand to admonish my heedlessness and improvidence. To her I owe whatever I am, to her whatever I shall be."

It detracts somewhat from the romance of the case, perhaps, that Sir James became consoled for his loss, in just *one year* from the time of his great bereavement, by a second marriage. And here we may venture the somewhat obvious remark, that the domestic histories of remarkable men are the most pleasing records of literature, for the reason that, in these matters, every reader, however humble, has a sort of personal interest in the narrative, readily recalling his own feelings in similar circumstances, or the history of his own friends, and so having a community of joy or sorrow with distinguished personages of other times. It must be confessed, too, that the cool and business-like way in which biographers sometimes dispose of affecting domestic events is noticeable, especially when, as in the case just mentioned, the reader has hardly got over his emotions of sadness at the end of one chapter, and is told at the commencement of almost the next one of the happy marriage of the man for whose intense grief his eyes are still moist. It rarely happens that a man who is his own Boswell does not manage this matter with more delicacy. The case of the Rev. Dr. Spring may be regarded as a remarkable exception. This well-known octogenarian has recently favored the public with lively Personal Reminiscences of his Life and Times, in which he copies extracts from his private journal that are not seldom "rich and rare." Thus, under date Aug. 7, 1860, he writes: "This morning, at half-past 8 o'clock, my sweet wife was released from this scene of debility and suffering." And, after a particular account of her sickness, and a statement that she was the mother of fifteen children, he indulges in a strong expression of his feelings—not unnatural, but perhaps as well suppressed in the printed volume—and winds up with some verses in which the soundness of doctrine is more remarkable than the poetic expression. Just five pages further on, in the very next entry in the diary, the worthy Doctor, after admitting that his "sweet wife was too valuable a woman ever to be forgotten," and that he "never thought he could love another," says that he had advanced beyond threescore years and ten, was partially blind, and needed a helper fitted to his age and condition:—

"No one needs such a helper more than a man in my advanced years. I sought and God gave me another wife. A few days only more than a year after the death of Mrs. Spring, on the 14th of August, 1861, I was married to Abba Grosvenor Williams, the only surviving child of the late Elisha Williams, Esq., a distinguished member of the bar. She is the heiress of a large property, and retains it in her own hands. She is intent on her duty as a wife, watchful of my wants, takes good care of me, is an excellent housekeeper, and instead of adding to the expenses of my household, shares them with her husband."

In addition to which remarkable circumstance, the autobiographer asserts, that

"Not until after our mutual engagement was entered into, did we know that we were descended from the same stock, and that our grandmothers were sisters."

A French author gives an account of a nobleman who lost his wife, to whom he was tenderly attached, and with thoughts occupied only with the hope of joining her in another world, shut himself up for three years in a religious retreat. He uttered a prayer to God, which some may be surprised to find in the mouth of a French marquis: "*d'accroître mon courage et de me laisser ma douleur.*" Give me strength, but diminish not my sorrow! Certainly a most delicate and poetical sentiment. But the bereaved husband was still young, and after three years of retirement, he quits it, marries again, and plunges into political intrigues and the worldly ambition of his class. The writer from whom we derive the account remarks, with calmness and placidity: "This is one type of our inconstant nature. But here the very intensity of one feeling seemed to forebode the reaction of the opposite; and the change appears so natural, so almost inevitable, that we rather sympathize with it than otherwise." In other words, those widowers who apparently and demonstratively suffer the most under such circumstances are the surest to be early consoled by a new arrangement. They may not, like Dr. Spring, "ask God for another partner," but they are pretty sure to find one, nevertheless.

The dedication of Mill's book on Liberty is familiar to all:—

"To the beloved and deplored memory of her who was the inspirer, and in part the author, of all that is best in my writings—the friend and wife whose exalted sense of truth and right was my strongest incitement, and whose admiration was my chief reward—I dedicate this volume. Like all that I have written for many years, it belongs as much to her as to me; but the work as it stands has had, in a very insufficient degree, the inestimable advantage of her revision; some of the most important portions having been reserved for a more careful re-examination, which they are now never destined to receive. Were I but capable of interpreting to the world one-half the great thoughts and noble feelings which are buried in her grave, I should be the medium of a greater benefit to it than is ever likely to arise from any thing that I can write, unprompted and unassisted by her all but unrivaled vision."

Horace Mann thus wrote of his deceased wife—the daughter of Rev. Dr. Messer, of Brown University, who lived but two years after her marriage:—

"She supplied me with new strength for toil and new motives for excellence. Within her influence there could be no contest for sordid passions or degrading appetites; for she sent a divine and overmastering strength into every generous sentiment, which I cannot describe. She purified my conceptions of purity, and beautified the ideal of every excellence. I never knew her to express a selfish or an envious thought; nor do I believe that the type of one was ever admitted to disturb the peacefulness of her bosom. Yet in the passionate love she inspired, there was nothing of oblivion of the rest of mankind. Her teachings did not make one love others less, but differently and more aboundingly. Her sympathy with others' pain seemed to be quicker and stronger than the sensation of her own; and with a sensibility that would sigh at a crushed flower, there was a spirit of endurance that would uphold a martyr. There was in her breast no scorn of vice, but a wonder and amazement that it could exist. To her it seemed almost a mystery; and though she comprehended its deformity, it was more in pity than in indignation that she regarded it; but that hallowed joy with which she contemplated whatever tended to ameliorate the condition of mankind, to save them from pain or rescue them from guilt, was, in its manifestations, more like a vision from a brighter world, a divine illumination, than like the earthly sentiment of humanity. But I must forbear; for I should never end were I to depict that revelation of moral beauties which beamed from her daily life, or attempt to describe that grace of sentiment, that loveliness of feeling, which played perpetually, like lambent flame, around the solid adamant of her virtues." The period which elapsed before Mr. Mann's second marriage is not stated in his biography. It appears to have been something over ten years—a length of time which is very unusual in such cases.

CHAPTER XLIII.

MOURNERS AND CROAKERS.

OMNISCIENCE has implanted a propensity in the principles of man's mind—and to discern it clearly is to be benefited, and not defeated, by it—in the selfish gratification of which all men, consciously or unconsciously, wisely or otherwisely, are full of lamentations and croakings for what in story is called "spilled milk."

I croak, thou croakest, we croak. Yea, we *mourn* the degeneracy of the human family. ("Present company always excepted.") There is, in these days of mediocrity, of mental shallowness, nothing, nothing, and nobody, to compare with even the babies of the Past! As poets, we mourn, yea, we *croak*, that, in these days of soft sentimentality and silly rhyming, we find no Homer, no Æschylus, no Cervantes, no Shakspeare, no Milton, no Cowper. Our Bryants, Longfellows, Whittiers, Lowells, Emersons, Brownings, are nobodies. *They* cannot furnish the great poetry demanded by our great minds. And we mourn and mourn, and we croak and croak!

Carlyle is mourning for the good old heroic days of Frederick the Great. Military gentlemen gaze away admiringly, adoringly, to the era, departed era, of the great Napoleon. As artists, we croakingly mourn that *we* did not live in the days of Angelo, Rubens, Titian, and the great masters of the mediæval ages. No artists in these times! The great-minded contemporaries of Shakspeare cared so little about "The Great Dramatist," and left in books so little in his favor, that it is now, as some scholars affirm, exceedingly difficult to demonstrate by the laws of history that there ever was any such man. But *we* mourn and mourn, and we croak and croak!

Religionists mourn that they did not live in the glorious and holy days of Jesus, and John, and Paul. Then they could have heard language and witnessed miracles in keeping with their lofty tastes and great capacities for comprehending such things. The so-called inspired utterances and spiritual manifestations of these weak days cannot meet the religious demands of minds so exalted, and hearts so full of truth. And they mourn and mourn, and they croak and croak!

Politicians mourn the departed days of Washington, Jefferson, Jackson, Adams, Clay, Webster — days of giant intellects — men capable of constructing arguments and using language adapted to the great abilities of their living mourners. Lincoln, Sumner, Wade, Wilson, Washburn, Julian, Chase, Stanton, and the others—no-bodies, mere political nothings, compared with the wondrous greatness of departed giants—and we mourn and mourn, and we croak and croak!

And have we not reason for mourning? The case is this: We (the mourners) have been moving forward, untrammeled and free, ever active and always harmonious, with just and natural admiration for great minds like our own; meanwhile the mass of men has been "degenerating," losing the "conservative" grandeur of character, becoming inflamed with a shadowy belief in "progression;" and so we mourn and mourn, and we croak and croak!

There are, this moment, half a million of beautiful babies crying in their cradles, who, when they shall have reached that ultimate mark of manhood known in law as "the age of discretion," will, because they are (I trust) our *legitimate* descendants, keep up the family trait of mourning and croaking, because there will be about them no Garrisons, no Phillipses, no Emersons, no Bryants, no Parkers, no Beechers, no Greeleys, no Whittiers. Oh, the stores of wisdom they would have gathered in, had they lived "in those glorious days!" They wonder, possibly, why their ancestors (*i. e.*, *we*, the present great mourners and croakers) did not more vividly and more reverently realize that they had, within their immediate grasp, the rare wisdom and varied experiences of great men—for "there were *giants* in those days!" But until those babies attain the "years of discretion," we must do our best, and so—we mourn and mourn, and we croak and croak!

Already an accomplished gentleman has written "The Bequest of Spiritualism," as though it were a religious movement of the gigantic past, calling for a respectful obituary notice; whereas, viewed with less historic and more intuitive eyes, Spiritualism is yet like a child, whose little feet are not poised to the earth's center, who has been dressed in its pretty clothes, and tumbles, and bumps its head, and cries with wide-open mouth, and calls in a loud voice for its mother, or for vigilant nurses, all which happens to it in making the tour of the sitting-room. What it is, or what it is to do, or how long it will live untranslated, or to what institutions it will be married, or how many sect-descendants it will propagate—are questions, with answers, too far in the non-existent future to merit more than speculative meditation. But *this* we know:—Our progeny will be mourners and croakers. They will, with their capacious intellects and high culture, spurn and neglect and defame the characters of their contemporaries; and, looking back upon these hallowed days, so redolent with inspirations, and so opulent with mediumistic demonstrations (and through persons, too, about whom none but the persecuting religionists could utter a contumacious word), will exclaim: "Oh, that we could have lived in the times of the Hares, and Edmondses, and Chases, and Owens, and Harrises, and Davises, and Ballous, and Howitts, and Coopers, and Ashburners, and Higginsons, and Finneys, and Brittans, and Willises, and Tuttles, and Hardinges, and Dotens, and Scotts, and Homes, and Newtons, and a host of others equally worthy; for then, Oh, *then*, in that great departed epoch of gigantic intellects, and living inspirations, and reliable mediums, and disease-curing miracles, we could have been fed and gratified, in accordance with our refined tastes and cultured abilities—but, alas! alas! we live in an age of mediocrity in regard to all these things; and so we mourn and mourn, and we croak and croak!"

And our modern ladies, too, and even those who are not only ladies, but greater than ladies—the *women* of our day—are mourning and croaking because they do not find among their acquaintances a Queen Bess, a Margaret of Anjou, a Madame Roland, a De Staël, a Guion, a Somerville, an Edgeworth, the Countess of

Derby, Grace Darling, a Siddons, a Maria Theresa, an Elizabeth, a Jeanne d'Albert, or an Isabella of Castile. Instead of these noble specimens of the race—warriors, poets, historians, actors, novelists, and rulers of empires—our moderns have to contemplate the mere nothings of this century—a Browning, a Fuller, a Bremer, a Howitt, a Hosmer, a Childs, a Hunt, a Fowler, a Miller, a Mitchell, a Mott, a Nightingale, a Bonheur, a Swisshelm, a Victoria, a Ristori, a Lander, a Farnham, a Stone, a Stanton, a Dale, a Dix, and a thousand others—all mere non-entities. Oh, so *far behind* the genius of our educated man! and so *far below* the abilities of our modern ladies! that they cannot help treating them with indifference, or openly denouncing them, and thus they mourn and mourn, and they croak and croak.

The *moral* of it all is: While justly reverencing the memories of those who have lived and worthily wrought in the Past, and while erecting magnificent monuments, and writing obituaries in Greek and Latin, over the dead skeletons, once the lime-foundations of human temples, whose proprietors have long since found better company in the Summer Land; we, their successors and historical administrators, should not deprive ourselves of the current manifestations of Arabula, as they appear and reappear in the poetry, painting, music, morals, religions, governments, inspirations, revelations, reasonings, ideas, and reforms of our own day and generation.

CHAPTER XLIV.

DEATH OF MY FATHER.

Look with pure Reason's pure eyes—which is the clairvoyance of the whole superior spiritual consciousness—and you will perceive plainly, and *not* as "through a glass darkly," impressed on all things, the truth-tracks of immutable omniscience. In nothing is the infinite goodness more beautifully manifest than in the government of what blind and grave-dreading intellect entitles "The King of Terrors."

Death is no enemy to mankind; rather a servant of Life. He carries the key to the door which opens wide upon the templed grandeur of the imperishable Universe. It is impossible that he should ever travel to "where the soul wanders in sublimest thought." His government is of the earth, earthy. His breath is never felt across "the hallowed plains where angels dwell." He is sovereign pontiff in the lower kingdoms of life and organization. But he has no throne in the higher realms of existence.

Your reason tells you this: The Spirit can, by experience, know absolutely *nothing* of the "King of Terrors." He falls a supplicant, yea, a driveling imbecile, at the feet of Spirit. The Spirit goes happily, exultingly, through the wreaths of worlds to the Summer Land, which is lighted by a belt of suns and constellations, which are forever rolling musically in the boundless sky. But Death! Oh, joy! joy! he drops powerless at the base of the "Mountains of Life," with no eyes to see the path of the Spirit; which, guided by the pole-star of love and wisdom, rises through the welcoming heavens triumphantly, unshackled by terrestrial gravitation, and sweeps onwardly, singing the excelsior songs of eternal progression.

Furthermore, Death is a screening process to some extent. Beecher, under the afflatus of Arabula, said: "How strange and blessed must be that emancipation which passes upon every man when the great deliverer, Death, puts his ordaining hand upon the heart and head."

And like a philosophical Spiritualist he affirms: "We shall enter upon another life divested of many of the hindrances and encumbrances of this. We shall, however, lose none of the things that one should wish to retain. We are double in this life; for the problem of our existence here seems to be to develop a blossom of spirituality out of the stem of materiality; to develop out of the physical body, and to ripen a spiritual soul. * * * *

"It seems to me that much that mars life is what we call infirmity; and that when we die we leave behind us many things that we call faults, and follies, and sins, as the trees shed their leaves when winter comes. When the body dies, oh, *how much will perish that is the result of the forces of those passions which sleep with the flesh!* When we go from this world, how shall we be released from ten thousand things that belong to our physical state, and that tend to *hinder* our spiritual development. * * * *

And when, in departing from earth, we shall be stripped of the flesh and all its influences, we shall find in ourselves beauties and glories more than we have ever dreamed that we possessed. * * * *

"And so there are many passions, many appetites, many lower faculties, that are indispensable to our physical conditions, which we can easily imagine will drop away from us when we pass out of this life, and yet leave the soul unimpaired. *The reason, the affections, all the higher faculties, will go forth into immortality;* but it will be no small thing to have left behind those things which belong to the body exclusively, and from which come largely the distemperature and trouble that afflict us in this life. If there may be a hope that in part we shall leave behind the appetites and passions, and that those which we carry with us shall no longer be turned downward, as here, to minister to evil, but shall be evermore turned upward as auxiliaries of the higher feelings, then the thought of departing, the thought of going forth, should not be one of loss, but one of essential gain."

Readers of the "Magic Staff," by returning in memory to the earlier chapters, will recall the image and characteristics of my father. Here, it is only needful to remark that the last few years of his life were comfortably spent under the roof of our "Orange Home." There was gratitude in Mary's heart, as much as in mine, because it was within our power to afford him this retirement and independence.

It was precisely a quarter before six o'clock, Monday afternoon, April 10th, 1865, when my venerable father closed his physical eyes forever. Those eyelids which had been raised and dropped, opened and closed, in keeping with the laws of action and rest, during eighty-three years of earthly existence, went down over the fixed gaze for the last time. He "died," externally, when "life" in the temple became heavy and a burden.

For years his chief source of entertainment consisted in books and the liberal publications of the day.* He had no taste for landscapes and rambling walks in the parks. Society had no attractions. Before his sight grew dim with age, and while his hand remained steady, there was nothing so attractive as industry. When he laid aside his apron and packed away his tools, under the pressure of his own senses, that they were no longer capable of serving him in his accustomed labor, he was a very sad and dissatisfied man. For over a year after "closing up" his bench, his eye was restless, and his tongue was ever asking for "something to do to fill up time."

Many hours of each day, during the last three years, his thoughts were devoted to subjects concerning the "inner life," and especially concerning the prospect of existence in the "Summer Land." Independent in his temperament, and naturally strong in his moral attributes, and fond of mental liberty in every particular, he

---

* *The Banner of Light*, published in Boston, was my father's favorite paper. It is the only Spiritualistic organ that was ever unflinchingly and unswervingly devoted to the advocacy and demonstration, through facts of mediumship, of the Central Idea of Individual Immortality. My father used to read every week the communications through Mrs. J. H. Conant. And many times he said: "As soon as I can, I will go to Boston; and you'll hear from me through Mrs. Conant."

was fed and satisfied with the principles of the Harmonial Philosophy. They were a light to his understanding and an anchor to his soul. He fully investigated the claims of old theology, and therefore for himself *ascertained* the absolute truth of harmonial principles.

With reference to "death," he invariably expressed himself perfectly satisfied. Several times, during the last twenty months of his life, he had "visions" of the higher and better. His only anxiety seemed to be, that, owing to a naturally healthy and vigorous body, he might be compelled to "live too long." His standing saying was: "When I can no longer be useful, then I want to be off." His last days were a perfect fulfillment of every prayer I ever heard him utter with regard to the closing scenes of his terrestrial pilgrimage.

It was my privilege to witness the rolling down of life's curtain, which shut from his material senses the outer world of effects in which we yet dwell; but I was not prepared, just at that hour, to withdraw to the secret closet of clairvoyance. Therefore, like others present when he ceased to breathe, I saw the usual external, grand, solemn fact. Of the locality or condition of his spirit I had no perception, but supposed that, as in most of the numerous instances I had witnessed, he would probably depart from the Orange home to the Summer Land in the course of from one to three hours.

On the subsequent morning I arose somewhat earlier than usual, and was the first to open the north door of the hall looking upon the garden. I walked out upon the stoop, and halted at the second step of the short flight of stairs outside, and leaned lightly against the west banister, musingly looking at the flowering fruit-trees and beautiful verdure of the vines and shrubbery, and listening to the music of song-birds.

At this moment, I felt a commotion in the atmosphere at my right hand. This aërial agitation was so surprising to my sensation, that, in less time than I can write this sentence, it had reversed the poles of outer consciousness. In a word, I was translated into a most perfect state of clairvoyance. This state, so far at least as personal sight and consciousness are concerned, is identical with the condition of a person fully awakened "after death." It is unlike the state of the departed in one essential particular, that while the clairvoyant is still an inhabitant of the physical body, the departed one is wholly emancipated from the organic structure. The clairvoyant can, for the time being, see things and principles with the same sight that is natural to those who no longer dwell in the earthly body, but who live in the Spheres.

The incoming of clairvoyant perception at that moment, and by means of what seemed to be an atmospheric disturbance wholly external, proved of great advantage. The movement of the air was like that caused by a body passing with great swiftness through the immediate space. With my attention thus attracted I turned to the right, and at once *saw my father* in the act of passing out from the hall into the atmosphere, on a plane level with the floor of the stoop! Imagine my surprise, because I had somehow settled into the conviction that he had left the Orange home even before the undertaker had performed his first kindly offices. True, my sister Eliza once said, during the evening, that to her it seemed that "father's spirit had not gone out of the house."

The face was his own in every essential feature and line of expression. In stature he was perhaps four inches shorter, and in general proportions about the same as I remember him thirty years ago, being consistent with the remarkable alteration in the height of his person. His motions seemed to be the result of some will-power or intelligence outside of his consciousness. He walked out with a kind of indecision, or languidly, and with the step of unconsciousness peculiar to one moving about in a somnambulic state. There was, however, an expression upon his countenance of complete repose. No child in the slumber of innocence ever looked more serene and happy. It was the expression of "rest" and profound satisfaction; and along down over his shoulders and new-born body there flowed and shone the same indescribable atmosphere of contentment and beauty.

On reaching the open space in front of the stoop, without seeming to notice that I was observing his movements, or indeed without taking any particular interest in any thing that was going on with himself, he turned to the east, and rapidly glided to the side of a person, who, until that instant, I had not observed. The moment I saw this manly, intelligent personage, I was satisfied that *his* will, and not my father's, had developed all the voluntary movements I had witnessed. Unquestionably, his state was like that known as somnambulism; and he did not awaken on touching the side of the spiritual man, who stood waiting for him on the northeast corner of the house. Their heads were about level with the window-sills of the second story. Immediately after he reached the other's side, the twain rose rapidly toward the east, and passed beyond the reach of my already retiring vision. Thus my father withdrew from his earthly entanglements!

In my joyousness and gratitude I hastened within to tell the "angel of the house" what had transpired but a few moments before. "Mary! I have just seen father go out of the hall, and around the corner of the house." For a moment she appeared overcome with astonishment, thinking of the possibility of the fact being external; but, quickly gathering her thoughts to my meaning, she began to enjoy with me the glorious laws of resurrection, by which the old are made youthful and the sick healthful—by means of which all are prepared for progress and usefulness in the higher realms of existence. On going up-stairs, to the room where reposed the cast-off body of the departed one, I chanced to step into a small bedroom at the south end of the upper hall, which at that time was not used for any purpose, and there most distinctly I realized that, in that unoccupied spot, the final spiritual organization which my father bore aloft, on the wings of the morning, was formed and prepared for the eternal pilgrimage. The atmosphere was still warm with the constructive process, which had been so beautifully carried forward during the night. In the whole temple of the Father's wisdom and the Mother's love, I know of no spot more sacred than that where the Spirit is clothed upon for immortality.

* * * * * * * * * *

* * * * * * * * *

For months and months, until two years had nearly passed, we received no tidings from the departed. How strange that no word, no sign of existence, came to our waiting senses! To those who are less in communication with the Summer Land, such continued *silence* must indeed be painful, if not the cause of skeptical misgivings and vague distress. But to me these "misgivings" and this "vague distress" are strangers. Patience and Time brought the long-looked-for communication. Taking up the *Banner of Light* bearing date "May 28, 1867," and glancing over the names and addresses in the "Message Department"—as you go to the window aperture of the post-office and hopingly ask the clerk to "look over the package of letters, and see if there is n't one for you"—so, running over the published messages from the departed to their friends on earth, my eye was suddenly arrested by the following: [The questions and remarks in brackets are by the gentleman (Mr. White) who, I am informed, presides at all the public sessions of Mrs. Conant.]

I am Samuel Davis, and I've come to send a message to my boy, Jackson. I want to tell him that the philosophy that the spirits teach through him is true. I know he 's aware of it, but I feel like coming back here and telling him *I* know it's true. And I want to tell him, too, that I was right close by him when he was standing beside my body, before it was laid away. And I was so near that I could understand the remark he made to a friend of his who stood near. It was this: "He has n't yet ascended; he 's here."*

---

* This remark *I* do not recall. But I am assured by persons present at the time, that the expression is *correct.*

That was true; I had n't entirely separated myself from the body; I was there, and I seemed to hear what he said, through waves of sound that conveyed the meaning to me.

I 'm very happy in the spirit-world; perfectly satisfied; and I 'm proud to be able to come back and declare that he was right; that the intelligences who took him when he was a little boy are wise and good, and they have instructed me in many things since I came to the spirit-world, and assisted me a great deal.

I have met his mother, although we 're not together. She is entirely different from me, so we are satisfied to live apart. She 's better, better than I am.

And I hope he'll be spared here on the earth to do good, a great deal more good than he has done, and never get out of the way of doing well.

[How long have you been away?] Only a few months. You know my boy Jackson? [Andrew Jackson Davis?] Yes. [Of course we do.] Well, then, you 'll see he has my message. [He 'll get it.] I suppose so, because he takes the *Banner*. Good-day.

My Reader! Have you a vacant chair at the hearthstone? Have you in solemn sorrow, wearing the mantle of mourning, walked to the Silent Garden and wept, as the men shoveled the cold earth upon the painted casket, which contained the form of one dearly beloved? Did you feel desolate and bereft? If so, there is in the world a balm for you. It is the *truth* of the Spiritual Philosophy. When walking through the cemetery at Orange, you may, perchance, observe a white stone bearing the name of "Samuel Davis," and under it this immortal motto:—

"*Death is but a kind and welcome servant, who unlocks with noiseless hand life's flower-encircled door, to show us those we love.*"

CHAPTER XLV.

THE QUINTESSENCE OF THINGS.

A FORMIDABLE and fearless writer exclaimed: "O, Truth of the earth! O, Truth of things! I am determined to press my way toward you. Sound your voice! I scale the mountain, or dive in the sea after you!"

Thus, too, was I determined; but not in the forces of my will; for my intellect, now in the resurrection, was drawn by a divine *attraction*. I was now recovering from the physical prostration mentioned in a previous chapter. "What and where is God?"—a frequent question of my intellect in its former unresurrected state, was now unceasingly answered in the deep, deep *rest* of my entire consciousness. My conscious spiritual identification with *the quintessence of things* enabled me to say, in the language of the Arabula—"I AND MY FATHER ARE ONE." The profoundness of this experience made "expressive silence" the only appropriate expression. This, and this only, was my whispered acknowledgment:—

"Seldom upon lips of mine,
Father! rests that name of Thine
Deep within my inmost breast,
    In the secret place of mind,
    Like an awful presence shrined,
Doth the dread idea rest!
Hushed and holy dwells it there,
Prompter of the silent prayer,

Lifting up my spirit's eye,
And its faint but earnest cry,
From its dark and cold abode,
Unto Thee, my Guide, and God."

Language cannot picture the fullness of my private "life with God." The tranquillity and happiness of this state surpassed any and all of my other experiences. But one day, all was changed! And why? Because, as I have explained to you before, I was becoming *selfish* in my sequestered happiness. All at once I realized that seven-tenths of the intellectualized part of mankind were at that very moment "without God, and without hope in the world"—skeptical, miserable, unprincipled, straying, and restless as evil itself.

Contemplating the world, I saw that, where *intellect* was unbound, there was little or no perception of, or faith in, a Divine Existence. But that, in countries where intellect was yet trammeled by ignorance and fear, *faith* and superstition sustained the millions. And that every people, country, and age, had a name for its *Idea* of God. Allah, Chur, Addi, Zain, Ezsi, Adad, Odin, Gott, Theos, Deus, Dieu, "Jehovah, Jove, or Lord"—but that, associated with the name, I could perceive no corresponding knowledge of how such a Being exists in the constitution of things. "Hence," I thought, "does not man's intellect *need* some rational, scientific, and mathematical *basis* on which to erect a true and lasting temple of knowledge of God?" Is it not *within* the grasp of man, intellectually, to trace the facts and follow the principles of "Nature up to Nature's God?" I recalled the significant recorded astronomical fact, that, from the year 1821 to 1845, it was becoming more and more certain that there was a planet outside of Uranus, because there were irregularities in the motion of Uranus which were otherwise unaccountable. After a careful investigation, Leverrier announced, in 1846, that those irregularities would be accounted for by a planet of a certain size in a certain place in the heavens, but so distant as to be invisible without telescopic aid. The planet Neptune was found in consequence of that announcement, corresponding in position and appearance with the prediction. And although it was subsequently shown that the orbit of Neptune did not correspond with the orbit of the predicted planet, yet the fact remains, that the existence of Neptune was determined with a considerable degree of certainty by astronomical theory, before it had been proved by ocular demonstration.

I meditated that scientific discoveries and philosophical triumphs were never so numerous or so prophetic as now. And it further seemed to me that, upon grounds of induction, similar to Leverrier's process of reasoning, the human intelligence might make its own discovery, and establish its own demonstration of God. These thoughts led me to the following philosophical argument. It was published in the *Spirit Messenger* without its author's name, and subsequently copied into the *Herald of Progress*. It is reproduced in this volume, because the line of argument and the illustrations are strictly in accordance with the necessities of every intelligent mind.

CHAPTER XLVI.

GOD REVEALED TO INTELLECT.

THE construction of the following argument, in my own mind, originated in the necessity of my nature. Some years ago, I had the misfortune to meet the fallacies of Hume, on the subject of causation. His specious sophistries shook the faith of my reason as to the being of a God, but could not overcome the fixed repugnance of my heart to a negation so monstrous; and consequently left that infinite, restless craving for some point of fixed repose which atheism not only cannot give, but absolutely and madly disaffirms.

Through the gloom of utter skepticism, I turned for relief to the Treatise of Paley, and other reasoners, on the mere mechanical hypothesis, but there found, as I deemed, an impassable hiatus in the logic of the argument itself. I was forced to admit that every machine must have had at first a machine-maker; but I saw clearly, that the fact of its being a machine must, first of all, be proven, before the reasoning could hold at all; and thus the argument was worthless. For as it is based on the assumed postulate of an actual creation, and as such a postulate is any thing but self-evident, it needs to be demonstrated. And no logician of the whole mechanical school has ever attempted to furnish such a demonstration. Indeed, were creation once proven, there would be no necessity for more argument on the subject, since a Creator would on that supposition be proven also.

But I saw a still more fatal defect in the reasoning of Paley. I said to myself, Suppose that we admit the world to be a machine; still, we have no evidence that the machine-builder exists now. The watchmaker of Paley's example may have ceased to be, countless centuries ago, and still the watch remain as perfect as ever. And thus the mechanical conception of the universe could afford me no ray of light.

And yet I sought with eager solicitude for some solution of this vast world-enigma. I resembled a child who, in the crowd, had lost its parent. I went wildly, asking of every one, "Where is he? have ye seen him?" But there was no answer. I teased philosophy, science, and literature with endless questionings, but all in vain. I plunged in fierce excitements, but no solace was there. The infinite void in my want-nature would not thus be filled. I was as an Arab, washing himself with sand instead of water. Neither the heat of the heart, nor the impurity of even the surface, diminished by any such lavation. I will not attempt to paint the intense gloom of my situation. Death seemed to ride on the *present* hour as a race-steed of destruction. The *past* was a grim waste, strewn with the ruins of worlds, men, and things. The future was a chill mist hovering over incalculable sepulchers. Every voice in creation seemed to me a wild wail of agony. The godless sun and cold stars glared in my face. I turned often to the pitiless sky, which no longer wore the poetic hue of my credulous boyhood.

One beautiful evening in May I was reading by the

light of the setting sun in my favorite Plato. I was seated on the grass, interwoven with golden blooms, immediately on the bank of the crystal Colorado of Texas. Dim in the distant west arose, with smoky outlines, massy and irregular, the blue cones of an offshoot of the Rocky Mountains.

I was perusing one of the Academician's most starry dreams. It had laid fast hold of my fancy without exciting my faith. I wept to think that it could not be true. At length I came to that startling sentence, "God geometrizes."—"Vain revery!" I exclaimed, as I cast the volume on the ground at my feet. It fell close by a beautiful little flower that looked fresh and bright, as if it had just fallen from the bosom of a rainbow. I broke it from its silvery stem, and began to examine its structure. Its stamens were five in number; its green calyx had five parts; its delicate corol was five-parted, with rays expanding like those of the Texan star. This combination of fives three times in the same blossom appeared to me very singular. I had never thought on such a subject before. The last sentence I had just read in the page of the pupil of Socrates was ringing in my ears—"God geometrizes." There was the text written long centuries ago; and here this little flower, in the remote wilderness of the West, furnished the commentary. There suddenly passed, as it were, before my eyes a faint flash of light. I felt my heart leap in my bosom. The enigma of the universe was open. Swift as a thought I calculated the chances against the production of those three *equations* of five in only one flower, by any principle devoid of the reason to perceive number. I found that there were one hundred and twenty-five chances against such a supposition. I extended the calculation to two flowers, by squaring the sum last mentioned. The chances amounted to the large sum of fifteen thousand six hundred and twenty-five. I cast my eyes around the forest; the old woods were literally alive with those golden blooms, where countless bees were humming, and butterflies sipping honey-dew.

I will not attempt to describe my feelings. My soul became a tumult of radiant thoughts. I took up my beloved Plato from the grass where I had tossed him in a fit of despair. Again and again I pressed him to my bosom, with a clasp tender as a mother's around the neck of her sleeping child. I kissed alternately the book and the blossom, bedewing them with tears of joy. In my wild enthusiasm, I called out to the little birds on the green boughs, trilling their cheery farewells to departing day—"Sing on, sunny birds; sing on, sweet minstrels; Lo! ye and I have still a God!"

Thus perished the last doubt of the skeptic. Having found the Infinite Father, I found also myself and my beloved ones—all, once more. By degrees I put together the following argument. I tried it by every rule of logic; I conjured up every conceivable objection against all its several parts, and grew thoroughly satisfied that it contained an absolute demonstration. But I rested not here. I resolved to have it tested to the uttermost. For this purpose I journeyed all the way to Boston last winter. I presented it to the most eminent pantheists, atheists, and skeptics of that literary city. Not one of them attempted to point out a flaw in its logic.

Thus I became convinced that the demonstration is utterly unassailable; and I therefore offer it without hesitation to the criticism of the world.

The aggregate argument is my own; though many of the particular elements have been freely borrowed from others.

The principal consideration, however, is not as to authorship, but validity. And this may readily be determined. Let the objector designate its fallacy, and I will be among the first to renounce it altogether. Until this is done, I hold myself pledged to maintain it in fair controversy against all adversaries; though I will not debate the question with any person unacquainted with algebra, geometry, and the rules of strict logic.

"God Geometrizes."—*Plato.*

The following argument assumes a bold tentative. It undertakes to demonstrate, in an absolute manner, not only the being, but ever-present agency of the Deity in all the phenomena of the material universe. It professes to solve the old problem that has puzzled philosophy in every age, ever uttered by human curiosity, but perhaps never, as yet, answered by pure reason—"What is the true nature of causation?"

Beyond all controversy, this must be regarded as the fundamental problem of all real science; for we know nothing, we never can know any thing, but causes and effects. All time and eternity form but one vast flowing stream, where these come and go like waves of the sea. All space is but the expanse where these rise and fall in oscillations, as of some ethereal fluid of infinite extent, vibrated by a viewless force. Well has a distinguished pantheist of the modern German school worded this profound idea: "The soul will not have us read any other cipher but that of cause and effect." All scientific treatises, however pompous their nomenclature, contain but generalizations of these, expressed in mathematical formulas, with greater or less accuracy. I am stating a simple fact, admitted on all hands. Cause and effect are thus correlatives in language and thought. The former is first, both in logic and chronology. It is, therefore, the necessary exponent of the latter. Unless its true nature be comprehended, nothing else can possibly be understood. If we err at this great starting-point, every subsequent step must prove a blunder in every process of philosophical inquiry. And accordingly, universal history shows that the false solution of the radical problem has been the fruitful source of all pestilential heresies, both in philosophy and religion.

To the mighty question, "What is causation?" four different answers, and no more, can be given—the skeptical, the material, the pantheistic, and the rational, or Christian.

To assert that man is utterly ignorant of the true nature of causation, is total skepticism.

To predicate the doctrine of invariable sequence, as did Hume and Brown, presents the formula of materialism. Idealism is but another phase of the same false view; for both idealism and materialism are at a certain depth identical, as they both take for granted that all Nature is but a dream-show, a mere conjurer's trick of fleeting appearances, where phenomena have only the tie of antecedent and consequent, to bind them together in a union that touches nowhere and produces nothing.

If we answer, that *emanation* is the only causation, we are landed in pantheism. All individual existence vanishes away, and with it all proper ideas of right and wrong, of truth and falsehood; and, in fine, all logical predicates of every name and nature; for if nothing remains but indivisible unity, proposition is impossible, since it would be absurd to assert unity of itself.

The only remaining conceivable answer I deem the rational, the Christian, the true one—that causation alone resides in mind; that matter never can be a Cause; and, therefore, every phenomenon in the universe is, and ever must be, but the effect of intellectual force exerted by pure volition.

This view we now proceed to demonstrate, after the rigorous method of the geometricians, and discarding, as much as practicable, all loose and rhetorical digressions.

Proposition I.

We may lay it down as a general proposition, *that the perception of mathematical truth evinces mind of a lofty order.*

It is for this reason the universal consent of mankind has placed Pythagoras and Plato, Archimedes and Kepler, Newton and La Place, among the very foremost of the species. We would not exalt beyond due bounds the dignity of mathematical studies. We have long since awoke from the dream of our youth, that supposed a vain distinction of high and low among the sciences, which ought to be like the halo of a star, bright all around. But, beyond question, there is no good reason for the neglect of those ennobling, strict, and severely logical exercises in our elementary education. Far wiser was the lesson taught by the great Plato, in the inscription engraved over his immortal academy—"Let no one presume to enter *here* who does not understand geometry."

However this may be, even in this age of light studies, no enlightened mind will deny that the power to perceive mathematical truth is essentially an attribute of no mean intellect.

Corollary.

Hence it follows, *à fortiori*, as a self-evident corollary, *that to evolve mathematical motions*—or, in plainer terms, *to work mathematically, evinces mind of a still loftier order.*

For to evolve mathematical motions unquestionably implies their perception. No person will assert for a moment that an analyst can reduce algebraic equations, or solve geometrical problems, and demonstrate theorems, without comprehending in the one case the meaning of the terms, and in the other the axioms and definitions on which the operations hinge.

To present this view in the clearest possible light, we beg leave to offer an obvious illustration.

Suppose that John and James sit down to work out a knotty question in decimal fractions; John passes from one operation to another with the skillful rapidity of an accomplished arithmetician, adding and subtracting swift as thought, and balancing tangled columns of vast numbers into a definite and accurate result; while James can understand the explication of it when it is stated in luminous order on the sheet before his eyes, but finds it wholly impossible to accomplish the task for himself. Now, which of the two, in the given case, manifests the superior intellect? The veriest skeptic must answer—"He who has not only the penetration to perceive, but the mental power to perform the processes assigned him." Thus, undeniably, to evolve mathematical motions implies not only their distinct perception, but the additional faculty of an active power also. Finally, I put the question home, and the entire controversy betwixt the believer and the atheist turns upon the answer—Can any one work out all the sublime problems of mathematics, from the simplest in the first book of Euclid to the most complex in conical sections, without the mind to comprehend what he is doing? He who responds in the negative must crucify reason and betake himself to utter insanity.

The discussion of our second proposition will place this averment above all dispute. To that we will now attend.

Proposition II.

All the motions of the material universe, in all their wondrous variety and unity, are strictly mathematical.

The foregoing proposition is susceptible of proof by an immense induction. The field for its exercise has absolutely no other limits than the frontier line that encircles the domain of science. A hundred volumes might be filled with instances, and still the materials would remain unexhausted in their infinite richness. Every new discovery in the abyss of unfathomable

Nature adds to the store, which is as vast as the immensity of creation.

We have only room in this hasty dissertation for a few out of incalculable millions of examples. Our choice will be only embarrassed by the teeming profusion that crowds upon our eye, and almost overwhelms every sense of the soul, from the circles of light that spread in decreasing intensity and augmented distance around the candle, near which we are now writing these paragraphs, to yonder remote pale star that twinkles through the open window, immeasurable leagues away, in the midsummer's night of a cloudless sky.

Induction I.—Myself.

I will begin with my own organism.

I survey my right hand; it has five fingers. I look at my left; it has five also. There is another member of an algebraic equation. This is singular. I turn down to each foot, and on each behold five toes. There is another equation. This is still more singular. I then think of my bodily senses; there are five again. The wonder is increasing. And now all the millions of my fellow-men rise up before the mind's eye—and in rapid succession. Lo! the countless millions of millions that have lived and died pass along the great world-stage, in the view of astonished meditation; and they all, with unimportant exceptions, possess the miraculous five fingers on each hand, five toes on each foot, and glorious five senses. If this be not a God-announcing miracle, then is human reason itself a dream, and all truth a worthless fiction.

But let me apply to myself the rigorous doctrine of the calculation of chances, lest I suffer my judgment to be deceived by undue excitement of the organ of wonder.

In this calculation of chances, let me bear in mind an ingenious remark of Archbishop Whately, that "the probability of any supposition is not to be estimated by itself singly, but by means of a comparison with each of its alternatives."

Now there are but two suppositions possible as to this mysterious combination in the human organism, by which the number five is five times repeated, not only in myself, but in all the myriads of mankind. For these wondrous equations there must be a Cause; and that Cause, whatever may be its nature, and by whatsoever name you see fit to express its existence, be it necessity, law, order, physical force, or God, must either possess intelligence to perceive its own marvelous results, or else be destitute of such intelligence, and work blindly through all its processes. There is no means to evade the force of this statement. These two are positively the only alternatives which logic allows us. For in abstract, definitive division, a perfect affirmation and negation always exhausts the subject divided. Every thing, in the whole compass of thought, must be either a tree or not a tree; and as there is nothing that can be neither, so nothing can be both at the same time. Just so, every Cause, or assemblage of Causes, must possess intelligence or not.

Therefore this wonderful combination of fives must be produced by either a rational Cause, or one wholly irrational—by a Cause that can perceive the relations of number, or otherwise—in fine, by a Cause that can *count*, or one that cannot *count* five, or any other numerical amount whatsoever.

Let me now assume the first alternative. If the Cause that arranged the relations of my several organs be sufficiently intelligent to understand the mathematical harmonies, then all is luminous. There is no chance to be calculated against their production, since he who comprehends the relations of number, can, of course, evolve such relations to any extent, and indefinitely, nay, infinitely, if he be granted to be infinite himself.

Let me now take up the only remaining alternative which the given case permits.

I will assume that the Cause, call it what you please, which produced this even combination of fives on my hands, feet, and in my corporeal senses, be not mathematical mind at all, but unconscious force—what, on such a supposition, are the chances against one single combination of fives, in a pair? Let the fixed laws of eternal mathematics answer the question. Suppose we had two dice with five faces each, marked in arithmetical order, one, two, three, four, five; we shake them in a box—what are the chances against turning up the number five on each? Every gambler will answer, "the chances against such an event are just twenty-five, the square of the numbers on the several faces; or the total number of ways in which two separate series of fives can possibly be arranged."

Apply this analysis to the given case of the human organism. If the Cause which made me, man, be indeed destitute of mathematical reason, the chances against my possessing five fingers on each hand are twenty-five; add the five toes on each foot, and the chances are six hundred and twenty-five. Then incorporate into the calculation the five senses, and the chances are three thousand one hundred and twenty-five. Let me now get a larger sheet, for the full flow of infinite numbers is fast pouring in upon me. Now calculate the chances against this combination of fives in two men; they swell to the enormous sum of nine millions seven hundred and sixty-five thousand six hundred and twenty-five. Then calculate the chances for four men like myself. They will be the square of the last number, and so on forever. But the immense sums overpower all the most magnificent processes of our algebra, and no logarithmic abbreviations can aid us to grasp what soon stretches into immensity.

The attempt to apply the calculation to all the innumerable millions of mankind now living, and all that have lived and passed away, were as idle as to essay the enumeration of sunbeams shed during sixty centuries of solar years. The algebra of an archangel, with infinite space for his balance-sheet, and eternity for the period of solution, were insufficient, perhaps, for the overwhelming computation.

I would advise the atheist, before he dares grapple in this argument, to refresh his memory with the doctrine of the calculation of chances, in his favorite La Place—or, at least, to look into his common arithmetic. No acquaintance, however profound, with Fichte, Hegel, or other German mystics, will avail him aught in such an inquiry as the present.

In relation to my single self, I might pursue the subject much further. Throughout all the members of my body there runs a wondrous *duality*—in my eyes, arms, hands, feet, ribs, and the convolutions of the brain, where equal numbers balance each other.

The simple question that settles the controversy on its true basis is this: Could any cause without the intellect to perceive—the reason to count, produce all these invariable equations? Shrink not from this simple problem, I beseech thee, O, my brother! The infinite hopes hang upon it, and all time and eternity—the life everlasting, and the loves dearer than life itself. Fly not for refuge to barren logomachies. It will not thus be resolved. Answer me not, that these are only the effects of law! Say not, with Ralph Waldo Emerson (who thus responded when I presented the demonstration in private conversation), that "It is Order which *does* all this!" That is no solution of the problem at all, but only its statement in a different form. The enigma cannot be read by a mere repetition of the same idea crouched in other words. The difficulty remains as inexplicable as ever. For these equations, this sublime universal harmony, is the order itself—neither more nor less. Could the order constitute itself? Can there be order without intellect?

But even supposing that we allow a reality to the abstractions. Let us admit, for the argument's sake, that Law, or Order, or any idea you please, caused these mathematical harmonies of equation, in every series and degree; the same question rebounds upon us with undiminished force: "Is that wonderful order, that mysterious law, self-conscious? Knows it what it doeth? Can it count? Hath it mathematical reason?"

If ye answer "Ay," very well; ye believe in God,

though ye misname him. But if ye say "No," the vailed Sphinx repeats her riddle. "How, then, can blind force produce heavenly harmony, and midnight darkness gild all worlds with ineffable radiance? Whence come these iris-winged splendors that flash up through all immensity? Yonder are the halos, but where is their sun?"

I know the beggarly sophism to which the skeptic ever flies as his dernier resort. He will reply, "Suppose we acknowledge a God to account for this magnificent order, we only postpone the difficulty indefinitely, without attaining the required solution. For then we must attempt the greater problem, to account for the existence of Deity himself." This objection is plausible only in appearance, and can never satisfy any but very shallow minds. The acute logician sees through it at a glance. It is one of the most pitiful specimens of *ignoratio elenchi.* It is founded on a total misapprehension of the true difficulty.

The reason why we set about accounting for the present order and harmony of Nature is, because we see with our own eyes its finite evolutions passing immediately before us. We see many millions of them begin; we watch their progress, as in some gorgeous panorama; and we behold them terminate. The flower puts forth in spring and perishes with the advance of autumn. Yonder great oak on the Alleghanies was once a little acorn, and shall again be nothing as an organized form. The child was born to-day; last year it was not, and next summer it may die. We are made acquainted with indubitable tokens of commencement in the whole material universe. We read those infallible signs in the first leaf of the Bible of creation, scorched, as it were, among the primitive rocks, by the mighty fire-pen of world-volcanoes. The star that shoots from the midnight sky proclaims as it falls :—" Look, mad atheist! Lo! I had a beginning *once*, as *now* I have an end!"

For this reason we seek to *account* for these passing, present events—these mathematical motions, which it were worse than lunacy to deny. We are irresistibly forced to the predication of a Cause by a fixed necessity of our rational nature. Failing to do so would be, not to over-soar the condition of living men, but to sink below the moral *status* of even brute instinct.

But the idea of a God presents no such problem. Here the necessity of the intellect does not hold. There is not a token, in all time or throughout all known space, of his commencement. He is not revealed to us by Eternal Reason in the character of an effect at all. In the mere conception of his whole being and attributes there is nothing whatsoever *phenomenal*. Therefore, to assert for the Divinity a producing Cause, were as foolish as to affirm a like predicate of the infinite space, his everlasting and unchangeable habitation.

We say, then, to the atheist, show us only the slightest proof that God ever began to be, and then, but not till then, can you, with any show of philosophical consistency, demand of us to account for his being. We admit that every phenomenon must have a Cause. Present us, then, some evidence that the Deity is a phenomenon, and we will hear you with patience, when you inquire for a pre-existent producing power. Nothing but phenomena implies causation. No one thinks of proposing such a question in relation to any eternal truth. Who is so silly as to ask why the three angles of a triangle are always equal to two right angles? We have dunces enough in this world of ours, beyond all doubt, but the darkest of them all never conceived such a problem as that. Give us the actual evolution of an undeniable effect, and its origin must be explained—some casual force is necessarily assigned. But to assert such an evolution, and then seek for the evolving power, is an act, not of philosophy, but madness.

In the works of material nature the transient manifestations pass immediately before our eyes, and therefore we must, in spite of ourselves, attempt to account for them. No one but a fool will ever ask, "What was before the Eternal? What is greater than the Infinite?" But every one endowed with one pale ray of human reason cannot help but ask, "What caused the transient? What is above the finite?" This is the first question of infancy, and the last of old age. The savage puts it to his reason in the earliest glimmerings of reflection; and it glances like a sunbeam, gilding the loftiest meditations of the sage. And all science is but an actual or ideal answer to this great radical problem of the universe.

Thus we have sufficiently shown the folly of atheism as an objector, as well as her insanity as a constructor of syllogisms. And now we return to our main argument, by which we are attempting to demonstrate that all motions in Nature are strictly mathematical.

Induction II.—Chemistry.

We will take our next comparisons from Chemistry,

that youngest daughter among the sciences, the beautiful child of the Galvanic Battery, brought forth in splendor and cradled on rollers of fire.

Go, analyze me a cup of water; you find it composed of two parts of hydrogen to one of oxygen, by volume, and eight parts of oxygen to one of hydrogen, by weight. And these numerical ratios never vary. Freeze it into ice, hard as the granite of the eternal hills; dissipate it into vapor of such exquisite tenuity that it would take a million acres of the floating mist to form a single drop of dew; bring it from the salt solitudes of the ocean, or from the central curve of a rainbow, and submit it to the test of analysis; and still the pale chemist, as he watches the developments of his laboratory, calls out, "Two to one and one to eight, now and forever." And will any one be mad enough to affirm that the mighty Cause, who rolled out yon dark blue expanse of ocean, and bade the liquid crystal bubble in multitudinous springs from the fissures of cleft limestone, and sing in the innumerable flowing rills, was and is himself unconscious of the mystic numbers by which the separate elements that compose its dual essence are married to eternity? I would be loth to judge any man's heart; but it does seem to me that the head which can credit an hypothesis so monstrously absurd must have exchanged brains with a baboon. It may be argued that I express myself too strongly. I can only say, in reply, that I do not utter the half of what I feel. Nor can I be made, very easily, to believe that any decorous terms are too severe, in denunciation of the moral felons of the universe, who would rob humanity of its dearest hopes.

But to proceed with the argument. Go again, and analyze me a gallon of atmospheric air. You find it composed of twenty parts of oxygen to eighty of nitrogen in every hundred, by volume, nearly.

And these proportions never vary. Bring it from the high billows of the distant seas, or from the depths of the Lybian deserts, or with Guy Lussac in your balloon, bottled up twenty-two thousand feet above the earth's surface, and still the mystic numbers keep their exact count. And was the Cause of this numerical harmony—the Author who rolled this ocean of the breath of life, forty-five miles deep, around the globe—destitute of the reason to perceive the ratio of its union? Can that Cause count—yea or nay—which ever works in magnificent numbers?

But still again, go analyze me a bit of limestone. You discover that its elements bear a quadruple ratio. There are twenty-two parts by weight of carbonic acid, and twenty-eight of lime. Lime is composed of twenty parts of the white metal calcium, and eight parts of oxygen gas. Carbonic acid is composed of sixteen parts of oxygen, and six of carbon. And these proportions, too, are of unchanging uniformity. They are the same in the stalactite, icicle-shaped and crystal-grained, torn from the roofs of coral caves, and in the rifled slab, hurled up from the heart of the earth by the volcano's hand, mailed with thunder, and in the glittering pebble that a child picks out of the brook in which it plays with naked feet. What a field is here for the calculation of chances! What a theme for devout and transcendent wonder! What a Bible is this among the old rocks! What magic hieroglyphics on the mountains!

But not only are numerical characters here; symbolical angles are traced in splendor also. All the hundred forms of carbonate of lime split into six-sided figures, called rhombohedrons, whose alternate angles measure 105 deg. 55 min. and 75 deg. 05 min. Let the mathematician come with his plane trigonometry, fresh from the schools, and study a higher lesson. But if he be wise, he will study it as the great Linnæus studied flowers—on bended knees!

Induction III.—Botany.

We will make our next comparisons in that science so charming to all lovers of Nature. Not over smoky furnaces, or in darkened chambers, will we read this division of our lecture; but out among the silken sisterhood of sweet-scented flowers, where the blue-eyed heavens smile love down in our faces, and the winds whisper through our sunny hair.

The first ten classes of Linnæus are arranged simply according to the number of stamens in each flower.

Let us analyze a flower of the tobacco-plant. It is of the fifth class, and of course has five stamens. Its corol has five parts, and its calyx five points. It is so with every tobacco-flower on the earth. It ever was, and will ever remain so.

Now let us suppose that every flower is produced by a Cause that cannot count; what are the mathematical chances against this combination of fives, three times in a single flower? The answer is obviously: "One hundred and twenty-five;" while the chances against a like combination in two flowers amount to the great sum of fifteen thousand six hundred and twenty-five.

Let the atheist answer me, What must the chances be in one large field? in all the fields throughout the world during one solar summer? and extending the view still wider, so as to embrace all the summers ever shed by yonder bright sun?

He who can shut his eyes to the overwhelming force of this demonstration, deserves never more a single glimpse of the green fields, with their coronals of golden bouquets floating in their own perfume.

Look at the lily in her snowy robes. All over the world, and throughout all times, it numbers but six stamens, and its delicate corol is six-parted.

Some of those beautiful flowers are vegetable clocks and watches, and keep time with the revolutions of the world, and sublimer roll of the twinkling orbs in their eternal movements. Some open to the morning sun; some beneath the blaze of noon; others at purple twilight, when the soft dews begin to fall; and one in the wild West, the magnificent flower discovered by Captain Bonneville, near the base of the Rocky Mountains, lifts its gorgeous eye alone to gaze on the midnight stars! Do these blooms of Nature's garden know the divisions of day and darkness, or the seconds and minutes of recorded time, that they thus equal our best pocket chronometers in taking note of the fast-flowing hours? Can the Cause of all this order be unintelligent? He who can believe so may safely be set down in the category of those who are beyond the reach of all argument.

Induction IV.—Light.

We shall not hazard a single remark as to the nature

of light, that wonderful agent that plays so important a part in the processes of creation, and which is so beautiful in itself, and moves with a velocity so immense, that, with a slight poetic license, it might be regarded as a smile of the omnipresent Deity. We have only to do, at present, with its mathematical evolutions.

Its first law is a strict algebraic formula, and may be expressed thus: The intensity of light decreases as the square of its distance increases, and *vice versa.* Does the Cause, whatsoever we may suppose it to be, which produces this mathematical ratio, understand the evolution of numbers? If not, how, in the name of reason, can it be supposed to form those miraculous squares that often sweep, in many circles, embracing billions of leagues, in the stellar spaces? Let me pledge faith in the wildest fictions of fairy land, the most impossible fables of false theology, sooner than in such inconceivable absurdities as an hypothesis like that. But it is ever thus; when the human mind once rejects the general belief of mankind, there is nothing then too monstrous for its voracious credulity.

The second law of light is stated mathematically, in a form equally luminous, and conveys a truth equally magnificent. *The angles of incidence and reflection are always equal.* Thus, if a ray of light from the sun fall on the table before me, at an angle of forty-five degrees, it is reflected again at a like angle; and so of all other lines of every possible obliquity. These angles never vary so much as a single hair's breadth. Euclid or Legendre has none so perfect. Try, we entreat you, Oh, rational reader, with all your skill; and see if you can trace any equally exact, with the pen, on the smoothest paper! And is it possible that, after all, the Cause which thus *geometrizes* is devoid of all knowledge of geometry? If so, then may a blind mole—nay, a nonentity itself, compose a treatise superior in splendor and accuracy to Newton's world-renowned *Principia!*

But apply the doctrine of chances to these angles now being formed, every instant, all over the universe, and even imagination staggers under the immensity of the idea. Only pause here for a moment. Think of all the beams that emanate from the sun during one long summer day—of all the rays that flash out from the stars for only a single night. Then let your mind travel back over the march of dim, distant centuries, gathering age upon age, and cycle on cycle, in vast segments of eternity, where *platonic years* vanish into insignificant vibrations of the pendulum, and the duration of galaxies are seen but as shadows on the dial-plate of infinitude. Then bid imagination lift her lightning wing away on high, from world to world remote, as far beyond the reach of the telescope as the glance of that magic tube transcends the vision of a flitting insect, and behold the horizon of the space that knows no limits, still opening forever, onward, and upward, and all around, and thickening with columns of suns, and breaking into nebulous starry haze, and undulating, like some shoreless sea, with waves of light, and then tell me the number of all the rays ever shot athwart the great immensity since the first fire-sons of heaven sang their choral hymn in the morning of creation—and then answer me, who shall calculate the chances against the perpetual, universal observance of the law in relation to angles, in and by all *these*, on the supposition that there is no God? Only God himself may solve the mighty problem!

We may here note a remarkable law, in reference to light of different colors, only discovered recently. [Children's Lyceum colors have high meanings.]

If two rays, from two luminous points, be admitted in a dark chamber, and falling on white paper, or other suitable reflecting surface, differ in their length by .0000258 part of an inch, their intensity is doubled. A like result is produced if such difference in length be any multiple of that nearly infinitesimal fraction by a whole number. But, strange to say, a multiple by $2\frac{1}{2}$, $3\frac{1}{2}$, $4\frac{1}{2}$, &c., gives the result of total darkness! While a multiple by $2\frac{1}{4}$, $3\frac{1}{4}$, &c., gives an intensity equal to one ray only. In one of these cases the fact is seen, which, from the beginning of the world, has been regarded as the extreme of impossibility—light actually produces darkness!

Corresponding effects are witnessed in violet-rays, if the difference in their lengths be equal to .0000157 part of an inch. And the like results are given by experiments on all other rays, the difference in length varying with a steady uniformity of increase, from the violet to the red. Who shall reckon the chances, in two cases only, in such vast number as these?

Let not shallow sciolism answer me by a pitiful evasion, "that all this is accounted for on the principle of mechanical vibrations." Cannot the merest tyro in logic see that the difficulty remains the same? For the question immediately presents itself: What causes the vibrations? And how can unintelligent vibrations be supposed to arrange such wonderful combinations of arithmetic?

Uniformity of colors in refracted light is equally marvelous.

See yon dark cloud, only a moment ago one thick mass of gloom, lurid, almost appalling to the gazer's eye! Suddenly the sun breaks forth in the western sky; and lo! in an instant the rainbow is born, and stretches afar the curved wings of its prismatic plumage, as if to play around the world! Count well its gaudy colors. There is the sacred number seven, composed by the blending of the mystic three. And never, either on the land or sea, in city or solitude, hath a single cloud blushed to the kiss of the sunbeam without the colors of the sacred seven, painted by the Divine ray-brush, in heavenly enameling there. O, golden-haired sun! "O, airy vapor! Father and mother of that beatiful child of the sky, brought forth in purple, cradled in vermilion, baptized in molten gold, and swathed in dun," know ye what ye do? Are ye indeed blind? Can ye count without arithmetic? without the algebra of a Euler?—ay, without even the poor instinct of the eagle, that dips his wing in the checkered cloud—would ye undertake to teach the whole world mathematics?

Were there no other proof of the existence of a Deity, this one consideration would settle the question forever. Every rainbow is an exact mathematical equation of every other rainbow in the universe!

Awake, ye dreaming metaphysicians! Arouse from your darkling dormitories, and those pale lucubrations which are more than half slumber. Come away to the floods and fields, the flower-banks and the forests—out *here*, in open space and the free air, where sea and earth and sky mingle in mutual embraces, like the greeting of youthful lovers! Listen to the pine-songs, which are chants of praise, and the wind-warblers, which are hymns of hallelujah! Look up yonder on the fire-dance of innumerable rolling worlds, and then answer me, before the sun and all the stars—"is there no God?"

We will take our next inductions from the science of ASTRONOMY, which is only another name for sublimity itself.

For countless centuries, the stars, high and mysterious, had shone on in the blue vault of immensity; and ignorant man knew nothing of the nature of their movements—could not divine even what they were. But although knowledge may sleep, the eye of curiosity never closes while the heart of the human reckons one beat. And so the eager question was repeated in every age, and over all lands—"What do these lights mean?" But neither to Magian on the plains of Shinar, nor to the prince of philosophers in the "city of the violet crown," came forth any answer from the silent solitudes of the sky.

At length a little boy was born. His dark eye inherited some rays from the light of the stars, and flashed with wild meaning from his childhood; and as he grew up, he became a gazer at all things beautiful, and a questioner of all things dim. He saw all eyes turned to those "isles of light" that gem the seas of the upper firmament; and he heard all lips repeat the earnest inquiry,—"What do these lights mean?" But he heard no whisper in reply. He looked at them with his naked eye, but the God's type of their far-off letters could not be read so far. He ruminated on the mystery day and night, and, either waking or sleeping, he dreamed of the power of lenses; and then set about constructing glasses to read the riddle of the lofty stars. He succeeded; for there are no impossibilities to patient attention—there never was a bar unconquerable to the will that dares all things! And then for the first time the vail of Egyptian Isis was lifted up, and the secret of ages was out. The stony eyes of the Sphinx melted with tears of joy!

What a miracle is this of the telescope! Never a poet lived, but in his heart wished for pinions to soar and mingle with the stars. Lo! Here are the plumes. The telescope gives not the wings to us; but it ties them with lines of light to the stars, which thus fly down to us, and tell us all their hidden laws! Is there any thing in the golden dreams of fable—in all the tales of fairy enchantment, to be compared to this sublime result, evolved by mathematical reason?

Next came the great Kepler, and erected his triangular pyramid of the three laws, on the summit of which Newton stood, to fix forever the true theory of the universe.

Let us glance a moment at these laws.

1. All the planetary orbits are regular ellipses, in the lower focus of which the sun is placed.

Propose the problem to yonder intelligent school boy. Tell him to trace on the paper, with his pen, an elliptical curve, and dot the two foci. Can he do it? Come, sage skeptic, with all your boasted reason, can you do it yourself? The planets are masses of blind matter. Who, then, will dare assert that such may trace perpetually, for thousands of years, mathematical lines, with a regularity that no college professor can ever hope to equal?

2. The times occupied by any planet, in describing any given arcs of its orbit, are always as the areas of sectors, formed by straight lines drawn from the beginning and end of the arcs to the sun, as a center.

Let no one attempt the solution of this problem, in any specified case, unless he be a thorough mathematician. God solves it for all the planets.

3. But the third law of Kepler is still more astonishing. Hear! The squares of the periods of the planets' revolutions vary, as the cubes of their distance from the sun. What wonderful operations are these, to be the work of unthinking masses of matter! What music is this among the stars, to be sung by tongueless atoms!*

Well might the inspired old man exclaim, "I have stolen the golden secret of the Egyptians. I triumph. I will indulge my sacred fury. I care not whether my work be read now or by posterity. I can afford to wait a century for readers, when God himself has waited six thousand years for an observer!"

Some cold critics have called this insanity. The man must be insane to say so! I never perused the passage without tears. It is the language of reason and imagination, which, at their sublimest depths, are but one.

We will not speak of chances here. We may not even think of them, unless we might pilfer the algebra of the morning star.

---

* See a recent volume by the author, entitled, "*The Stellar Key to the Summer Land.*"

Promiscuous Inductions.

1. Some years ago it was keenly debated whether the sea was not receding and the dry land gaining ground; and the general opinion of scientific men leaned strongly in favor of such an hypothesis.

At length a Swedish astronomer struck out a novel method of settling the controversy. He cut down a large pine tree that grew at the water's edge on the Gulf of Bothnia, and on counting the concentric circles, found that it was five hundred years old; and, consequently, during all that time the ocean must have remained stationary. This was decisive. And yet how wonderful the fact! Millions had lived and died; nations had flourished and fallen; genius had sung its flame-songs, and love had breathed its burning sighs, and all had passed away—and still the forest-born grew on, buffeted by tempests, and chilled by freezing frosts, but nurtured always by genial summers, and fed on silver-singing rains, and listening to the bird-music in its branches, till half a millennium is gone; and still all that time it had kept an exact account of its age, never losing a single year, all noted in beautiful circles, amid the fine woof of its own fibers. It is so with every cone of wood in the wide world. And again we ask, Can aught but reason trace circles, or reckon the count of passing time?

2. But let us select a last example. If anywhere we might suppose the absence of mathematical motion, we would expect to find it in those air-fiends that often desolate whole countries—the hurricanes of the tropics.

But modern science teaches us "that hurricanes are

only whirlwinds on a larger scale. That they all have a regular axis of rotary motion, which axis is itself progressive, like a planet in its orbit, tracing an elliptical or parabolic curve." Sometimes the vortex of storm covers an area of over five hundred square miles, and sweeps over distant seas for hundreds of leagues; but ever this *dual* motion is preserved. Ay—beyond all question, the hand that launches the tornado, and girds its dark bosom with thunder, is the same that originally "weighed the hills in scales, and the mountains in a balance;" and not poor, blind, and utterly impossible chance!

Thus it is plain that all motions in nature are mathematical.

But the skeptic may object:

The proposition is not proven. For although we may admit that such a truth holds within the sphere of our actual observation, still, what right have we to extend the predicate beyond the limits of that sphere? What right can we show to carry it back to the everlasting ages of the eternity without a beginning, and down to the incalculable years of that time which shall never end? What right have we to break over the impassable limits of the sense of sight, and assert a law that we know only to appertain to a little segment of the circle of infinitude, of all the untrodden fields that may bloom with worlds, like flowers in the unexplored spaces, of which we behold but a twinkling point?

We have stated the objection in its full force; because it is much easier to answer than to state it.

We reply thus: All the forms of matter must be, of

necessity, mathematical, simply because it is matter; as all its motions must likewise be so, for the reason that matter is inert.

We ask the reader to pursue the second scholium to the nineteenth proposition of the fourth book of Legendre. He will there find that all the figures possible in space are resolvable into the triangle, and of course must be mathematical.

Then let him turn to Arnott's Elements, where it is demonstrated that all motion must be in a straight line, unless controlled by some interfering force, when it takes the direction of a curve. So all motion must be mathematical, or not be at all.

The simple answer that demolishes the whole objection is this: We see nothing but mathematical harmony in all the motions that occur within our own sphere—we can conceive of nothing but mathematical harmony in any other sphere. We see the unequivocal footsteps of a God within our sphere; and every fresh gush of light from the remotest suns adds to the evidences that it is so everywhere else in the wide universe. And this is enough. We are not called upon to roam over all space, and ascend the heights of all eternity, merely to answer a supposition destitute of even a shadow of proof, and verging close on the confines of absurdity! If we have a God ourselves, that is sufficient, if we but pay him the proper adoration. We need not stop to inquire whether some little mote or molecule of sand does or does not gyrate without a God, somewhere in the vast void of immensity!

Now let us put together, syllogistically, the two propositions heretofore demonstrated, and note the logical result.

1. Nothing but mind can work mathematically.

2. All the motions of Nature are strictly mathematical.

Then must it follow, as a conclusion utterly unassailable, that every effect in the universe is produced by the immediate agency of Mind.

To this, however, a plausible but false objection may be made. It was put against my argument last winter, by a distinguished Pantheist of Boston.

It may be said, that although it be demonstrated that matter cannot geometrize, still we are not entitled thence to infer that mind alone can; since there may be other substances in space beside matter and mind. What right, the objector may say, have we to assume duality only in substantial existence? It is true that we are acquainted within our own sphere with nothing but these. But our sphere is scarcely so much as an infinitesimal fraction of the whole universe. The entire concavity of the sky is a mere point, dotted in a space of inconceivable extent. The totality of our historical time is not a second in that eternity without bounds, which expands both behind and before us. And how can we know but beyond this paltry sphere there may exist millions of substances that are neither material nor mental, but of an altogether different, nay, contradictory nature? And even as to that, we are limited in our own fragmented sphere by the solid wall of impassable sensation, that shuts us up as in a cage or prison of iron bars, in this our little world of fleeting appearances. For aught we can say to the contrary, here, where we now dream our philosophical reveries, perhaps no loftier than those the oyster excogitates in his shell; yea, immediately here, in the very space occupied by this poor grain of earth, and yonder evanescent bubbles of air and sky, there may be now substances indefinite in number, the very opposite of matter and mind, and with which we have no sense fitted to converse! To deny this, says the sophist, were as unreasonable as for the animalculæ in the dew-drop to assert that there is nothing but insects in the whole creation.

We cannot forbear remarking what a marvelous amount of credulity it implies to put with a grave face such objections. The skeptic refuses to credit the existence of the God who made him, though the splendor of the divine attributes shines on the face of all Nature brighter than the blaze of the myriad suns; and yet he finds no difficulty at all in affirming the reality of innumerable beings, the impossible brood of a wild imagination, as devoid of all proof as the fairies of Scottish fable—the veriest of all moonshine.

And yet even scientific men of eminent fame have entertained such vagaries, and gravely uttered them on the printed page. Dr. John Mason Good was absurd enough to give the hypothesis a place in that strange medley of fact and fiction, so pompously denominated "The Book of Nature." I cannot but attribute such crude inanities to the general neglect of logic, mathematics, and true metaphysics among the moderns.

No person the least acquainted with logical analysis ever could have seriously started such an objection. It is founded on the sheerest ignorance of division. We showed, at an earlier stage of this inquiry, that the *abscisio infiniti* always exhausts the subject divided.

Every thing in the whole compass of thought must be either a tree or not a tree. It is so with matter and mind. We define mind, that which possesses reason; and we define matter, that which doth not so possess reason. And it is evident to a schoolboy that every object that ever was, or will be, or possibly can be, must either possess reason or not possess it. He who fails to see this distinction may rest assured, that whatever may be his talents, the faculty of logical investigation is not to him an attainable accomplishment.

For surely, unless reason itself be a dream, and insanity the only wisdom, every substance must be either active or passive, have intelligence and volition, or not. And, therefore, matter and mind are two logical categories that encompass all thought and exhaust all Nature. We demonstrate, then: 1. That matter is passive, and consequently cannot be supposed to originate its motions. 2. That no effect in Nature can possibly occur without motion. We must, therefore, seek for casual force in the category of universal substance, or nowhere. We find it in mind; and this is confirmed by our own inner consciousness, which assures us, by the exercise of our voluntary activity, that the mind within us can and does produce motion, and cause effects as astonishing as they are beautiful. We next demonstrate that nothing but the reason, which perceives its own operations, can possibly work mathematically. And then we show by inductions, as wide as the generalizations of science, that all natural motions are mathematical. Hence, they must be produced by a cause possessing reason. And the calculation of chances proves most conclusively that to deny this is an absurdity a thousand times worse than the ravings of utter madness.

As to all that exuberant sophistry about the impossibility of predicating any thing out of our own actual sphere, we may observe that it is but a common trick of skeptics when driven from the field of fair argument. They assume a feigned humility, meeker than the most pious believers. Creation becomes a mere point, and life the flutter of a leaf in the sunbeam. They claim affinity with the blind worm and droning beetle, and can do nothing but shiver with awe at the immensity above and beyond them. They ape all the ignorance of the child, without any of its trusting confidence, its ardent, innocent love, or its eager, soaring hope.

We admit the grandeur of eternity—we wonder at the infinitude of space ; and we freely confess our own littleness when compared, not with those mighty masses of moving matter that wheel on high over our heads, but with that Omnipotent Being who guides them in their courses.

For although our life is fleeting, and our globe but a dot on the map of the universe, we have thought, that wanders throughout eternity, and, "before creation peopled earth," even now "rolls through chaos back;" and with a glance dilates o'er all to be in the vast fields of futurity, and climbs with winged feet the golden ladder of all the stars. Nothing material can do that—not the beam of light, shot from equatorial suns—not the lightning, which darts from heaven to earth in a moment. May we not assert, that although we be as nothing in the presence of that God "who wheels his throne upon the rolling worlds," yet one human soul of the countless millions of our species is superior to all the worlds that God ever made or can make? *It* inherits the divine attribute of reason. *They* never knew the sublime "geometry of their own evolutions!"

But it is utterly untrue that we can predicate nothing beyond the sphere of our own sensation. That is one of the follies of exploded materialism. Do we not know that everywhere a triangle must have three and only three angles? Can we not affirm this truth as certainly of the space a million leagues beyond the orb of solar day, beyond the farthest star that twinkles in blue ether, as of the little figure on the paper but six inches from our eyes? Must not the radii of every circle in the universe be equal? Is not the whole everywhere greater than any of its parts? Can there be any phenomenon without a cause?—in any, the wildest of the wilderness?—in any, the remotest cycle of eternity? Can love be a crime, or murder virtue, in any conceivable sphere of existence? Can truth become a lie for any being to whom atheism is not reason? All spheres alike belong to the soul, when it puts on its beautiful wings, and goes forth through the open door of universal faith to universal triumph. Then the stars beckon it to their bosom, and legions of angels fly down to meet it. Then it becomes a note in the eternal anthem of sphere-melodies that hymn the universal Father; and in affirming God, it conquers even death, and is already one of the immortals.

But again, it may be objected, that although no mass of matter can be supposed to move itself, yet two masses or elements, when brought sufficiently near, may move each other.

But this is too shallow for a serious answer. For how shall the given masses, or elements, or separate atoms, be ever brought near without first of all moving? And what cause may move them? Not other matter, for that would be to shift the difficulty without solving it. Such are all the arguments of atheism—fallacies that are their own refutation—quibbles that a modest monkey, were it gifted with speech, would blush to utter!

Another and very common objection of scientific skeptics may be expressed thus: It is true, say they, that we are irresistibly forced by our intellectual constitution to affirm a Cause for this vast flowing stream of phenomenal events that together constitute the universe. But we find that Cause in Nature; it is Nature which does all this. She builds up and tears down her own systems. She evolves at once the life and the death, which are but two different phases of one and the same fact, or as the opposite sections of all are, where the universe plays as a pendulum betwixt birth and dissolution.

See how easy it is to use words without meaning. The shadows of language do not embarrass each other —do not impinge, so to speak, at all, when they have lost the substance of ideas that gave them soul.

Let us ask the objector—Tell us seriously, what do you mean by the term Nature? Is it a reality, or only a relation? Hath it a substance? and if so, that substance, as we have seen, must be either matter or mind—must possess reason or not. And if it be without reason, how doth its mimicry of the attribute so far transcend all known originals? The difficulty loses nothing of its force by predicating Nature as the cause of any conceivable operation. The question still comes up, whence this exquisite harmony, which intellect alone could order? That will not down at the bidding of a lifeless word—that will not be solved by the art of a juggler, that merely shifts his penny covertly from one hand to the other.

All men of sense now agree that Nature is but a general term—a mere abstraction. It means but the totality of phenomena that constitutes the universe. It is the very order which it is used by the sophist to account for—nothing more. It is an ideal exponent, a symbol in the mind's algebraic notation for all the motions of the universal whole. It does not and cannot give the unknown X which lies beneath them.

It is the same with the phrase, "Laws of Nature." No philosopher, since the publication of Bacon's Organon, has regarded these as any thing other than the very facts themselves *generalized.* They are merely classifications of observed phenomena. How ridiculously absurd is it, then, to use the word law to account for the facts that constitute the law, and without which it were not. It is a law of Nature that the sun rises in the morning. But that is nothing more than a general assertion of the particular fact; and to say the fact is so because it is a law of Nature, is precisely equivalent to the identical proposition, "the sun rises because the sun rises!"

Nor is the case at all different, if we use the word *property* instead of the word law. For recollect, that Matter and Mind are the only two substances possible, even in imagination. And when you affirm that a certain property in one body causes motion in another, before you look wise, and raise a shout of gratulation at the fancied success of your own ingenuity, pause a moment and ask yourself the short, simple question—What is property? Is it matter, or is it mind? Is it an entity, or an abstraction? Has it color and form, or hands and feet? Has it consciousness and a will? And above all—for that will touch, as with a ray of electrical light, the secret heart of the matter—be sure and ask, "Has the given or supposed property Reason, and does it understand mathematics?"

But we feel that on this part of our argument among these skeptical objections, we have wandered far from the sunlight of the common earth and air, into a dim world of empty abstractions. A cold wind breathes in our faces, like "the difficult air of the iced mountain-tops, where the birds dare not build, nor insect's wing flits o'er herbless granite;" or rather like the stifling vapors of sepulchral vaults, where shadows come and go, as in a dance of mocking wild-fires. Never mind; let us proceed. The children of the mist will vanish before the torch of Reason, and the firmest pillars of the capital of atheism melt away into mere negation.

I will now state an objection to the mathematical argument, urged in a private conversation, by an eminent atheistical writer of Boston, during a recent visit to New England.

He said: "It is true I cannot pretend to answer your demonstration by laying my finger on a palpable logical flaw in the reasoning. But I can do more. I can show that it must be false, since it contradicts the evidence of the senses. You undertake to prove that one body cannot move another. Every man's eyes behold the contrary. Yonder is a barrel of gunpowder. Let a spark fall on its surface, and the whole detonates instantaneously with a deafening explosion, producing light, heat, and sound."

To this we reply, that in such cases as these, and all others of sensible motion, our eyes truly see nothing but the visible phenomena. We behold the appearance, not the power which produced it. The surface is plain enough to view; the solid center eludes our vision. Yet we know there is a producing power—we believe with absolute certainty in a center. We cannot help doing so, unless we would turn maniacs. The veriest atheist does the same. Ask him what causes the gunpowder to deflagrate on the application of a spark of fire? He will not answer—unless in the last stage of lunacy—" there is no cause for it, in good sooth." That would be too much for even an atheist of the Modern Athens. He will respond, " there is a secret property in the spark to ignite the powder, and therefore it must be ignited;" and ten to one he will launch boldly out into a learned dissertation concerning the chemical composition of the powder, and the hidden qualities of fire, showing, with consummate ingenuity, how well suited they are to be joined in wedlock—how much they desire to be married, and what a flame-progeny they must necessarily beget between them! Now ask him what is that secret property in the spark which evolves such results? He will surely respond—" It is the unknown cause, which has the power of production." One more question and the problem is solved. Is that property or cause matter or mind? Doth it know what it doeth? Hath it a will to originate motion? Can it move itself? And so still on and forever, there can be but one solution for the universal enigma, and that alone is afforded in the infinite reason. We can never hope to meet with action, save in that which is essentially active. The purely passive cannot furnish it.

But finally, as a last resort, the skeptic flies in a sudden panic, as it were, from his own objections, and takes refuge in blasphemy. "If there be a God," says he, in the maddened language of Shelley, "that God must be the author of all evil; and such a proposition is more revolting than the worst forms of atheism. I would rather," he continues to urge, "credit any absurdity, or commit any conceivable folly, than acknowledge a creed like that. Can we suppose that a God of infinite reason and unlimited power would voluntarily create such a universe as this? Would he give life to beings, only to confer an acquaintance with its exquisite sweetness, and then almost instantly take it away? Would he plant in quivering hearts not only those burning tortures which are of the very essence of hate, but those sorrowy stings that follow the rosy feet of gliding love also? Tell me that God made some other world, where perfection is the order of Nature, and I may, perhaps, believe you. But ask me not to admit a divine origin for such a desolate sphere as this. Somewhere else, for aught I know or care, there may be harmony. Here I behold nothing but sin and disorder. Pestilence and famine—volcanoes and devouring war—tempest and earthquake, alone reign around us. A wild, wailing howl of agony resounds throughout all lands; and even brute instinct echoes the appalling cry of the human. Vanity is written, in fire-letters of ruin, even on yon starry azure, where pale suns burst in shivered bubbles, and vanish away. Urge not that a Deity dug, in void space, this universal sepulcher, haunted alone by the ghost of mourners, by the incalculable millions. Say that it is the work of some dreadful demon, and I may entertain the proposition!"

Such blasphemies are horrible to hear. * * * * I can listen to any other man with patience. I can bear with the poor Pagan, who honestly bows the knee to his idol, painted with blood though it be. I can sympathize with the Polytheist, who beholds a separate god in every object of beauty and of wonder. I recognize a brother man struggling through the deep gloom of superstition, striving to reach the light. But I recoil instinctively from an unprincipled atheist. I realize the fearful presence of some dark spirit of a different order.

But let us trace the objection seriously, according to the strictest rules of logic.

We remark, in the first place, that it is not an objection to the argument, as such, but a mere truculent tirade against the conclusion established. And even so to this, it is wholly irrelevant. It lies, if it be of any worth at all, not against the being, but the attributes of the Deity. The presence of evil may, or may not, furnish a valid reason for pronouncing as to the moral character of a power. It certainly does not touch the question of existence at a single point whatsoever. The dullest intellect must perceive this at once, without illustration, on the bare statement. The problem of the origin of evil has positively nothing to do with the proposition that God is. It belongs to a very different category—the inquiry as to whether God is good.

The problem of evil has been professedly solved in many opposite ways. Every creed presents its own solution. Free-will, predestination, optimism, the fall of man, transitive progress, and several minor theories, are so many methods of explanation. We shall not presume to attempt an account of it. Such a tentative, however ingenious, can at least be but pure hypothesis. Nay, it is demonstrably insolvable without a direct revelation from heaven; and for the obvious reason that the existence of evil is a contingent, not a necessary truth, in the metaphysical sense. It is not based upon any principle of eternal reason, from which it may be educed and expressed in analytical formulas. It is, on the contrary, a fact of experience, the origin of which can only be comprehended by actual or historical survey. But when, or where, or how it originated, who shall declare? The true question, embodying the whole difficulty, is this—"Why did the Deity purpose to permit it?" or to cause it, if the wording suit you better? And this, beyond all controversy, no one in the universe, not the oldest seraph of knowledge, can possibly tell, unless the Deity see fit to reveal it to the intellect.

For this cause, all metaphysical solutions of the origin of evil must ever continue to be mere hypotheses, and, as such, founded on very meager data. We have not framed such; we have essayed to do better—to demonstrate their insufficiency, and unfold the reasons why they are so. But with this frank admission to back it, the objection, even as to the divine attributes, remains as futile as ever.

We cannot judge the moral character of the Deity from one manifestation of his power alone, unless we are thoroughly familiar with the whole compass of its design. The act reveals the attribute only in connection with the purpose that put forth the act. This is evidently true of even the finite fellow-creature. Suppose that the history of some ancient nation simply informs us that "Zanoni killed Uelika," and informs us nothing more. Can we, therefore, pronounce with unerring, or even probable certainty, that Zanoni must have been a bad man? Assuredly not, unless we know also, in addition to the fact, the cause and motive of the killing. Uelika may have been a traitor to his country, and Zanoni put him to death as a minister of the law. The slaying may have been in self-defense, or in open and honorable war; nay, on some glorious field of victory, where the heroic patriot fought for the redemption of his race, and to protect the hearth of his home and the wife and children of his bosom. It may have been, for any thing we can allege to the contrary, an act of the loftiest virtue, rather than one of the lowest criminality, or, indeed, of any guilt at all. Thus we reason in relation to our finite fellow-men. Wherefore, then, apply a totally different sort of ratiocination to the ways and purposes of the Infinite Father?

He may have permitted evil as a condition of the greatest good. He may have suffered it in order to the necessary display of that wondrous mercy which could be revealed alone through its partial or general prevalence. Nay, he may have ordained it, in order to enhance our everlasting happiness hereafter. The shooting pang of this fleeting moment of life may form the point of comparison by which to reckon the raptures of the whole eternity. In fine, a thousand suppositions may be conceived to avoid the follies of atheism and the sins of blasphemy. Doth the skeptic get rid of evil by denying God? On the contrary, he affirms its endless perpetuity—the utter impossibility of its termination. He does not circumscribe its boundaries—he cures not one pain in the bleeding bosom of humanity; but he extends the grisly terror into all other spheres of existence; since what blind matter, and crude, unconscious force has accomplished here, it must accomplish everywhere and forever!

But the shuddering horror we experience at the bare idea of God's willing evil for its own sake is proof positive of the divine benevolence, which has thus constituted our inner nature to love virtue and abominate vice, even were such vice possible in Deity himself!

Besides, we know innumerable evidences of Infinite goodness around us. In the boundless beauty that ever lives from age to age on the earth below, and in the splendors of the firmament above us, we see and feel it. We behold it in the ecstasies of youthful love, in the serene joys of friendship, in the cherished sympathies and endearing recollections of sweet home. It bubbles up even in the gratifications of sense, and mingles with the coarse luxuries of animal instinct. We hear it in the songs of birds and the evening hum of the bee-hive. Sickness adds a new zest to convalescence. Never is the light of heaven so enchanting as after a night of cloud and tempest. And even the grave itself is sometimes sought after by philosophy as well as religion, as a not unwelcome bed of repose. It is only the sin that has wrought its own keenest sufferings, which throws such gloomy colors on the features of Nature. The little innocent children, and all true poets, as well as enlightened Christians, and the great mass of mankind, love this same Nature so well that they are very loth to bid her farewell, even for the revealed bliss of life everlasting!

We will notice only one more objection, and speedily bring our argument to a close. It is not an atheistical objection, but one that will doubtless be made by many intelligent and pious Christians to one idea expressed in our conclusion, and demonstrated, as we cannot but deem most fully, in our whole course of reasoning. The idea is the immediate ever-present agency of the Deity, in all the phenomena of Nature. One class of writers on natural theology view the universe of worlds as a grand machine, that was, to be sure, originally put together by the divine hand and set in motion, since which time it continues to run of its own accord, like other mechanical constructions of a similar kind, though under the general superintendence and control of Providence.

Such is the mechanical conception of the universe, as opposed to the dynamic or atheistical. It allows the presence and agency of God: 1. At the period of creation; and, 2. His occasional intervention at the periods of miracles. It allows, too, his general supervision, to keep the machine of Nature from falling into pieces. But it denies altogether that every phenomenal evolution of matter—every motion produced, either in molecules or masses, is the immediate effect of a present volition of the Divine mind.

This conception prevails to a considerable extent among scientific men; and is embraced, perhaps, by at least one-half of the Christian world.

We have no doubt that the almost material, certainly sensual, philosophy of Locke, contributed mainly to this result in the first instance—a result still further strengthened by the strictly mechanical argument, presented with such admirable clearness, in Paley's Natural Theology. The exceedingly eloquent writings of the late lamented Dr. Chalmers also aided the advance of this general tendency.

We are compelled to regard the prevalence of such an opinion as injurious, though not designedly so, to the general interests of religion and science both; while we must feel that it strips Nature of her most highly poetic ornaments, and reduces her most gorgeous works to the condition of mere lifeless contrivances. We have no sympathy whatever for "celestial mechanics." Indeed, it seems to us that the word is a strange misnomer, when applied to the magnificent creations of the Deity, either on the earth or in the sky. To render this evident, let us consider the meaning of the term when used in reference to the works of human art.

In such structures we do not create any new material nor any new force. We simply apply the old to the new purposes, by giving them a new direction. It is a settled law in mechanics, that no arrangement of parts can possibly, under any combination of circumstances, add one particle of power to the original stock of Nature. The screw, the lever, the wheel and axle, always lose in time exactly what they gain in intensity. And thus it is true, beyond all controversy, that the mightiest art of man can neither create a single new atom of matter, or add to the universe one iota of active force. It merely plans special collocations of parts, and adapts them to the action of existing forces. Thus it prepares the water-wheel, and places it in the running stream, where the revolutions are performed by an ever-present power. Thus is human mechanics an arrangement of means, where the human intellect co-operates with the uniform motions perpetually evolved by the Divine volition.

Now, we may be permitted to inquire, In what sense can the Deity be said to fabricate such contrivances? He is the direct Creator, not only of the matter and collocations, but of all the forces whatsoever. He cannot possibly, then, adapt arrangements of means to the action of pre-existing forces, which is the sole meaning of the word mechanics with us. Thus is the conception of a mechanical Deity as false in theory as it is, in our humble opinion, degrading to the proper idea of God, which is that of an infinite free activity, the cause of all conceivable effects which are not the voluntary products of the finite activities created and preserved by him.

The mechanical argument is also defective as a mere piece of reasoning, for—

1. A machine doth unquestionably prove a machine-builder, if it be granted that the given structure be indeed a machine, and that it was actually created. But deny this—deny that a given apparatus ever began to be at all, and until the fact of its beginning be proven,

the argument opens an hiatus that no extent of ingenuity can possibly bridge over.

This is the first and radical defect in the reasoning of Paley. It is based on the postulate (not proven, or attempted to be proven, in his treatise) of an actual historical creation. The moment the question comes up —"But what if this earth and yonder heavens be from eternity?" the argument of Paley can furnish no answer, but silently crumbles into pieces. Atheists never were logicians, and they have, therefore, all failed to notice this ruinous flaw in Paley's Treatise. The piercing sagacity of Dr. Chalmers detected its existence, and he essayed to supply the *desideratum* by considerations deduced from the facts of geology. It might, perhaps, be difficult to say whether he did or did not partially succeed. One response, however, to all his eloquent dissertation renders it utterly impotent to work conviction in a thoroughly logical mind—that if *present* physical powers can *now* form the individual organized vegetable or animal, the presumption is strong that *past* physical powers may primarily have created the genus and the species. To this there can be no answer.

2. But in the second place, an equally fatal defect in the argument of Paley is, that it affords no shadow of even presumptive proof of the present existence of God at all! His favorite example of the watch demonstrates this so clearly that we need refer to no other.

No watch ever constructed by the art of man can possibly furnish the slightest proof of the present existence of its maker. It may continue to keep the record of passing time with the most admirable regularity and precision long after the hand that wrought and arranged its springs and wheels had moldered into dust. He may have ceased to be for a day, a year, a millennium of ages, and it still beat on, ticking its metallic teeth, but telling no news of him who first polished them, nor of the very fingers that wound up its slender chain but yesterday. May it not be so with the world, with all worlds, on the mechanical hypothesis? God may have exhausted his power in the creation, for aught a cold machine may say to the contrary. He may have ceased to exist six thousand years ago; nay, the very moment He rested from his labors, and we be none the more apprised of the fact by the utterance of all the mechanical suns and systems which, as to this point, are dumb as the coarsest clods of inorganic matter.

Nothing can prove *present* power but *present* motion, or the unequivocal signs of its *present* being.

But no such objections hold as to the mathematical and rational argument, of which we have presented the brief outlines in the foregoing pages. It appeals only to the past as witnessed in grand hieroglyphics, seen at the present hour, sculptured on the limestone of the mountains, and engraven in the soft wood of every tree in the forest, and written among the silken corals of all the flowers of the fields.

For the most part, our argument appeals to present motions—the sublime evolutions that are each moment being manifested before our eyes. It points to the past, and proves that a God was. It turns to the present, and demonstrates that He is NOW. It calls to mind the eternal uniformity of Nature, and infers with indubitable certainty that He will continue to be forever. It leaves no *desideratum* to be wished for by its friends, and no weakness assailable by its foes. By its application of the doctrine of chances to the mathematical equations which Nature presents in ever-recurring series, this argument renders the creed of atheism impossible without actual insanity.

And, viewed in this radiant light, how wonderfully luminous and beautiful doth the face of the universe become! We behold the Deity enthroned in splendor everywhere, and on all things alike. We see his love-smiles on the petals of flowers and the wings of birds, as well as in the brightness of the sky and deep azure of the ocean. We hear his voice in the octaves of all our music, pealing in the deep bass of our Sabbath-organs, out-preaching all our priests, and tolling the bell of thunder, hung in clouds that float higher than the Andes. He weaves the fibers of the oak, he twines the gleaming threads of the rainbow, he vibrates the pendulous sea-waves, he calls to prayer from the heart of the storm. But sweeter, oh, sweeter far than all, soft and clear, and without ceasing in our own souls, for ourselves, and those whom we are permitted to love as dearly as ourselves, he whispers infinite hope and life everlasting.

All this follows from the admission of the immediate and universal agency and providence of God throughout all the realms of Nature. Despair can fling no dark shadow on the soul in the presence of that sunshine which gilds all things. There is no room for doubt when faith fills immensity. Atoms and worlds alike become transfigured in the new and cryptic light which beams out, as from beneath a transparent vail, in objects the most insignificant, in scenes the most unpoetic.

Even the cold eyes of death ray ineffable effulgence, like stars rising upward to their zenith. Pale fear, appalled at his own shadow, flies over the confines of creation, and leaves all hearts alone with love and joy. We know that we cannot be lost out of the bosom of God; for the root of the soul is in God, and therefore cannot die. The iron chain of necessity releases its coil around the world, and its clanking links of dark circumstance melt away in receding mists, as in the presence of a sun shivered into spangles of glory. The tears of sorrow turn on the faded cheek of the mourner into priceless pearls; and prayer and praise breathe out among blooming roses on white lips quivering with agony. The old familiar faces of the "long, long ago," the loved, the lost, ay, the long lost but never forgotten, are around us once more.

> "Their smile in the starlight doth wander by,
> Their breath is near in the wind's low sigh"—

In music's divinest tone. The endless ages are crowded into a luminous point. There is no past or future. The faith that asserts God proclaims all things present to the soul. We repose on the bosom of our Father with a confidence nothing can shake. Friends may grow cold and change around us; enemies may band together for our destruction; lovers may fly away and leave us, like sunny birds when the cloud lowers, and the voice of thunder is heard remote. But we have one immortal Friend who stands between us and all foes, encircling our souls in his arms of everlasting love.

For shall not he who preserves, and blesses, and beautifies all things, take good care of all these, his human children, especially created in his own image of power, wisdom, and love? He paints the wings of the little butterfly. He gilds the crimson flower-cups where the tiny insect sips honey-dew at morn. He launches every beam of light. He adds plumes to every wandering zephyr. Every sparrow that falls from its leafy boughs with a chill-pain in its dying heart, falls to sleep on his kindly breast. Never a grain of sand, nor a drop of dew, nor a glimmer of light, has been lost out of his embrace of infinite tenderness since the beginning of time, nor will be while eternity rolls on. Shall he, then, lose me? Can I lose myself?

Then "will I trust him though he slay me." On the summit of this exalted faith, which is certainty, I rest secure. Nothing can move me more. The sensuous world has vanished from beneath my feet. I live already in the Spirit Land. The immortal dead are around me. I hear them holding high converse in the translucent clouds. It is no night-vision, although brighter than all dreams. I am become a king, for I am now a son and heir of the universal empire. My throne stands on a pyramid of mathematical principles as old as God himself. I have ascended a demonstration that carries me into the heavens. I have bid adieu to fear. What is there to harm me in the presence of my Almighty Father in a universe of brethren? There can be nothing more to desire. Other want is impossible. I have found God, who owneth all.

Here, then, will I take my repose. The vessel in which I am embarked may drift whithersoever it will on this immeasurable sea of being. It may run riot on the giddy waves; lightning and tempest may rend every sail, and leave its masts bare. Impenetrable storms may hide every lodestar in heaven; the angry spirit of the waters may shriek till the whole world is deaf. What care I? Let the storm howl on—God guides it! And on whatsoever shore the wreck is thrown, he is sure to be there, with all my loves and hopes around him; and wherever he is, there is the open gate of heaven—for there is the everlasting love, which *is* heaven!

CHAPTER XLVII.

MORE EXPLICIT DEFINITIONS.

KIND READER, do we begin to approach and lift each other's consciousness? Are we strangers still, not understanding one another's mind; or, are we becoming *interiorly* acquainted? Have our minds yet met and mated? Do our thoughts meet and intermingle, and flow *together* in the new channel, which is stretching away so beautifully through the infinite landscape? If we have not yet met, why not? Am I obscure? Or, are you obtuse? "Come, let us reason together." Can we not, at least for one short golden hour, live together like sunshine and flowers, reciprocating each other's inner sentiments, and faithfully reflecting each the other's deep convictions, as sky and sea?

Let us meditate together, and prepare our minds for the discourse of Arabula. Are my definitions clear? Let us review them. To begin, here is a tree. Call it "Intellect." Now analyze it: first, its myriad *roots* are the *Facts* (or phenomena) of the universe without; second, its mighty solid *body* is *Experience* (or sensation); third, its outspreading *branches* are *Reflections* (or reasonings); fourth, and lastly, its *fruits* are *Memories;* and the whole is called "Intelligence," or "Judgment," or (in the Harmonial Philosophy) "Knowledge." All this we mutually understand, do we not? Even if we do not logically meet and delightfully mate on this classification of man's mentality—which, for promoting the ends of independent private growth, may not be desirable—yet, by the understanding, we unquestionably stand each before the other clearly defined. Well, now let us take another step.

Here is another tree. Call it "Wisdom." First, its myriad *roots* are *Instincts* (or, the radical fundamental elements and basic principles of all mentality); second, its great powerful *body* is *Affection* (or, the instincts arisen to the height of unselfish manifestation); third, its divinely beautiful *branches* are *Intuitions* (or, the unselfish, impersonal, immortal principles of conscious identification with *the* PRINCIPLE of all Principles, GOD); fourth, and lastly, its perfect *fruit* is pure *Reason* (or, the full and complete resurrection and harmonization of all instincts and passions, of all affections and attractions, of all intuitions and sentiments, and of all the powers of thought and understanding); and the whole is called "Harmony," or "Spirituality," or "the state of resurrection," or (in the Harmonial Philosophy) by the all-embracing and immortal name, "WISDOM."

In this "light," who is worthy of being called the possessor of "Reason?" He, only, whose whole nature is lifted into the presence of Arabula; wherein *self*, being elevated (not "crucified," remember, but *elevated* into sympathy with divine principles), the individual Spirit can, with the voice of truth, say—"I AND MY FATHER ARE ONE!"

What, then, shall we call that condition in which most men live? This question is answered by this central fact: All mankind are becoming! They have not yet arrived. What the Harmonial philosophers call "Reason," is yet *a sealed book* to the advancing millions. The ignorant look upon that state as "supernatural." One in the Superior Condition, even during the entrancement of a single hour, is, to the mass of selfish and superficial sensuous observers (who are non-experienced in spiritual things), a "wonder," a strange "phenomenon," a human "miracle," a dangerous "witch," a troublesome "prince of devils," an angel of "light," a great sign of "spirit," the discoverer of "heaven," only little less than an "angel."

No selfish man can see the *light* of Arabula. No selfish man is ever a *wise* man. No selfish man can understand what is meant by the terms "Pure Reason," or the higher term, "Wisdom." The mind is in "outer darkness"—in the realm of discord, divisions, and ever-recurring causes of unhappiness—until its interiors are open to the love, light, law, liberty of Arabula. It is the angel presence of this unselfish Guest that causes the soul to love its neighbors, to overcome all enmities, and to reverence the Eternal Good with all its heart and might.

And so it must be said that, measured by this standard, the world's Ideal of the heavenly state of "Pure Reason" is yet far, far future; for which all naturally aspire; to which all spiritual eyes are turned; unto which few appeal for baptism and purification. Syllogistically, how does this look to you? First, all selfish thoughts are derived from these two sources—the unresurrected instincts and the fact-rooted, materialistic, atheistic Intellect; second, that which is selfish, or of selfish origin, cannot be productive of the highest good and happiness; third, man's selfishness is derived from his instincts and intellect; fourth, therefore, intellect and the instincts are selfish, and the *cause* of the world's evil, disease, and misery. Or, from another syllogistic stand-point, look at the question: First, the state called "Wisdom" is the embodiment of all Reason, all Harmony, all Happiness in the individual or in the world; but the infinite Mother (Nature or Love) and the infinite Father (God or Reason) are the source of Wisdom; therefore, Nature and God (always in our philosophy interchangeable terms) are the *causes* of all instincts, all affection, all intelligence, all harmony, and all happiness.

CHAPTER XLVIII.

ARABULA'S DISCOURSE ON WISDOM.

"Writing by means of Light," is the English translation for the Greek word "Photography," so commonly spoken in these days of chemical and imitative art. In this book the quality of this "light" is appropriately called "Arabula." Plato, a true spiritual philosopher, exalted this light above the intellect. Theætetus and Plotinus cognized this principle of interior illumination as "that which *sees*, and is itself the thing which is seen." It is called the "Good," the "Unite," the "One," the "Virgin," the "Love," the "Undefinable."

"The Arabula, as revealed to the good Plotinus, is described as the "One that is not absent from any thing, and yet is separated from all things; so that it is present and yet not present with them. But it is present with those things that are able, and are prepared to receive it, so that they become congruous, and as it were pass into contact with it, through similitude and a certain inherent power allied to that which is imparted by the One. When, therefore, the soul is disposed in such a way as she was when she came from the One, then she is able to perceive it, as far as it is naturally capable of being seen. He, therefore, who has not arrived thither . . . may consider himself as the cause of his disappointment, and should endeavor by separating himself from all things to be alone. . . .

"We denominate it the ONE from necessity, in order that we may signify it to each other by a name, and may be led to an indivisible conception, being anxious that our soul may be one."

The language of the poet is recalled—

> —"God is God!
> Mistake, and accident, and crime,
> Are but man's growth in earth and time;
> And upward still life's spiral turns
> To where the Love Eternal burns."

Light! the prime cheerer "of all beings first and best." Efflux divine! "without whose vesting beauty all were wrapt in unessential gloom." Let us hear thy voice, overflowing with the very quintessence of truth; tell us in thine own sweet words, of thy mystical journeyings; speak to us of the Mother and the Father; teach us to *love* Wisdom; and lift us, we beseech thee, to thy holy presence.* Listen! from afar, as over the troubled bosom of unnumbered seas of centuries, I hear the voice of Arabula:—

"Happy is the man that findeth wisdom, and the man that getteth understanding. For the merchandise of it is better than the merchandise of silver, and the gain thereof than fine gold. She is more precious than rubies: and all the things thou canst desire are not to be compared unto her. Length of days is in her right hand; and in her left hand riches and honor. Her ways are ways of pleasantness, and all her paths are peace. She is a tree of life to them that lay hold upon her; and happy is every one that retaineth her. . . My son, keep sound wisdom and discretion: so shall they be life unto thy soul, and grace to thy neck. Get wisdom, get understanding: forget it not; neither decline from the words of my mouth. Forsake her not, and she will preserve thee: love her, and she shall keep thee. Wisdom is the principal thing; therefore get wisdom. . . . Exalt her, and she shall promote thee: she shall bring thee to honor, when thou dost embrace her. She shall give to thine head an ornament of grace: a crown of glory shall she deliver to thee. . . . Doth not wisdom cry? and understanding put forth her voice? She standeth in the top of high places, by the way in the places of the paths; she crieth at the gates, at the entry of the city, at the coming in at the doors: Unto you, O men, I call; and my voice is to the sons of men. O, ye simple, understand Wisdom; and ye fools, be of an understanding heart. . . . Receive my instruction, and not silver; and 'Knowledge' rather than choice gold. For Wisdom is better than rubies; and all the things that may be desired are not to be compared to it. I find out knowledge. . . . Counsel is mine, and sound wisdom; I am understanding; I have strength. By me kings reign, and princes decree justice. By me princes rule, and nobles, even all the judges of the earth. I love them that love me; and those that seek me early, *shall find me*. . . .

"Wisdom is more moving than any motion: she passeth and goeth through all things by reason of her pureness. For she is the breath of the power of God, and a pure influence flowing from the glory of the Almighty: therefore can no defiled thing fall into her. For she is the brightness of the everlasting light, the unspotted mirror of the power of God, and the image of his goodness. And being but One, she can do all things: and remaining in herself, she maketh all things new: and in all ages entering into holy souls she maketh them friends of God and prophets. . . For she is more beautiful than the sun, and above all the order of the stars: being compared with the light, she is found before it. . . . Wisdom reacheth from one end to another mightily; and sweetly doth she order all things. He that holdeth her fast shall inherit glory; and wheresoever she entereth, the Light will bless. They that serve her shall minister to the holy One: and them that love her the Lord [Light (?)] doth love. Whoso giveth ear unto her shall judge the nations: and he that attendeth unto her shall dwell securely. If a man commit himself unto her, he shall inherit her; and his generation shall hold her in possession. For at the first she will walk with him by crooked ways, and bring *fear* and *dread* upon him, and *torment* him with her *discipline*, until she may trust his soul, and try him by her laws. Then will she *return* the straight way unto him, and *comfort* him, and shew him her mysteries. But if he go wrong (i. e. if he is selfish, living continually in the instincts and intellect) she will forsake him, and give him over to his own ruin. Observe the opportunity, and beware of being selfish and evil; and be not ashamed when it concerneth thy soul. For there is a shame that bringeth sin; and there is a shame which is glory and grace. . . . In nowise speak against the truth; but be abashed of the error of thine ignorance (and selfishness). . . . My son, if thou wilt, thou shalt be taught. If thou love to hear, thou shalt receive understanding: and if thou bow thine ear, thou shalt be wise."

Arabula's voice is thus full of Wisdom and overflowing with Love. The true follower from early youth, exalted to the Superior Condition by her magnetically entrancing hand, thus acknowledges benefits prayerfully: "When I was yet young, or ever I went abroad, I desired Wisdom openly in my prayer. I prayed for her before the temple, and will seek her out even to the end. Even from the flower till the grape was ripe hath my heart delighted in her: my foot went the right way, from my youth up sought I after her. I bowed mine ear a little, and received her, and got much learning. I profited therein, therefore will I ascribe the glory unto him that giveth me wisdom. For I purposed to do after her, and earnestly I followed that which is good; so shall I not be confounded. My soul hath wrestled with her, and in my doings I was righteous. I stretched my hands to heaven above, and bewailed my ignorance of her. I directed my soul unto her, and I found her in pureness. I have had my heart joined with her from the beginning; therefore shall I not be forsaken. My heart [being so full of selfish instincts] was troubled in seeking her: therefore have I gotten a good possession. The Father hath given me a tongue for my reward, and I will praise him therewith. Draw near unto me, ye unlearned, and dwell in the house of learning. Wherefore are ye *slow*, and what say ye of these things, seeing your souls are very thirsty? [Is it because ye are in bondage to self?] I opened my mouth, and said, 'Buy her for yourselves without money.' Put your neck under the yoke, and let your soul receive instruction."

CHAPTER XLIX.

DEBATE ON THE BIBLE.

About this time I experienced a peculiar and powerful attraction toward the "interior sense" of all inspired poetry and serious volumes. "The letter killeth," reasoned I; "but the *spirit* of a thing is its very life, and it can impart 'life' to those who perceive and accept it." Perhaps, methought, the skeptics approach the investigation of the Bible with hostile prejudices—predetermined, so to speak, to see errors in its pages, as evil-minded men find in the conduct of those they hate numerous falsehoods, contradictions, immoralities; and, so thinking, I at once resolved upon a candid and calm analysis of the law, the letter, and the testimony.

And first, in this connection, let me take down the testimony of a skeptic; once an influential preacher in "Merry England." The question which I now wait for you to answer fully and solemnly, is this: Did you, or did you not, lose your faith in the plenary inspiration of the Bible by being overcome, in some undefinable manner, with selfish and atheistic temptations of intellect—under the baneful mood of which you became first prejudiced against, and then bitterly hostile to, the letter and teachings of the Testaments?

The gentleman promptly answered: "The truth is, so far from coming to the investigation of the Bible with prejudices against the Bible, or with feelings of hostility to the Bible, my prejudices and feelings all leaned the other way. My prejudices were all in *favor* of the prevailing doctrine, the doctrine of the superhuman origin and divine authority of the Bible. I was taught that doctrine from my earliest childhood. I received it as eternal truth. I looked on those who dared even to doubt it with the most painful suspicions. I reverenced the Bible next to God himself. The reverence with which my parents regarded the Bible; the solemn manner in which they spoke of it; the tones with which they read it; the horror with which they regarded those who doubted or disbelieved it; all tended to strengthen my belief in its divinity. All those whom I loved and revered, believed in its divinity. None but those whom I regarded as outcasts and profligates, as enemies of God and goodness, called its divinity in question. Every sermon or speech that I heard, and every book that I read, were in favor of the prevailing doctrine. My strongest passions were enlisted in its favor. I was taught that a belief in it was essential to eternal salvation; that doubt of it was to run the risk of eternal damnation. My prejudices grew with my growth, and strengthened with my strength. I sought to strengthen my belief by reading books on the subject, written by the ablest and most learned defenders of the divine authority of the Bible. I read every book on the subject I could find, on the popular side. I believed the books. I supposed the writers of them to be learned and honest, and my assurance was increased. I preached and advocated the common doctrine. I defended it against unbelievers. I wrote several books in its favor. I received praise and rewards for my labor. My reputation, my friends, my interests, as well as my prejudices, affections, and passions, all joined to keep me to the Orthodox faith. When light at length compelled me to modify my belief, I yielded with the greatest reluctance. As long as I could, I *resisted* the light. I would fain have closed my eyes against it. To change seemed horrible. The thought distressed me beyond measure. The consequences which threatened me in case of change were truly terrible. My agony was often intense. Through the night, it deprived me of sleep; through the day, it filled me with gloom. Nothing but an ardent love of truth, and an ever-anxious wish to be right, could have carried me through the struggle."

"In your investigations," I inquired, "did you search the letter or the spirit of the Bible?"

"It was the *spirit* within the letter that first aroused my faculties to independent inquiry!"

"Indeed! What, pray, did you find in the *spirit* of the Bible that troubled you?"

"Before I investigated the texts and the spirit of the Bible for myself," he replied, "I held, firmly, that the volume was a collection of miraculous books, written by supernaturally inspired men, at different periods of history; and that, according to all established rules of reasoning, it must be from the all-wise and all-perfect God, and, being so derived, would show its divine origin on its very face, but more vividly in its spirit; that, in short, the Bible was as wise, as perfect, as consistent, as unchangeable, and as harmonious as God himself."

"Well, did you not find the Bible as consistent and as perfect as you supposed?"

No! The more carefully I read it, the more I compared chapter with chapter and passage with passage, the further I got from the recognition within it of the Supreme Being."

"What first arrested your attention?"

"The first thing that disturbed me was the 109th Psalm, written by King David, said to be a man 'after God's own heart.' It seems that he had been slandered and unjustly treated by some one, and this is what he asked God to do by way of punishment:

"Set thou a wicked man over him, and let Satan stand at his right hand. When he shall be judged, let him be condemned, and let his prayer become sin. Let his days be few, and let another take his office. Let his children be fatherless, and his wife a widow. Let his children be continually vagabonds, and beg; let them seek their bread also out of their desolate places. Let the extortioner catch all that he hath; and let the stranger spoil his labor. Let there be none to extend mercy unto him; neither let there be any to favor his fatherless children. Let his posterity be cut off, and in the generation following let their name be blotted out. Let the iniquity of his fathers be remembered with the Lord; and let not the sin of his mother be blotted out. Let them be before the Lord continually, that he may cut off the memory of them from the earth. As he loved cursing, so let it come unto him; as he delighted not in blessing, so let it be far from him. As he clothed himself with cursing like as with his garment, so let it come into his bowels like water, and like oil into his bones. Let it be unto him as the garment which covereth him, and for a girdle wherewith he is girded continually. Let this be the reward of mine adversaries from the Lord, and of them that speak evil against my soul."

Nothing can exceed the bitterness, the cruelty, the

murderous malignity and revengefulness of this prayer. David is not content with the torment and ruin of the person who had offended him, but must pray for all imaginable curses and calamities on his widowed wife, his fatherless children, and even the unborn offspring of his children. Thus—

"Let his children be fatherless, and his wife a widow. Let his children be continually vagabonds, and beg; let them seek their bread also out of their desolate places. Let there be none to extend mercy unto him; neither let there be any to favor his fatherless children. Let his posterity be cut off, and in the generation following let their name be blotted out. Let the iniquity of his fathers be remembered with the Lord; and let not the sin of his mother be blotted out. Let them be before the Lord continually, that he may cut off the memory of them from the earth."

"Yes," said I, "David was exceedingly angry, no doubt, but David was not Deity; and it seems to me that you should make the discrimination."

"Indeed, I *did* make the very discrimination which you suggest, but it did not help me; because the volume abounds in absolutely conflicting ideas and irreconcilable teachings."

"Can you give me a few examples, where the *spirit* and texts of teachings in different parts of the Bible are positively contradictory?"

"Nothing can be easier, for the volume is full of inconsistencies, proving that an all-wise, an all-perfect, and a perfectly harmonious Being could not have dictated the contents of the Hebrew and Christian Scriptures. For example (See Ex. 3 : 21, 22, and 12 : 35, 36), *robbery* is commanded by God, thus:

"'When ye go, ye shall not go empty; but every woman shall *borrow* of her neighbor, and of her that sojourneth in her house, jewels of silver and jewels of gold, and raiment; and ye shall put them upon your sons, and upon your daughters; and ye shall spoil the Egyptians. . . . And they borrowed of the Egyptians jewels of silver, and jewels of gold, and raiment. . . . And they spoiled the Egyptians.'

"But in Lev. 19 : 13; and Ex. 20 : 15, the same God is reported to have said:—

"'Thou shalt not defraud thy neighbor, neither rob him. . . . . . Thou shalt not steal.'

"Again, by the same God, slavery and oppression were ordained in a curse! Thus: 'Cursed be Canaan; a servant of servants shall he be unto his brethren' (Gen. 9: 25). Of the children of the strangers that do sojourn among you, of them shall ye buy. . . They shall be your bondmen forever; but over your brethren of the children of Israel, ye shall not rule with rigor (Lev. 25: 44, 49). I will sell your sons and daughters into the hands of the children of Judah, and they shall sell them to the Sabeans, to a people afar off; for the Lord hath spoken it (Joel 3: 8).

"But in other passages, by the same God, all slavery and oppression are positively and forever forbidden. Thus: 'Undo the heavy burdens. . . Let the oppressed go free. . . break every yoke. (Is. 58: 6.) Thou shalt neither vex a stranger, nor oppress him. (Ex. 22: 21.) He that stealeth a man, and selleth him, or if he be found in his hand, he shall surely be put to death' (Ex. 21: 16).

"Neither be ye called masters (Mat. 23 : 10)."

Again, the Lord is reported to have engaged in spreading falsehood among the people. Thus: "I will go forth and be a lying spirit in the mouth of all his prophets. And he said : Thou shalt persuade him and prevail also; go forth and do so." (1 Kings 22: 21, 22.)

But elsewhere the same Lord positively condemns lying. Thus: "Thou shalt not bear false witness (Ex. 20: 16). Lying lips are an abomination to the Lord (Prov. 12: 22). All liars shall have their part in the lake which burneth with fire and brimstone." (Rev. 21 : 8.)

Again, God is reported to have considered hatred to kindred a part of religion. Thus: "If any man come unto me, and hate not his father, and mother, and wife, and children, and brother, and sisters, yea, and his own life also, he cannot be my disciple." (Luke 14: 26.)

But in other places we read that nothing can be more wrong than this hatred to kindred. Thus: "Honor thy father and mother. (Eph. 6: 2.) Husbands, love your wives. . . . For no man ever yet hated his own flesh. (Eph. 5: 25, 29.) Whosoever hateth his brother is a murderer." (John 3 : 15.)

Again, marriage is approved by God. Thus: "And the Lord God said, It is not good that the man should be alone: I will make an help-meet for him. (Gen. 2: 18.) Be fruitful and multiply, and replenish the earth. (Gen. 1 : 28.) A man shall leave father and mother and shall cleave unto his wife." (Matt. 19: 5.)

But in other passages the same God, through Paul, says: "It is good for man not to touch a woman. (1 Cor. 7: 1.) For I would that all men were even as I myself. . . It is good for them if they abide even as I." (1 Cor. 7: 7, 8.)

Again, the Lord teaches the inferiority of woman to man, and denies to her the right to speak in public, or to be independent of her husband. Thus: "And thy desire shall be to thy husband, and he shall rule over thee. (Gen. 3: 16.) I suffer not a woman to teach, nor to usurp authority over the man, but to be in silence. (1 Tim. 2: 12.) They are commanded to be under obedience, as also saith the law. (1 Cor. 14: 34.) Even as Sarah obeyed Abraham, calling him Lord." (1 Pet. 3: 6.)

But in other chapters the same Lord favors the supremacy of woman, and compels her to appear and to speak in public. Thus: "And Deborah, a prophetess, judged Israel at that time . . And Deborah said unto Barak, Up, for this is the day in which the Lord hath delivered Sisera into thy hand . . And the Lord discomfited Sisera, and all his chariots, and all his host, with the edge of the sword before Barak." (Judges 4: 4, 14, 15.) The inhabitants of the village ceased; they ceased in Israel, until I, Deborah, arose, a mother in Israel. (Judg. 5: 7.) And on my handmaidens I will pour out in those days my spirit, and they shall prophesy. (Acts 2: 18.) And the same man had four daughters, virgins, which did prophesy." (Acts 21: 9.)

Again, the institution and observance of the Sabbath is thus set forth: "For in six days the Lord made heaven and earth, the sea, and all that in them is, and rested on the seventh day; wherefore the Lord blessed the Sabbath day and hallowed it. (Ex. 20: 11.) Remember the Sabbath day to keep it holy." (Ex. 20: 8.)

But in other parts of the Bible the same God, through the Apostle Paul, considers the Sabbath of no account. Thus: "One man esteemeth one day above another; another esteemeth every day alike. Let every man be fully persuaded in his own mind. (Rom. 14: 5.) Let no man therefore judge you in meat and drink, or in respect of a holy day, or of the Sabbath days." (Col. 2: 16.)

Again, by command of God, no work should be done on the Sabbath under penalty of death. Thus: "Whosoever doeth any work on the Sabbath day, he shall surely be put to death. (Ex. 31: 15.) And they found a man that gathered sticks upon the Sabbath day . . And all the congregation brought him without the camp and stoned him."

But in John 5: 16 it is recorded that the same God was himself disregarding the Sabbath. Thus: "Therefore did the Jews persecute Jesus, and sought to slay him, because he had done these things on the Sabbath day." And the case is thus stated: "At that time Jesus went on the Sabbath day through the corn; and his disciples were a hungered, and began to pluck the ears of corn, and to eat. But when the Pharisees saw it they said unto him, Behold, thy disciples do that which is not lawful to do upon the Sabbath day. But he said unto them, . . Have ye not read in the law, how that on the Sabbath days the priests in the temple profane the Sabbath, and are blameless?" (Matt. 12: 1, 2, 3, 5.)

Again, in Matt. 6: 13, the God of Heaven is thus addressed in prayer: "Lead us not into temptation." But the same Lord elsewhere is called a *tempter*. Thus: "And it came to pass after these things, that God *did tempt* Abraham." (Gen. 22: 1.) And yet, in the same volume we read: "Let no man say when he is tempted, I am tempted of God; for God cannot be tempted with evil, neither tempteth he any man." (James 1: 13.)

Again, in one place (Heb. 6: 18) we read: "It is impossible for God to lie." But in another place it is said: "For this cause God shall send them strong delusion, that they should believe a lie." (2 Thes. 2: 11.)

Again, in Matt. 19: 26, we are told by one of the supernaturally inspired penmen that "With God all things are possible;" and elsewhere that he is all-powerful, thus: "Behold, I am the Lord, the God of all flesh; is there any thing too hard for me?" (Jer. 32: 27.)

But in the forepart of the Bible you will find the following curious contradictory passage: "And the Lord was with Judah, and he drave out the inhabitants of the mountain; but *could not drive out the inhabitants of the valley*, because they had chariots of iron." (Judg. 1: 19.)

Again, it is unqualifiedly said: "No man hath seen God at any time. (John 1: 18.) Ye have neither heard his voice, at any time, nor seen his shape." (John 5: 37.)

But the same God said unto Moses: "And I will take away my hand, and thou shalt see my back parts. (Ex. 33: 23.) And the Lord spake to Moses face to face, as a man speaketh to his friend. (Ex. 33: 11.) And the Lord called unto Adam, and said unto him, Where art thou? And he said, I heard thy voice in the garden, and I was afraid. (Gen. 3: 9, 10.) For I have seen God face to face, and my life is preserved." (Gen. 32: 30.)

Again, in one place I read that God is perfectly satisfied with his works. Thus: " And God saw every thing that he had made, and behold it was very good." (Gen. 1: 31.)

But in the sixth chapter and sixth verse of the same book, I read: " And it repented the Lord that he had made man on the earth, and it grieved him at his heart."

Again, I read in the following passages that signs, wonders, and miracles are a proof of divine mission or supernatural power: " Now when John had heard in the prison the works of Christ, he sent two of his disciples, and said unto him, Art thou he that should come, or do we look for another? Jesus answered and said unto them, Go and show John again those things which ye do hear and see; the *blind* receive their *sight*, and the *lame walk*, the *lepers* are *cleansed*, and the *deaf hear*, the *dead are raised.* (Matt. 11 : 2–5.) Rabbi, we know that thou art a teacher come from God; for *no man can do these miracles* that thou doest *except God be with him.* (John 3 : 2.) And Israel saw that *great work* which the Lord did upon the Egyptians; and the people feared the Lord, and believed the Lord, and *his servant Moses.*" (Ex. 14 : 31.)

But elsewhere I read that signs, wonders, and miracles, are not only *no* evidence, but are absolutely condemned, or are considered of little account. Thus: "And Aaron cast down his rod before Pharaoh, and before his servants, and it became a serpent. Then Pharaoh also called the wise men and the sorcerers; now the magicians of Egypt, *they also did in like manner* with their enchantments, for they cast down every man his rod, and *they became serpents.* (Ex. 7 : 10–12.) If there arise among you a prophet, or a dreamer of dreams, and giveth thee a *sign* or a *wonder*, and the sign or the wonder *come to pass* wherein he spake unto thee, saying, Let us go after other gods which thou hast not known, and let us serve them, thou *shalt not hearken* unto the words of that *prophet* or that dreamer of dreams. (Deut. 13 : 1–3.) If I by Beelzebub *cast out devils*, by whom do your *sons* cast them out?" (Luke 11:19).

Again, in 2 Tim. 3:16, I read the affirmation that all scripture is inspired: "*All scripture* is given by *inspiration* of God." "But I speak this *by permission and not by commandment.*" (1 Cor. 7–6.) But Paul, one of God's inspired writers, who wrote the most popular parts of the New Testament, said: "But to the rest speak I, *not the Lord.* (1 Cor. 7:12.) That which I speak, I speak it *not after the Lord.*" (2 Cor. 11:17.)

"For Heaven's sake!" I exclaimed, "do not quote another passage; I am dreadfully tired; and, besides, I cannot see what more you can possibly say on the subject."

"What more! What more! Why, man alive, you have not heard a twentieth part of the absurdities and inconsistencies and errors of history, of fact, of morals, of doctrines, of principles, &c., which I found in the Bible upon thorough investigation."

"But," said I, "why did you not find out all these contradictions *before* you entered the ministry?"

"Oh, I studied the Bible *with the eyes of other men*—that's the reason why. Dr. Clark's commentary, and the writings of the Christian philosophers and other Bible believers, were the *spectacles* I wore when studying for the pulpit profession."

"If you have any thing further—that is, if you have facts and conclusions condensed and understandable by the common intellect—I will patiently give another hour to the subject."

"Well, then, with your permission I will read from a certain 'Discussion'—which shall be nameless—the objections of skeptics to the popular doctrine that the Testaments are plenarily inspired, and leave to you to judge whether we have any *just* grounds for skepticism.

1. We know that books *generally* are the productions of men, and it is natural to conclude that *all books* are so, the Bible included, till proof is given to the contrary.

We *know* of no proof to the contrary. We can find neither *internal* nor *external* evidence that the Bible had any higher origin than other books, or that it is entitled to any higher authority. We have examined what has been brought forward as proof of the superhuman origin and divine authority of the Bible, but have found it, as we think, wanting.

II. Even our opponents, who believe in the divine origin of the *Bible*, do not believe in the divine origin of the books deemed sacred by other people. They smile at the credulity of the Mohammedan, who believes in the superhuman origin of the Koran; they are even disposed to scold the Latter-Day Saint, for believing in the superhuman origin of the Book of Mormon.

They are sure the Turk and the Latter-Day Saint are in error. We are confident that our opponents themselves are in error. They have hardly patience to read the arguments of Mohammedans and Mormonites in behalf of their Bibles. We have read to some extent the arguments of all, and found them all equally unsatisfactory.

III. We have, as we think, proof that the Bible is *not* of divine origin—proof, instead, that it is of *human* origin.

1. The Bible in common use is a *translation*, made by men as liable to err as ourselves; men who *did* err, grievously. The translation bears marks of their liability to err on almost every page.

2. The Christian world bears witness to the imperfections of the translation, by its demand for new and better translations. No sect is satisfied with it. Many of the sects have made new translations.

The Greek and Hebrew scriptures, of which the translators profess the common English Bible to be a translation, were compiled by men, weak and erring like ourselves, and they, too, are acknowledged to bear the marks of human imperfection and error.

3. The Greek and Hebrew Bibles were compiled from pre-existing manuscripts. Those manuscripts are human transcripts of still earlier manuscripts, which are also human transcripts. Those manuscripts are all imperfect. They differ from each other. The manuscripts of the New Testament, alone, differ in more than 150,000 places.

4. The *originals* are lost—the manuscripts cannot, therefore, be compared with them. No means remain of ascertaining which is least corrupted. A perfect Bible, therefore—a Bible thoroughly divine—a Bible free from error and uncertainty, is a thing no more to be hoped for, even supposing such a Bible once existed. But there is no evidence that such a book ever did exist. If, therefore, we *had* the originals, there is no reason to believe that we should find them less imperfect, less erroneous, than our common translations. We have, therefore, to do chiefly with the contents of the common version. These contents furnish *internal* evidence, evidence the most decisive, that the Bible, like other books, is the work of erring and imperfect men. To this "internal" evidence we call attention. . . .

The form, the arrangement, the language, the style of the different portions of the Bible are all manifestly human. The Grammar, the Logic, the Rhetoric, the Poetry, all bear marks of human weakness. We see nothing "supernatural" anywhere in the book, but human imperfection and error we see everywhere.

But the moral, theological, and philosophical portions of the Bible have the principal claim on our attention, and on these we should chiefly dwell. We can see no traces of any thing more than human in the morality, theology, or philosophy of the Bible; but the plainest traces of imperfect humanity.

Bishop Watson, in his letters to Thomas Paine, has these words: "An honest man, sincere in his endeavors to search out truth, in reading the Bible, would examine, first, whether the Bible attributed to the Supreme Being any attribute repugnant to holiness, truth, justice, goodness; whether it represented him as subject to human infirmities."—*Bishop Watson*, p. 114.

We have followed out this course, and will now state the result. We find that the Bible *does* represent God as subject to human infirmities, and that it *does* attribute to him attributes repugnant to holiness, truth, justice, and goodness.

1. It represents God as subject to human infirmities. It represents him as having a *body*, subject to wants and weaknesses like those of our own selves. When he appears to Abraham, he appears, according to the Bible, in three men. These three talk to Abraham. Abraham kills for them a calf, Sarah bakes them some bread, and they eat and drink. They wash their feet, soiled with their journey, and sit down to rest themselves under a tree. God is also represented as appearing to Jacob in the form of a man. He wrestles with Jacob all night. Jacob is too strong for him. He wants to go, but Jacob holds him fast. Jacob demands a blessing, and refuses to let go his hold of the Deity, till he obtains it. God, unable to free himself from Jacob's grasp, is forced, at length, to yield to his demand, and give him a blessing. He accordingly changes Jacob's name to Israel, which means the *God conqueror*—the man who vanquished God in a wrestling match. In other parts of the book, God is represented as tired and exhausted with the six days' work of creation, and as resting on the seventh day. In Exodus 31: 17, it is said that on the seventh day God rested, and was refreshed. In Judges 1: 19, God is represented as unable to vanquish some of the inhabitants of Canaan, because they had chariots of iron. "And the Lord

was with Judah; and he drove out the inhabitants of the mountains; but could not drive out the inhabitants of the valley, because they had chariots of iron."

2. God is further represented in the Bible as limited in knowledge. He did not know whether Abraham feared him or not, till he had tried him by commanding him to offer his son as a burnt-offering. But when Abraham had bound his son, and lifted up the knife to take his life, God is represented as saying: "*Now* I *know* thou fearest me; since thou hast not withheld thy son, thine only son, from me." He is also represented as having to use similar means with the Israelites to find out how *they* were disposed toward him. In one place he is said to try them by false prophets and dreamers, to know whether they loved the Lord their God with all their heart, (Deut. 13: 3.) In another he is said to have led them *forty years* in the wilderness to prove them, to know what was in their heart, and to find out whether they would keep his commandments or not. (8 : 2.) One passage represents him as putting the rainbow in the clouds to aid his memory—that he might look on it, and remember his engagement never again to destroy the world by a flood.

3. Other passages of scripture represent God as both limited in knowledge or limited in his presence—as dwelling somewhere aloft and apart from mankind—as receiving his information respecting the doings of men through agents or messengers, in whom he could not put confidence at all times, and as being obliged at times to come down and see for himself how things were going on. In Genesis 11 : 5, we read: "And the Lord came down to see the city and the tower which

the children of men builded.' So with regard to Sodom and Gomorrah, we read, Genesis 18: 20–21: "And the Lord said, because the cry of Sodom and Gomorrah is great, and because their sin is very grievous, I will go down now, and see whether they have done altogether according to the cry of it, which is come unto me: and if not, I will know." In all these passages, God is supposed to be subject to the same or similar limitations with ourselves.

The Bible further represents God as changeable, as repenting of his own doing. In one passage we are told that it repented him that he had made man, when he saw how badly he had turned out; and in another, that he repented of having made Saul king, for a similar reason. In many passages he is represented as being disappointed in men, and as repenting of the good he had promised them, or the evil with which he had threatened them.

5. The Bible gives still darker representations of God. It presents him to our view as subject not only to innocent human weaknesses, but to the most criminal and revolting vices. It represents him as partial in his affections and dealing toward his children. He is charged with a kind of partiality, which, in a human father, would be deemed most unreasonable and inexcusable. He is said to have loved Jacob and hated Esau, before either of them were born, and before either of them had done either good or evil. Thus we read, Rom. 9: 11–13: "For the children being not yet born, neither having done any good or evil, that the purpose of God, according to election, might stand, not of works, but of him that calleth; it was said unto her, The elder

shall serve the younger: as it is written, Jacob have I loved, but Esau have I hated." Some tell us that the Hebrew word translated '*hate*,' means only to '*love less*.' Suppose it does, it is still partiality to love one child less than another, before the children are born, or have done any thing to deserve peculiar love or hate. But the hatred here spoken of is something more than a less degree of love; it is positive ill-will, malignity, real deadly hate. Hear how Malachi expresses it. Malachi 1 : 2–4: "I have loved you, saith the Lord. Yet ye say, wherein hast thou loved us? Was not Esau Jacob's brother? saith the Lord: yet I loved Jacob, and I hated Esau, and laid his mountains and his heritage waste for the dragons of the wilderness. Whereas Edom saith, We are impoverished, but we will return and build the desolate places; thus saith the Lord of hosts, They shall build, but I will throw down; and they shall call them, The border of wickedness, and, The people against whom the Lord hath indignation forever." More cruel or deadly hate, a fiercer or more unrelenting cruelty, cannot be conceived. God is further represented as caring more for the Israelites than for any other people. He is represented as very much concerned for the health, the holiness, and the happiness of Israel; but as utterly careless what becomes of the rest of the world. Hence, he is represented as telling the Jews that *they* must not eat the flesh of any animal that dieth of itself, but that they *may* give it or sell it to the *stranger*. They must not run the risk of poisoning themselves, but they may poison as many others as they please. They are not to take usury for money of *one another*, but they may take it of others. They are not to hold each other as bondmen or bondwomen for more than six years at a time; nor are they to rule any of their brethren when in bondage with rigor: but they may hold the people of other nations as bondmen forever; take them and use them as property, buy them or sell them at pleasure; rule over them with rigor, and hand them down to their children as an *inheritance forever*.

6. Other passages represent God as grossly unjust and implacably revengeful. He is represented as punishing the innocent offspring for the sins of the parents—as visiting the sins of *idolaters* on their children—to the *third* and *fourth* generation. The sons and grandsons of Saul, to the number of seven, were hanged before the Lord, because Saul, many years before, had done wrong to the Gideonites. After this revolting butchery, the Bible says the Lord was entreated for the land. (2 Sam. 21: 1-14.) Because David did wrong in the case of Uriah, God is represented as saying, "The sword shall never depart from thine house." The sinner himself is spared, but his innocent child dies for his sin. Seventy sons of Ahab are beheaded for the sins of their parents. The prophet of God is represented as commanding their destruction. 2 Kings 9: 10: "The *whole house* of Ahab shall perish," saith the Lord, according to the prophet. God is represented as demanding the destruction of whole nations, for sins committed by their forefathers many generations before. He is represented as commanding Saul to destroy the Amalekites—to destroy them utterly—for a sin, if sin it was, said to have been committed by their ancestors, more than four hundred years before.

Hear the passage. It is in 1 Samuel, 15: 1-3: "Samuel also said unto Saul, the Lord sent me to anoint thee to be king over his people, over Israel; now, therefore, hearken thou unto the voice of the word of the Lord. Thus saith the Lord of hosts, I remember that which Amalek did to Israel, how he laid wait for him in the way, when he came up from Egypt. Now go and smite Amalek, and utterly destroy all that they have, and spare them not; but slay both man and woman, infant and suckling, ox and sheep, camel and ass." Saul went, it is said, and slew the Amalekites. He utterly destroyed all the people with the edge of the sword. He, however, spared Agag, the king, and some of the cattle, and so angry is God at this, that he repents of having made Saul king. Samuel takes Agag and hews him in pieces before the Lord, to prevent his wrath from consuming him. These are horrible and blasphemous stories. But they are not the worst. The Bible represents God as cursing, and as dooming to pain and agony, to servitude and death, whole races of his creatures, throughout all lands, and throughout all ages, for the sin of *one* individual. It represents him as cursing *all* serpents, making them cursed above *all* cattle, dooming them to go on their belly and eat dust, and putting enmity in men's hearts toward them, because one solitary serpent tempted Eve. It represents him as dooming *all* women, throughout all ages and all nations, to great and multiplied pains and sorrows, and making them all subject to the will of their husbands, because *Eve* did wrong, before any other woman existed. It also represents God as cursing the earth for the sin of one man; cursing it to bring forth thorns and thistles to annoy all future generations; dooming all mankind, throughout all lands and throughout all ages, to eat of the ground in sorrow all the days of their life; to eat the herb of the field; to eat their bread with the sweat of their brow; and lastly, to return to the dust. The thought is appalling. Countless millions mercilessly doomed to daily and hopeless misery, and then to death, for sins committed before any of them were born! As if this blasphemy were not enough, our Orthodox opponents assure us that the death here threatened was the death of the soul as well as the body, or the consignment of both to eternal torments in hell. The posterity of Ham are doomed to servitude through all the ages of time, for an alleged offense of Ham. The rest of mankind are, of course, doomed to slaveholding. The Israelites are destroyed with pestilence for the sin of David, and even David is said to have been moved by God himself to do the deed, for which the people were destroyed. The case of David deserves to be given at length. It is one of the most astounding, revolting, and blasphemous stories in the whole Bible. You may find it in 2 Samuel, 24: 1, 10: "And again the anger of the Lord was kindled against Israel, and he moved David against them to say, Go, number Israel and Judah. And David's heart smote him after that he had numbered the people. And David said unto the Lord, I have sinned greatly in that I have done; and now, I beseech thee, O Lord, take away the iniquity of thy servant; for I have done very foolishly." It seems strange that his heart should smite him for doing as God prompted him to do, and that he should charge himself with acting foolishly in yielding to God's impulse. But perhaps he was not then aware that it was God that made him do the deed. God probably kept his part in the matter a secret. Still, the account has a horrible look. "However, when David was up in the morning, the word of the Lord came unto the prophet Gad, David's seer, saying, Go and say unto David, thus saith the Lord, I offer thee three things; choose thee one of them, that I may do it unto thee. So Gad came to David, and told him, and said unto him, Shall seven years of famine come unto thee in thy land? or wilt thou flee three months before thine enemies, while they pursue thee? or that there be three days' pestilence in thy land? Now advise, and see what answer I shall return to him that sent me. And David said unto Gad, I am in a great strait; let us fall now into the hand of the Lord, for his mercies are great, and let me not fall into the hand of man. So the Lord sent a pestilence upon Israel, from the morning even to the time appointed; and there died of the people, from Dan even to Beer-sheba, seventy thousand men. And when the angel stretched out his hand upon Jerusalem to destroy it, the Lord repented him of the evil, and said to the angel that destroyed the people, It is enough; stay now thy hand. And the angel of the Lord was by the threshing-place of Araunah, the Jebusite. And David spake unto the Lord, when he saw the angel that smote the people, and said, Lo, I have sinned, and I have done wickedly; but these sheep, what have they done? Let thine hand, I pray thee, be against me, and against my father's house." The story bewilders us with its horrors. The sinner is *spared*, while seventy thousand *innocents* are *destroyed*. The *sinner*, we say. But who *is* the sinner? Is it a sin to do as God prompts us to do? The only sinner, according to the story, is God himself. Both David and his slaughtered people are victims to the unmerited anger of the great transgressor and destroyer. The blasphemy of the passage is truly horrible.

7. If possible, the Bible represents God in still darker colors. It attributes to him the direst cruelties—the most savage and revolting butcheries. Here is a story from Numbers 31: 1–7, 9, 15–18: "And the Lord spake unto Moses, saying, Avenge the children of Israel of the Midianites: afterward shalt thou be gathered unto thy people. And Moses spake unto the people, saying, Arm some of yourselves unto the war, and let them go against the Midianites, and avenge the Lord of Midian. Of every tribe a thousand, throughout all the tribes of Israel, shall ye send to the war. So there were delivered out of the thousands of Israel, a thousand of every tribe, twelve thousand armed for war. And Moses sent them to the war, a thousand of every tribe, them and Phinehas, the son of Eleazar the priest, to the war, with the holy instruments, and the trumpets to blow in his hand. And they warred against the Midianites, as the Lord commanded Moses; and they slew all the males. And the children of Israel took all the women of Midian captives, and their little ones, and took the spoil of all their cattle, and all their flocks, and all their goods. And Moses said unto them, Have ye saved all the woman alive? Behold, these caused the children of Israel, through the counsel of Balaam, to commit trespass against the Lord in the matter of Peor, and there was a plague among the congregation

of the Lord. Now, therefore, kill every male among the little ones, and kill every woman that hath known man by lying with him. But all the women-children that have not known a man by lying with him keep alive for yourselves." And the helpless women and the innocent children, even to the suckling born but yesterday, are all butchered. The exhausted mother, with her new-born babe on her breast, are slaughtered together without mercy; and the young untarnished daughters are given to the butchers of their fathers, their mothers, and their brothers. And neither God nor his prophet sheds a tear, or utters a word of regret or sorrow. And these the Bible represents as the doings of God!

In Joshua tenth and eleventh, we have a long list of such horrors. Joshua is represented as going forth under the command of God, and slaying men and women, children and sucklings without number, utterly destroying whole nations. His warriors put their feet on the necks of vanquished kings, then Joshua smites them, and hangs them on five trees. He slays the people with a very great slaughter. Even the sun and moon are made to stand still, until he makes the ruin complete. He takes city after city; smites them with the edge of the sword; utterly destroying all the souls therein—letting none remain. The Lord, it is said, delivered them into his hands. "So Joshua smote all the country of the hills, and of the South, and of the vale, and of the springs, and all their kings; he left *none* remaining, but utterly destroyed *all that breathed*, as the Lord God of Israel commanded." Then follows another string of horrible tragedies; whole nations, numbers of nations, all slaughtered; not one poor soul allowed to remain alive throughout their vast extent; and all is fathered on God. And now come other, longer, and more frightful lists of tragic and revolting deeds. Cities and nations, kings and people, men and women, old and young, all swept away. Not one is left to breathe. All, all are slaughtered, as the Lord commanded Moses. "There was not a city that made peace with the children of Israel save the Hivites," says the story. 'Ah! that explains the matter," says the believer. "Their destruction is chargeable on *themselves* if they would not make peace." What! must the women and children perish, because the rulers and the warriors refuse to make peace? But hark! the story adds: "Not a city made peace, for it was of the *Lord to harden their hearts* that they should come against Israel in battle, that he might *destroy them utterly;* that they might have *no favor*, but that he might destroy them, as the Lord commanded Moses." No book can give the Deity a darker character than this. None can throw out against him more atrocious blasphemies. Yet the book abounds in such stories.

God is said to have hardened Pharaoh's heart, that he might not let the children of Israel go, but bring down on his people, the innocent as well as the guilty, the most grievous plagues, including the destruction of the first-born in every family in the land. Of course we do not believe those stories; we regard them as false; but the blasphemy is none the less.

Then look at the story of the flood. God is represented as dooming to destruction the whole human race, with the exception of a single family. True, the story tells us man was very corrupt; but were *all* corrupt? Were there no good men? Were there no stainless women? No innocent children? Were all so lost to virtue as to be past hope? Impossible! But, supposing the degeneracy universal, is utter and unsparing destruction the only alternative? And shall the whole race be swept away without one word of pity, or one sign of sorrow or regret? It is thus the Bible represents the matter. The blasphemy could not be greater. Nothing worse can be attributed to God than what the Bible attributes to him. Nothing worse can be conceived.

8. The Bible represents God as demanding or accepting human sacrifices. It represents him as commanding Abraham to offer up his son Isaac as a burnt-offering, though the sacrifice was not completed. In 2 Samuel 21: 1–14, a sacrifice is demanded and made. The story is as follows: "Then there was a famine in the days of David three years, year after year; and David inquired of the Lord. And the Lord answered, It is for Saul and his bloody house, because he slew the Gibeonites. Wherefore David said unto the Gibeonites, What shall I do for you? and wherewith shall I make the atonement, that ye may bless the inheritance of the Lord? And the Gibeonites said unto him, We will have no silver nor gold of Saul, nor of his house; neither for us shalt thou kill any man in Israel. And he said, What ye shall say, that will I do for you. And they answered the king, The man that consumed us, and that devised against us that we should be destroyed from remaining in any of the coasts of Israel, Let seven men of his sons be delivered unto us, and we will hang them

up unto the Lord in Gibeah of Saul, whom the Lord did choose. And the king said, I will give them. But the king spared Mephibosheth, the son of Jonathan, the son of Saul, because of the Lord's oath that was between them, between David and Jonathan the son of Saul. But the king took the two sons of Rizpah, the daughter of Aiah, whom she bare unto Saul, Armoni and Mephibosheth; and the five sons of Michal, the daughter of Saul, whom she brought up for Adriel, the son of Barzillai the Meholathite. And he delivered them into the hands of the Gibeonites, and they hanged them in the hill before the Lord; and they fell all seven together, and were put to death in the days of harvest, in the first days, in the beginning of barley-harvest. And Rizpah, the daughter of Aiah, took sackcloth, and spread it for her upon the rock, from the beginning of harvest until water dropped upon them out of heaven, and suffered neither the birds of the air to rest on them by day, nor the beasts of the field by night."

"There!" said he, "I think the subject might be left right here. Of course there are 'doctrinal points' which might be debated. For example, take the doctrine of the Trinity: One God in three persons; three persons, each person God, and yet not three Gods. The first person is the father of the second, and the third proceeds from the father and the son, yet neither is before or after the other. All are of one age. The son is as old as his father, and the grandson is as old as either. The first of these persons demands satisfaction for man's sins; the others do not, though they are all one God. The second becomes man, suffers and dies; the others do not. The united Godhead and manhead are crucified and buried; go into hell; rise again from the grave on the third day. These are not a tenth part of the absurdities of this doctrine. The doctrines of original sin, the atonement, imputed guilt and imputed righteousness, justification by Christ's merits, &c., are as foolish, as absurd, as monstrous, as blasphemous, and as mischievous as any that can be found."

Several minutes passed in utter silence—I, reflecting on the influence of his criticisms on superstitious Bible-believers—he, watching the effect of his text and arguments upon my mind. And I reflected thus: The Bible, considered externally, is, like every other material book or form of matter, possessed of the properties of change, decay, contradiction, and darkness. The Bible is only a book compounded of changeable, fleeting elements; and this mutability is as true of its contents as of the paper, ink, and binding. But do not all books, as well as other forms of matter, proceed from spiritual fountains of causation? Are not material forms the mere shadows of interior harmonious principles? With earthly eyes we see externals; whilst with spirit eyes we see the interior sense and harmony. But did not every thing originate in the spiritual sources? The poet meant this when he said—

> "We do not make our thoughts; they grow in us
> Like grains in wood; the growth is of the skies;
> The skies are of nature: nature is of God."

Viewed from this central stand-point, may not all religious discourses and sacred books contain spiritual gospels? Why may not the sacred works of all nations be the coverings and viaducts of God's momentous truths to man? The laws of inspiration must be universal, and without variableness or shadow of turning; therefore that law, which demonstrates the Christian's Bible to be interiorly divine and authoritative, will apply, with equal consistency and cogency, to all sacred books of every other age or people.

At length, turning to the visitor, I remarked: "With you, sir, I have no belief in the miraculous origin or supernatural inspiration of any book or writing; neither do I think well of any priestly authority that is predicated on such false assumptions; but yet, unlike you, I discern in all *interiorly* written books, here and there, *the glorious presence of Arabula!* the lifting Light of divine Truth! shining and streaming through them all, as the sunlight of high heaven pours itself through the forest and flowers of nature; and to-morrow, if you will have the kindness to call upon me, I think I can furnish, for your special edification, passages of consistent and beautiful Scripture, taken from the uncanonized, but none the less real, Saints of past and present times."

He promised to give me his candid attention, as I had patiently given him mine, and so on the best of terms we parted.

CHAPTER L.

NEW COLLECTION OF GOSPELS.

Hail! gladdening Light of Arabula, thou beautiful and bountiful giver of joys unspeakable! I follow thee where'er thou lead'st; and where thou goest I will go; for my inmost nature *knows* that thou art the "light which lighteth every man that cometh into the world."

O, sacred Fire! blazing broad and high, "a consuming fire," beautiful and without vengeance, but powerfully armed with unchangeable Justice, perpetually flaming from the infinite heart of Love. O, pure, lambent Light! burning the roots and branches of all sin, and ignorance, and prejudice; and purifying all things, like "the refiner's fire," and separating the pure from the dross—the Light! who maketh seers of the poor and blind; who findeth saints among the so-called evil; who maketh the tongues of fools to confound the wise; who bringeth Prophets and Apostles out of darkness; who unfoldeth the heavens to the gaze of uncounted millions—unto Thee I come with open and beaming eyes, with a grateful heart, with an unprejudiced intellect, with reverential love for thy commandments, and unto Thee most gladly would I bring my patient, attentive, friendly reader. Take this earnest soul, whose wide-open eyes now tenderly dwell upon these sentences, and pour thy holy fire into the waiting intellect and sweet affections. Cause the reader's understanding to turn away from the prejudices of both association and memory. Expand and open the higher powers of mind, so that they shall magnetically *lift* the Intellect into the independent clairvoyance of the "superior condition," in which state alone can the pure impersonal principles of the Eternal be discerned by the reason, and their benefits taken like celestial food into the hungering affections.

Where art thou, patient Reader? Arabula says, "It is I, be not afraid." Courage, then, and tell, candidly, just *where* you are. Can you reason calmly and meditate, now, without "the heat of passion" and blindness of prejudice? Are you clear-sighted now, and can you "look truth in the face," and loyally say, "Lead on! I will follow Thee?" If you are still and exclusively under the "light of the Intellect," then you have pride and prejudices to intercept your progression in wisdom. Arabula knows no *meum et tuum*, for she is free from prejudice as "truth makes free," whilst Intellect, having all its eyes upon the world, the flesh, and the fleeting advantages thereof, gives nothing but *obstacles*.

Seneca, the truly moral philosopher, who lived at the beginning of the Christian era, said: "It is with most men as with an innocent that my father had in his family. One day she fell blind on a sudden, but nobody could persuade her that she was blind. 'I cannot endure the house,' she cried, 'it is so dark, so dark!' and so, fancying that it was light in the world without, she kept calling for liberty to go abroad." Thus it is with the *blindest* persons in the religious world—they fancy the darkness is in others, or possibly in their own circumstances, but never, O, no! *never in themselves.*

A new collection of Gospels is now imperatively demanded in the cause and interest of truth. With the light of Arabula before you, like a "pillar of fire," showing the path through the darkness of ignorance, you can see the footprints of the everlasting God through all the sacred writings of every age and people. Only the proud and prejudiced—only the ignorant and superstitious—are shut out of this beautiful and beneficent garden. Come, reader, let us enter and read.

THE GOSPEL ACCORDING TO

RISHIS, OR ANCIENT SAINTS.

CHAPTER I.

The Vedas are the Scriptures of the devout people of the Orient. The following passages declare the presence of the divine light in a very dark era of history. All Scripture-writing is given by inspiration.

ANY place where the mind of man can be undisturbed, is suitable for the worship of the Supreme Being.

2 The vulgar look for their gods in water; the ignorant think they reside in wood, bricks, and stones; men of more extended knowledge seek them in celestial orbs; but wise men worship the Universal Soul.

3 There is One living and true God; everlasting, without parts or passion; of infinite power, wisdom, and goodness; the Maker and Preserver of all things.

4 What and how the Supreme Being is, cannot be ascertained. We can only describe him by his effects and works. In like manner as we, not knowing the real nature of the sun, explain him to be the cause of the succession of days and epochs.

5 That Spirit who is distinct from Matter, and from all beings contained in Matter, is not various. He is One, and he is beyond description; whose glory is so great, there can be no image of him. He is the incomprehensible Spirit, who illuminates all, and delights all; from whom all proceed, by whom they live after they are born, and to whom all must return. Nothing

but the Supreme Being should be adored by a wise man.

6 He overspreads all creatures. He is entirely Spirit, without the form either of a minute body, or an extended one, which is liable to impression or organization. He is the ruler of the intellect, self-existent, pure, perfect, omniscient, and omnipresent. He has from all eternity been assigning to all creatures their respective purposes. No vision can approach him, no language describe him, no intellectual power can comprehend him.

7 As a thousand rays emanate from one flame, thus do all souls emanate from The One Eternal Soul, and return to him.

8 The Supreme Soul dwells in the form of four-footed animals, and in another place he is full of glory. He lives in the form of the slave, he is smaller than the grain of barley. He is the smallest of the small, and the greatest of the great; yet he is neither small nor great.

9 Without hand nor foot, he runs rapidly and grasps firmly; without eyes, he sees all; without ears, he hears all. He knows whatever can be known; but there is none who knows him. The wise call him the Great, Supreme, Pervading Spirit.

10 He who considers all beings as existing in the Supreme Spirit, and the Supreme Spirit as pervading all beings, cannot view with contempt any creature whatsoever.

11 God has created the senses to be directed toward external objects. They can perceive only these objects, and not the Eternal Spirit. The sage, who desires an immortal life, withdraws his senses from their natural course, and perceives the Supreme Being everywhere present.

12 This body, formed of bones, skin, and nerves, filled with fat and flesh, is a great evil, and without reality. It ought to perish. Of what use, then, is it, for the soul to seek corporeal pleasures?

13 The inhabitants of this body are cupidity, anger, desire for wealth, error, anxiety, envy, sadness, discord, disappointment, affliction, hunger, thirst, disease, old age, death. Of what use is it, then, to seek the pleasures of this body?

14 Through strict veracity, uniform control of the mind and senses, abstinence from sexual indulgence, and ideas derived from spiritual teachers, man should approach God, who, full of glory and perfection, works in the heart, and to whom only votaries freed from passion and desire can approximate.

15 Material objects have no duration. As the fruits of the trees grow and perish, so do these objects. What is there in them worthy to be acquired? Great things and small, commanders of powerful armies, kings who govern the earth, have relinquished their riches and passed into the other world. Nothing could save them. They were men, and they could not escape death.

16 The Gandharvas, the Sooras, the stars themselves, do not endure forever. The seas will one day be dried up, the high mountains will fall, even the polar star will change its place, the earth will be swallowed in the waves. Such is the world! Of what avail is it to seek its pleasures? One may perform meritorious works, from self-interested motives, during his whole life, he may enjoy all pleasures, still he must come back into the world. He can only continue passing from one world to another.

17 There is nothing desirable ex-

cept the science of God. Out of this there is no tranquillity and no freedom. To be attached to material things is to be chained; to be without attachment is to be free.

18 May this soul of mine, which is a ray of perfect wisdom, pure intellect, and permanent existence, which is the unextinguishable light fixed within created bodies, without which no good act is performed, be united by devout meditations with the Spirit supremely blest and supremely intelligent.

19 O thou, who givest sustenance to the world, unvail that face of the *true* sun which is now hidden by a vail of golden light! so that we may see the *truth*, and know our whole duty.

20 He who inwardly rules the sun is the same immortal Spirit who inwardly rules thee.

21 That All-pervading Spirit, which gives light to the visible sun, even the same in *kind* am I, though infinitely distant in *degree*. Let my soul return to the immortal Spirit of God, and then let my body return to dust.

22 By one Supreme Ruler is this universe pervaded; even every world in the whole circle of Nature. Enjoy pure delight, O man, by abandoning all thoughts of this perishable world; and covet not the wealth of any creature existing.

23 God, who is perfect wisdom and perfect happiness, is the final refuge of the man who has liberally bestowed his wealth, who has been firm in virtue, and who knows and adores the Great One.

24 To those regions where Evil Spirits dwell, and which utter darkness involves, surely go after death all such men as destroy the purity of their own souls.

25 Preserve thyself from self-sufficiency, and do not covet property belonging to another.

26 The way to eternal beatitude is open to him who without omission speaketh truth.

27 If any one assumes the garb of the religious, without doing their works, he is not religious. Whatever garments he wears, if his works are pure, he belongs to the order of pure men. If he wears the dress of a penitent, and does not lead the life of a penitent, he belongs to the men of the world; but if he is in the world, and practices penitential works, he ought to be regarded as a penitent.

28 No man can acquire knowledge of the soul without abstaining from evil acts, and having control over the senses and the mind. Nor can he gain it, though with a firm mind, if he is actuated by desire for reward. But man may obtain knowledge of the soul by contemplation of God.

29 Though man finds pleasure in that which he sees, hears, smells, tastes, and touches, he derives no benefit from the pleasure, because the soul, in attaching itself to external objects, forgets its high origin, which is The Universal Soul.

30 It is the nature of the soul to identify itself with the object of its tendency. If it tend toward the world, it becomes the world. If it tend toward God, it becomes God.

31 Saints wise and firm, exempt from passion, assured of the soul's divine origin, satisfied solely with the science of God, have seen God everywhere present with them, and after death have been absorbed in him.

32 To know that God *is*, and that *all* is God, this is the substance of the Vedas. When one attains to this, there is no more need of read-

ing, or of works; they are but the bark, the straw, the envelope. No more need of them when one has the seed, the substance, the Creator. When one knows Him by science, he may abandon science, as the torch which has conducted him to the end.

CHAPTER II.

"The following," says an author, "is one of the numerous prayers contained in the Vedas:"

WHERE they who know the Great One go, through holy rites and through piety, thither may fire raise me. May fire receive my sacrifices.

2 Mysterious praise to Fire! May air waft me thither. May air increase my spirits.

3 Mysterious praise to Air! May the sun draw me thither. May the sun enlighten my eye.

4 Mysterious praise to the Sun! May the moon bear me thither. May the moon receive my mind.

5 Mysterious praise to the Moon! May the planet Soma lead me thither. May Soma bestow on me its hallowed milk.

6 Mysterious praise to Soma! May Indra carry me thither. May Indra give me strength.

7 Mysterious praise to Indra! May water lead me thither. May water bring me the stream of immortality.

8 Mysterious praise to the Waters! Where they who know the Great One go, through holy rites and through piety, thither may Brahma conduct me. May Brahma lead me to the Great One. Mysterious praise to Brahma!

THE GOSPEL ACCORDING TO

THE ZEND-AVESTA.

CHAPTER I.

The Sacred Scriptures of the ancient Persians, contain many evidences that the Light was working its way into the World. Read the following sentences:—

WORSHIP, with humility and reverence, Ormuzd, the giver of blessings, and all the Spirits, to whose care he has intrusted the universe.

2 Men ought reverently to salute the Sun, and praise him, but not pay him religious worship.

3 Obey strictly all the laws given to Zoroaster.

4 Kings are animated by a more ethereal fire than other mortals; such fire as exists in the upper spheres. Ormuzd established the King to nourish and solace the poor. He is to his people what Ormuzd is to this earth. It is the duty of subjects to obey him implicitly.

5 It is the duty of children to obey their parents; for wives to obey their husbands.

6 Treat old age with great reverence and tenderness.

7 Multiply the human species, and increase their happiness.

8 Cultivate the soil, drain marshes, and destroy dangerous creatures. He who sows the ground with diligence acquires a greater stock of religious merit than he could gain by ten thousand prayers in idleness.

9 Multiply domestic animals, nourish them, and treat them gently.

10 Warriors, who defend the right, deserve praise.

11 Do not allow thyself to be carried away by anger. Angry words, and scornful looks, are sins. To strike a man, or vex him with words, is a sin. Even the intention to strike another merits punishment. Opposition to peace is a sin. Reply to thine enemy with gentleness.

12 Avoid every thing calculated to injure others. Have no companionship with a man who injures his neighbor.

13 Take not that which belongs to another.

14 Be not envious, avaricious, proud, or vain. Envy and jealousy are the work of Evil Spirits. Haughty thoughts and thirst of gold are sins.

15 To refuse hospitality, and not to succor the poor, are sins.

16 Obstinacy in maintaining a lie is a sin. Be very scrupulous to observe the truth in all things.

17 Abstain from thy neighbor's wife. Fornication and immodest looks are sins. Avoid licentiousness, because it is one of the readiest means to give Evil Spirits power over body and soul. Strive, therefore, to keep pure in body and mind, and thus prevent the entrance of Evil Spirits, who are always trying to gain possession of man. To think evil is a sin.

18 Contend constantly against evil, morally and physically, internally and externally. Strive in every way to diminish the power of Arimanes and destroy his works.

19 If a man has done this, he may fearlessly meet death; well assured that radiant Izeds will lead him across the luminous bridge, into a paradise of eternal happiness.

20 Every man who is pure in thoughts, words, and actions, will go to the celestial regions. Every man who is evil in thoughts, words, or actions, will go to the place of the wicked.

21 All good thoughts, words, or actions, are the productions of the celestial world.

CHAPTER II.

"A large portion of the Zend-Avesta," says the author of Progress in Religious Ideas, "is filled with prayers; of which the following are samples:"

I ADDRESS my prayers to Ormuzd, Creator of all things;

2 Who always has been, who is, and who will be forever;

3 Who is wise and powerful;

4 Who made the great arch of heaven, the sun, moon, stars, winds, clouds, water, earth, fire, trees, animals, metals, and men;

5 Whom Zoroaster adored. Zoroaster! who brought to the world knowledge of the law; who knew by natural intelligence, and by the ear, what ought to be done, all that has been, all that is, and all that will be; the science of sciences, the excellent Word, by which souls pass the luminous and radiant bridge, separate themselves from the evil regions, and go to light and holy dwellings, full of fragrance.

6 O Creator, I obey thy laws.

7 I think, act, speak, according to thy orders.

8 I separate myself from all sin.

9 I do good works according to my power.

10 I adore thee with purity of thought, word, and action.

11 I pray to Ormuzd, who recompenses good works, who delivers unto the end all those who obey his laws. Grant that I may arrive at Paradise, where all is fragrance, light, and happiness.

12 O Ormuzd! pardon the repentant sinner. As I, when a man injures me by his thoughts, words, or actions, carried away, or not carried away, by his passions, if he humbles himself before me, and addresses to me his prayer, I become his friend.

13 Grant, O Ormuzd! that my good works may exceed my sins. Give me a part in all good actions and all holy words.

14 I pray to Mithras! who has a thousand ears and ten thousand eyes; who never sleeps, who is always watchful and attentive, who renders barren lands fertile.

15 Thou Fire! son of Ormuzd, brilliant and beneficent, given by Ormuzd, be favorable to me.

16 I pray to the New Moon! holy, pure, and great. I pray to the Full Moon, holy, pure, and great. I gaze at the Moon which is on high. I honor the light of the Moon. The Moon is a blessed Spirit created by Ormuzd, to bestow light and glory on the earth.

17 I invoke the Source of Waters! holy, pure, and great, coming from the throne of Ormuzd, from the high mountain, holy, pure, and great.

18 I invoke the sweet Earth! I invoke the Mountains, abode of happiness, given by Ormuzd, holy, pure, and great.

THE GOSPEL ACCORDING TO

THE SON OF BRAHMA.

CHAPTER I.

The following Scriptures are from the writings of Menu. "It is believed by the Hindoos," says the translator, "to have been promulged in the beginning of time, by Menu, son or grandson of Brahma, and first of created beings. Brahma is said to have taught his laws to Menu in a hundred thousand verses, which Menu explained to the primitive world in the very words of the book now translated."

THE resignation of all pleasures is far better than the attainment of them.

2 Let man honor all his food, and eat it without contempt; when he sees it, let him rejoice and be calm, and pray that he may always obtain it.

3 Greatness is not conferred by years, not by gray hairs, not by wealth, not by powerful kindred; the divine sages have established this rule: "Whoever has read the Vedas, and their Angas, he among us is great."

4 Let not a sensible teacher tell what he is not asked, nor what he

is asked improperly; but let him, however intelligent, act in the multitude as if he were dumb.

5 The only firm friend, who follows men even after death, is Justice; all others are extinct with the body.

6 The soul is its own witness; the soul itself is its own refuge: offend not thy conscious soul, the supreme internal witness of men.

7 Food, eaten constantly with respect, gives muscular force and generative power; but, eaten irreverently, destroys them both.

8 The hand of an artist employed in his art is always pure.

9 Bodies are cleansed by water; the mind is purified by truth; the vital spirit, by theology and devotion; the understanding, by clear knowledge.

10 O friend to virtue, that supreme spirit—which thou believest one and the same with thyself—resides in thy bosom perpetually; and is an all-knowing *inspector* of thy goodness or of thy wickedness.

11 Action, either mental, verbal, or corporeal, bears good or evil fruit, as itself is good or evil.

12 Justice, being destroyed, will destroy; being preserved, will preserve; it must therefore never be violated. Beware, O judge, lest justice, being overturned, overturn both us and thyself.

13 Injustice, committed in this world, produces not fruit immediately, but, like the earth, in due season; and advancing, by little and little, it eradicates the man who committed it.

14 Iniquity, once committed, fails not of producing fruit to him who wrought it; if not in his own person, yet in his sons; or, if not in his sons, yet in his grandsons.

15 He grows rich for a while through unrighteousness; but he perishes at length from his whole root upwards.

16 If the vital spirit had practiced virtue for the most part, and vice in a small degree, it enjoys delight in celestial abodes, clothed with a body formed of pure elementary particles.

17 But if it had generally been addicted to vice, and seldom attended to virtue, then shall it be deserted by those pure elements, and, having a coarser body of sensible nerves, it feels the pains to which Yama shall doom it.

18 Souls, endued with goodness, attain always the state of deities; those filled with ambitious passions, the condition of men; and those immersed in darkness, the nature of beasts.

19 Grass and earth to sit on, water to wash the feet, and affectionate speech, are at no time deficient in the mansions of the good.

20 Let every Brahmin with fixed attention consider all nature, both visible and invisible, as existing *in the Divine Spirit;* for, when he contemplates the boundless universe existing in the Divine Spirit, he cannot give his heart to iniquity:

21 The Divine Spirit is the whole assemblage of gods; all worlds are seated in the Divine Spirit; and the Divine Spirit produces the connected series of acts performed by embodied souls.

THE GOSPEL ACCORDING TO

ST. CONFUCIUS.

CHAPTER I.

This wise and beloved Chinese philosopher lived five hundred and fifty-one years before the Christian era. The following passages show that the light of divine truth shone within him.

DO unto another what you would he should do unto you, and do not unto another what you would not should be done unto you. Thou only needest this law alone, it is the foundation and principle of all the rest.

2 We cannot observe the necessary rules of life, if there be wanting these three virtues: (1) Wisdom, which makes us discern good from evil; (2) universal love, which makes us love all men who are virtuous; and (3) that resolution which makes us constantly persevere in the adherence to good, and aversion for evil.

3 The love of the perfect man is a universal love; a love whose object is all mankind.

4 There are four rules, according to which a perfect man ought to square himself: I. He ought to practice, in respect of his father, what he requires from his son. II. In the service of the State, he ought to show the same fidelity which he demands of those who are under him. III. He must act, in respect of his elder brother, after the same manner he would that his younger brother should act toward himself. IV. He ought to behave himself toward his friends as he desires his friends should carry themselves toward him. The perfect man continually acquits himself of these duties, how common soever they may appear.

5 If you undertake an affair for another, manage and follow it with the same eagerness and fidelity as if it were your own.

6 Always behave yourself with the same precaution and discretion as you would do if you were observed by ten eyes, and pointed at by so many hands.

7 When the opportunity of doing a reasonable thing shall offer, make use of it without hesitation.

8 If a man, although full of self-love, endeavor to perform good actions, behold him already very near that universal love which urges him to do good to all.

9 He who persecutes a good man, makes war against himself and all mankind.

10 The defects of parents ought not to be imputed to their children. If a father, by his crimes, render himself unworthy of being promoted to honor, the son ought not to be excluded, if he do not render himself unworthy. If a son shall be of an obscure birth, his birth ought not to be his crime.

11 If a person has deviated from the path of integrity and innocence, he needs only to excite the good that remains to make atonement by pains and industry, and he will infallibly arrive at the highest state of virtue.

12 It is not enough to know virtue, it is necessary to love it; but

it is not sufficient to love it, it is necessary to possess it.

CHAPTER II.

An Exhortation to obtain Wisdom and to practice Virtue. Gluttony forbidden. He proclaimeth the glory of goodness, and showeth his admiration for the appearance of those who possess it.

IT is impossible that he who knows not how to govern and reform himself and his own family, can rightly govern and reform a people.

2 It is the wise man only who is always pleased; virtue renders his spirit quiet; nothing troubles him, nothing disquiets him, because he practices not virtue for a reward: the practice of virtue is the sole recompense he expects.

3 Endeavor to imitate the wise, and never discourage thyself, how laborious soever it may be; if thou canst arrive at thine end, the happiness thou wilt possess will recompense all thy pains.

4 Always remember that thou art a man, that human nature is frail, and that thou mayest easily fall. But if, happening to forget what thou art, thou chancest to fall, be not discouraged; remember that thou mayest rise again; that it is in thy power to break the bands which join thee to thy offense, and to subdue the obstacles which hinder thee from walking in the paths of virtue.

5 If a man feel a secret shame when he hears impure and unchaste discourses—if he cannot forbear blushing thereat—he is not far from that resolution of spirit which makes him constantly seek after good, and have an aversion for evil.

6 The wise man never hastens, either in his studies or his words; he is sometimes, as it were, mute; but, when it concerns him to act, and practice virtue, he, as I may say, precipitates all. The truly wise man speaks but little, he is little eloquent; I do not see that eloquence can be of any great use to him.

7 Those who constantly consult their appetites and palates, never do any thing worthy of their rank as men; they are rather brutes than rational creatures.

8 Eat not for the pleasure thou mayest find therein; eat to increase thy strength; eat to preserve the life which thou hast received.

9 Labor to purify thy thoughts, if thy thoughts are not ill, neither will thy actions be so. The wise man has an infinity of pleasures.

10 Give thy superfluities to the poor. Poverty and human miseries are evils, but the bad only resent them.

11 Riches and honors are good; the desire to possess them is natural to all men; but, if these things agree not with virtue, the wise man ought to contemn and renounce them. On the contrary, poverty and ignominy are evils; man naturally avoids them; if these evils attack the wise man, it is right that he should rid himself of them, but not by a crime.

12 The good man employs himself only with virtue; the bad only with his riches. The first continually thinks upon the good and interest of the State; but the last thinks on what concerns himself.

13 The way that leads to virtue is long [straight the gate and narrow the way], but it is the duty to finish this long race. Allege not for the excuse, that thou hast not strength enough, that difficulties discourage thee, and that thou shalt be at last forced to stop in the midst of thy course. Thou knowest nothing;

begin to run: it is a sign that thou hast not as yet begun.

14 It is necessary, after an exact and extensive manner, to know the causes, properties, differences, and effects of all things.

15 It is necessary to meditate in particular, on the things we believe we know, and to weigh every thing by the weight of reason, with all the attentiveness of spirit, and with the utmost exactness whereof we are capable.

16 He who in his studies wholly applies himself to labor and exercise, and neglects meditation, loses his time; and he who only applies himself to meditation, and neglects experimental exercise, does only wander and lose himself. The first can never know any thing exactly; and the last will only pursue shadows.

17 To the mind, virtue [chastity, integrity, uprightness] communicates inexpressible beauties and perfections; to the body it produces delightful sensations; it affords a certain physiognomy, certain transports, certain ways, which infinitely please. And, as it is the property of virtue to becalm the heart and keep the peace there, so this inward tranquillity and secret joy produces a certain serenity in the countenance, a certain air of goodness, kindness, and reason, which attract the esteem of the whole world.

THE GOSPEL ACCORDING TO

THE PERSIAN PROPHETS.

CHAPTER I.

THE PERSIAN LITANY.

LET us take refuge with Mezdam [God] from dark and evil thoughts which molest and afflict us.

2 O Creator of the essence of supports and stays! O Thou who showerest down benefits! O Thou who formest the heart and soul! O Fashioner of forms and shadows! O Light of lights!

3 Thou art the first, for there is no priority prior to Thee!

4 Thou art the last, for there is no posteriority posterior to Thee!

5 O worthy to be lauded! deliver us from the bonds of terrestrial matter! Rescue us from the fetters of dark and evil matter!

6 Intelligence is a drop from among the drops of the ocean of thy place of Souls.

7 The Soul is a flame from among the flames of the fire of thy residence of Sovereignty.

8 Mezdam is hid by excess of light. He is Lord of his wishes; not subject to novelties; and the great is small, and the tall short, and the broad narrow, and the deep is as a ford to him.

9 Who causeth the shadow to fall. The inflamer, who maketh the blood to boil.

10 In the circle of thy sphere, which is without rent, which neither

assumeth a new shape nor putteth off an old one, nor taketh a straight course, Thou art exalted, O Lord! From Thee is praise, and to Thee is praise.

11 Thy world of forms, the city of bodies, the place of created things is long, broad, and deep. Thou art the accomplisher of desires.

12 The eyes of Purity saw Thee by the luster of thy substance.

13 Dark and astounded is he who hath seen Thee by the efforts of the Intellect.

CHAPTER II.

Mezdam, the First Cause, or God, speaketh to the Worshiper.

MY light is on thy countenance; my word is on thy tongue. Me thou seest, me thou hearest, me thou smellest, me thou tastest, me thou touchest.

2 What thou sayest, that I say; and thy acts are my acts. And I speak by thy tongue, and thou speakest to me, though mortals imagine that thou speakest to them.

3 I am never out of thy heart, and I am contained in nothing but in thy heart.

4 And I am nearer unto thee than thou art unto thyself. Thy Soul reacheth me.

5 In the name of Mezdam, O Siamer! I will call thee aloft, and make thee my companion; the lower world is not thy place.

6 Many times daily thou escapest from thy body and comest unto me. Now, thou art not satisfied with coming unto me from time to time, and longest to abide continually nigh unto me; I, too, am not satisfied with thy absence.

7 Although thou art with me, and I with thee, still thou desirest and I desire that thou shouldest be still more intimately with me.

8 Therefore will I release thee from thy terrestrial body, and make thee sit in my company.

PROVERBS OF

SYRUS THE SYRIAN.

CHAPTER I.

In the translator's preface it is said that "like Terence and Phædrus, Syrus passed his early years in slavery. But as we have no evidence that he was born a slave, it is supposed he became one, when Syria, his native country, was reduced to a Roman province by Pompey (year of Rome, 690; B. C. 64). He was brought to Rome when about twelve years of age, by an inferior officer of the army, called Domitius, and thereupon received the name SYRUS, *in accordance with the custom by which slaves took a name derived from that of their province. The young Syrian was fair and well formed." These Proverbs were written about forty years before the Christian era.*

DO not find your happiness in another's sorrow. Receive an injury rather than do one.

2 Human reason grows rich by self-conquest. He has existed only,

not lived, who lacks wisdom in old age.

3 A wise man rules his passions; a fool obeys them.

4 Be not blind to a friend's faults; nor hate him for them. Friendship either finds, or makes, equals.

5 He sleeps well who knows not that he sleeps ill.

6 It is well to yield up a pleasure, when a pain goes with it.

7 Men are all equal in the presence of death. He dies twice who perishes by his own hand. The evil you do to others you may expect in return.

8 Happy he who died [in old age] when death was desirable.

9 We make the nearest approaches to the gods [the angels] in our good deeds.

10 A knave or a fool thinks a good deed is thrown away. The more benefits bestowed, the more received. Never forget a favor received; be quick to forget a favor bestowed.

11 There is no sight in the eye, when the mind does not see.

12 There is but a step between a proud man's glory and his disgrace.

13 The wounds of conscience always leave a scar. Consult your conscience rather than public opinion. Consider what you ought to say, and not what you think.

14 Wisdom had rather be buffeted than not be listened to. Folly had rather be unheard than be buffeted.

15 He who longs for death, confesses that life is a failure. A god [any thing external] can hardly disturb a man truly happy.

16 Patience is a remedy for every sorrow. What happens to one man may happen to all.

CHAPTER II.

Syrus rejecteth error, and showeth the folly of reliance upon externals. He exhorteth to a clear conscience, and showeth an empire to every man.

THERE is no safety in regaining the favor of an enemy. It is madness to put confidence in error.

2 The blessing which could be received, can be taken away. Whatever you can lose, you should reckon of no account.

3 Reflect on every thing you hear, but believe only on proof.

4 The less a mortal desires, the less he needs. Avoid the sweet which is like to become a bitter.

5 Control yourself, and you conquer a kingdom.

6 It is a kingly spirit that can return good deeds for reproaches. He who takes counsel of good faith is just even to an enemy.

7 Discord gives a relish for concord. Even calamity becomes virtue's opportunity.

8 For him who loves labor, there is always something to do. The hope of reward is the solace of labor.

9 The life which we live is but a small part of the real life. A great man may commence life in a hovel.

10 A prosperous worthlessness is the curse of high life. Many consult their reputation; but few their conscience.

11 Pardon the offense of others, but never your own.

12 The sinner's judgment began the day that he sinned. Would you have a great empire? Rule over yourself.

CHAPTER III.

He maketh plain the path of the noble and righteous. Good men he extolleth, and looketh for good even from the hands of the evil.

A TRULY noble nature cannot be insulted.

2 Slander is more injurious than

open violence. It is easier to do an injury than to bear one.

3 To forget the wrongs you receive is to remedy them.

4 The right is ever beyond the reach of the wrong. To do good you should know what good is.

5 In the art of praying, necessity is the best of teachers.

6 A noble spirit finds a cure for injustice in forgetting it. Mighty rivers may easily be leaped at their source.

7 The fear of death is more to be dreaded than death itself.

8 You will find a great many things before you find a good man. A great fortune sits gracefully on a great man.

9 The good man can be called miserable, but he is not so. The death of a good man is a public calamity.

10 A wise man never refuses any thing to necessity. There is no great evil which does not bring with it some advantage.

CHAPTER IV.

He rebuketh hypocrisy, and exhorteth the judges to be merciful as well as just. He explaineth misfortunes, and commendeth patience.

WHY do we not hear the truth? Because we do not speak it. Confession of our faults is the next thing to innocence.

2 He can do no harm who has lost the desire to do it.

3 You should not lead one life in private and another in public.

4 The judge is condemned, when the criminal is acquitted. Not the criminals, but their crimes, it is well to extirpate.

5 A good conscience never utters mere lip prayers.

6 Better please one good man than many bad ones. There is nothing more wretched than a mind conscious of its own wickedness.

7 The memory of great misfortunes suffered, is itself a misfortune.

8 The sweetest pleasure arises from difficulties overcome.

9 Misfortune is most men's greatest punishment. No man is happy who does not think himself so.

10 He is never happy whose thoughts always run with his fears.

11 God looks at the clean hands, not the full ones. Patience reveals the soul's hidden riches.

THE GOSPEL ACCORDING TO ST. GABRIEL.

CHAPTER I.

The inspired Russian statesman, Gabriel Derzhavin, who in the seventeenth century held a high place among the poets of his country, and who is now "wearing the garments of eternal day beyond this little sphere," wrote an ode to Deity, of which the following sentences form the substance:

O THOU Eternal One! whose presence all space doth occupy; all motion guide.

2 Thou only God! Being above all things, whom none can comprehend; who fillest existence with thyself alone: embracing all; supporting, ruling all; being whom we call "God."

3 Philosophy may measure out the ocean deep; may count the sands or the sun's rays.

4 But God! for Thee there is no weight nor measure. None can mount up to thy mysteries. Reason, though kindled by Thy light, in vain would try to trace Thy counsels; and thought, like past moments in eternity, is lost ere thought can soar so high.

5 All sprung from Thee—Light, Joy, Harmony—all life, all beauty Thine.

6 Thy splendor fills all space with rays divine. Thou art, and wast, and shalt be the life-giving, life-sustaining Potentate.

7 Thou the beginning with the end hast bound; and beautifully mingled Life and Death!

8 Suns and worlds spring forth from Thee! and as the spangles in the sunny rays shine in the silver snow, so the pageantry of heaven's bright army glitters in Thy praise!

9 A million torches, lighted by Thy hand, wander unwearied through the blue abyss.

10 What shall we call them? Piles of crystal light? A glorious company of golden streams? Lamps of celestial ether? Suns, lighting systems with their joyous beams? But Thou, to those, art as the noon to night.

11 Yes, as a drop of water in the sea, all this magnificence in Thee is lost. What are a thousand worlds, compared to Thee?

12 And what am I when Heaven's unnumbered host, though multiplied by myriads, and arrayed in all the glory of sublimest thought, is but an atom in the balance, weighed against Thy greatness—a cipher brought against infinity?

CHAPTER II.

The psalmist traceth his life to God. He acknowledgeth his own insignificance. God giveth all life, and receiveth perpetual praises.

BUT the effluence of Thy light divine, pervading worlds, hath reached my bosom. Yes, in my spirit doth Thy spirit shine, as shines the sunbeam in a drop of dew.

2 Therefore I live, and on Hope's pinions fly towards Thy presence; for in Thee I live, and breathe, and dwell.

3 I am, O God, and surely Thou must be!

4 Thou art directing, guiding all. Direct my understanding, then, to Thee! Control my spirit, guide my wandering heart, for I am fashioned by Thy hand.

5 I hold a middle rank 'twixt Heaven and Earth, on the last verge of being, close to the realm where angels dwell—just on the boundary of the spirit-land!

6 The chain of being is complete in me; in me is matter's last gradation lost. The next step is Spirit—Deity!

7 I can command the lightning, and am dust; a monarch and a slave; a worm, and a God!

8 Whence came I here, and how? so marvelously constructed and conceived, and unknown. This life lives surely through some higher energy; for from out itself alone it could not be.

9 Creator! Yes! Thy wisdom and Thy Word created me. Thou source of light and good! Thou spirit of my spirit, and my Lord!

10 Thy Light, Thy Love, in their bright plenitude, filled me with an immortal soul, so that I can spring over the abyss of Death.

11 There I shall wear the garments of Eternal Day, and wing my heavenly flight beyond this little sphere, even to its source—to Thee!

12 O thought ineffable! O vision
blest! God! thus alone my lowly
thoughts can soar; thus seek Thy
presence.
13 Being! wise and good! amid
Thy vast works I admire, obey,
adore. And, when the tongue is
eloquent no more, the soul shall
speak in tears of gratitude.

THE GOSPEL ACCORDING TO

ST. JOHN.

CHAPTER I.

The beloved prophet-poet of New England hath many inspired utterances; among them are these verses of hope for the world:

ALL grim and soiled, and brown with tan,
I saw a Strong One, in his wrath,
Smiting the godless shrine of man
Along his path.

2 The Church beneath her trembling dome
Essayed in vain her ghostly charm;
Wealth shook within his gilded home
With pale alarm.

3 Fraud from his secret chambers fled
Before the sunlight bursting in;
Sloth drew her pillow o'er her head
To drown the din.

4 "Spare," Art implored, "yon holy pile;
That grand old time-worn turret spare;"
Meek Reverence, kneeling in the aisle,
Cried out, "Forbear!"

5 Gray-bearded Use, who, deaf and blind,
Groped for his old accustomed stone,
Leaned on his staff, and wept, to find
His seat o'erthrown.

6 Young Romance raised his dreamy eyes,
O'erhung with playful locks of gold,
"Why smite," he asked, in sad surprise,
"The fair, the old?"

7 Yet louder rang the Strong One's stroke;
Yet nearer flashed his ax's gleam;
Shuddering and sick of heart, I woke,
As from a dream.

8 I looked: aside the dust-cloud rolled—
The Waster seemed the Builder too;

Upspringing from the ruined Old
I saw the New.

9 'Twas but the ruin of the bad—
The wasting of the wrong and ill;
Whate'er of good the old time had
Was living still.

10 Calm grew the brows of him I feared;
The frown which awed me passed away,
And left behind a smile which cheered
Like breaking day.

11 Green grew the grain on battle-plains,
O'er swarded war-mounds grazed the cow;
The slave stood forging from his chains
The spade and plow.

12 Where frowned the fort, pavilions gay
And cottage windows, flower-entwined,
Looked out upon the peaceful bay
And hills behind.

13 Through vine-wreathed cups, with wine once red,
The lights on brimming crystal fell,
Drawn, sparkling, from the rivulet's bed,
And mossy well.

14 Through prison walls, like heaven-sent hope,
Fresh breezes blew, and sunbeams strayed,
And with the idle gallows-rope
The young child played.

15 Where the doomed victim in his cell
Had counted o'er the weary hours,
Glad school-girls, answering to the bell,
Came crowned with flowers.

16 Grown wiser for the lesson given,
I fear no longer. for I know
That where the share is deepest driven
The best fruits grow.

17 The outworn right, the old abuse,
The pious fraud, transparent grown,
The good held captive in the use
Of wrong alone—

18 These wait their doom from that great law
Which makes the past time serve to-day;
And fresher life the world shall draw
From their decay.

19 Oh! backward-looking son of time!
The new is old, the old is new,
The cycle of a change sublime
Still sweeping through.

20 So wisely taught the Indian seer:
Destroying Seva, forming Brahm,
Who wake by turns Earth's love and fear,
Are one, the same.

21 As idly as in that old day
Thou mournest, did thy sires repine,

So, in his time, thy child grown gray,
Shall sigh for thine.

22 Yet, not the less for them or thou
The eternal step of Progress beats
To that great anthem, calm and slow,
Which God repeats!

23 Take heart!—the Waster builds again—
A charmèd life old goodness hath;
The tares may perish—but the grain
Is not for death.

24 God works in all things; all obey
His first propulsion from the night:
Ho, wake and watch!—the world is gray
With morning light!

CHAPTER II.

John, being full of the love of God, confesseth his humility. He waiteth for death, and knoweth that all will be right beyond.

I KNOW not what the future hath
Of marvel or surprise,
Assured alone that life and death
His mercy underlies.

2 And if my heart and flesh are weak
To bear an untried pain,
The bruisèd reed He will not break,
But strengthen and sustain.

3 No offering of my own I have,
Nor works my faith to prove;
I can but give the gifts He gave,
And plead his love for love.

4 And so beside the Silent Sea
I wait the muffled oar;
No harm from Him can come to me
On ocean or on shore.

5 I know not where His islands lift
Their fronded palms in air;
I only know I cannot drift
Beyond His love and care.

THE GOSPEL ACCORDING TO GULDENSTUBBÉ.

CHAPTER I.

[*These Scriptures were obtained by the Baron de Guldenstubbé and his inspired Sister. These sentences are selected from among a great number, which were produced on paper by the spirits alone, and not through the hand of a medium. The Baron discovered that, to gain this Scripture, it was necessary that there should be the male and female, or the positive and negative influences, present. The result is a little book, consisting of detached thoughts, in the French language. The account of how and when they were obtained may be found in a volume by the Baron, entitled, "Realité des Esprits et Phénomène Merveilleux—de leuer Ecriture directe."*]

PRAYER is the touchstone of the spiritual man.

2 Immortality is the Aurora which enlightens this world.

3 Wisdom is the garden wherein philosophy must cull her flowers.

4 Peace is the seal which the angel from beyond the tomb impresses on the forehead of her chosen.

5 Purity is the robe of the angels, and righteousness is the helmet of the wise.

6 In the beginning the spirit of man reposes within the bosom of Divinity.

7 Behold, oh men! the eagle rising in the air. He soars toward the heights of wisdom, leaving behind him the abysses of folly. The wise resembles him if he turn not his head earthward.

8 The vertigo of pride turns wisdom into folly. Humility is the basis of true grandeur. Great things are accomplished by her, and small things by pride.

9 Hatred only takes root in narrow hearts, and anger finds in little minds his sting.

10 The intelligence of man passes like lightning before the look of the Eternal.

11 Death is the sword-blade of the angel who guards the road to the tree of life, but already has the love of God blunted the point.

12 When immortality commences doubt ceases, the soul, emancipated from her chains, wonders, believes, and falls at the feet of Deity. Eternity! we cannot comprehend thee, till we have entered thy sublime portals!

13 Innocence is an aureole from the other world which decks the forehead of the child, but the dust of years effaces it.

14 The stoic knew how to escape the world; the disciple of Pythagoras how to *suffer* it.

15 Happiness loosens the bridle of strength.

16 The scenes of life pass like the shadow which flies before the sun.

17 The man who forever defers doing good is like the swamp of the desert.

18 The whirlwind of misfortune bears away the just to depose him in the bosom of the Divinity.

19 He before whom the depths are open, and who enables the eagle to balance himself on vacancy, can likewise fill with favors the depths of the human heart.

CHAPTER II.

THE prison of the body is most wearisome to the enlarged Spirit which aspires to immortality.

2 An ardent desire to tear the vail which hides from us the Divinity, is the ladder with which we ascend to heaven.

3 True love cannot exist without purity of heart. Barrenness of heart is the greatest of evils.

4 Oh, justice, truth, charity! royal mantle of the divine, how difficult is it to incarnate you into humanity!

5 Purity and humility should form the diadem which adorns the brow of woman.

6 Miracles, far from being contrary to the laws of Nature, are actually a necessary condition in the organization of the universe. Miracles merely manifest the power of spirit over matter by suspending for a time the effects of inert forces.

7 The universe is an immense book which the highest seraphim had not yet perused.

8 Prayer is the grand vehicle of the spiritual: time and space are absorbed in an infinite eternity, to the soul which is separated from matter.

9 Science, worthy of its name, never fails to discern the greatness of God in the laws of Nature.

10 In the last agony, man, instead of becoming unconscious, has, on the contrary, *a double consciousness*, perceiving things terrestrial and things invisible.

11 The passage through the valley of Gehenna [through the dark passages of selfishness and passion] is the most trying to man. The mercy of God alone can shorten it.

12 Death is no longer a mystery—nothing dies; all exists, and is only transformed. God is not the God of the dead, but of the living.

13 Oh, my God, send us (as to Elijah) thy celestial fire, and kindle in our hearts that sublime faith which can move mountains.

14 Charity is strong as death, and stronger than the walls of hell. Hope is the prospect of life eternal in thee.

15 The lily of the valley conceals itself between two large leaves, yet scents the air with the most delicate perfume. So should the Christian, though humble, fill the world with his good works.

16 Intolerance is a conformity with evil spirits. Alas! true tolerance reigns alone in the kingdom of the heavens.

17 The love of God is that heavenly flame [the light of Arabula] which enlightens each man who comes into the world. By losing the love of God we lose the love of good, faith in good, and even the hope of eternal life.

18 A lively desire is the spiritual railway which bears the spirits, by thought, toward those they love; *for the thought of a spirit is himself.*

19 Spirits incognizant of distance may perceive numberless happy states, in the different universes, as the rich man saw Lazarus, or as the lucid clairvoyant here sees at a distance.

20 State, in the spirit, depends not on place. Thanks to Thought! the state may extend to an ubiquity more or less complete.

21 Spirits have their existence where time flows into eternity, and space is inclosed in infinity, as the dew-drop is lost in the ocean.

22 Thanks to sympathy! that inner attraction, whereby a more advanced spirit can draw one less perfect toward himself, by inducing the latter to progress more quickly in the way of perfection.

23 All efforts made by philosophers and theologians to conciliate faith with reason have necessarily failed, not having been founded on the solid basis of a positive Spiritualism.

24 True liberty of heart consists in *obedience* toward Providence, and its ministers, the angels and genii, called "gods" in all revelations of religion.

25 Weakness of heart is the punishment of cowards. Adversity fortifies a noble heart.

26 The search for truth is the beginning of wisdom. Hope guides us to the threshold of eternity.

27 An enthusiasm for the love of good is the sacred fire of the soul! The profound conviction of immortality can alone produce a sublime death.

28 The union of two noble hearts is like a diamond dropped from the crown of God.

29 The fool is preoccupied with things of no moment. Mental slavery is the seal of infamy. A noble enemy ever admires his adversary.

CHAPTER III.

ACCORDING to so-called *orthodox teachers*, the demon is the sovereign master of the creation, whilst God is seated, like an old saint, impotent and superannuated, in a niche of the universe.

2 The supernatural world of in-

visible causes, of which the soul of man forms a part, is in continual and intimate rapport with the material and visible world.

3 The great ulcer of antiquity consisted in a tendency to Polytheism, whilst in our day humanity has fallen into the excess of Materialism.

4 The vice of ambition occasions the most suffering in the next world, because there are there neither thrones, nor prince, nor king, nor mighty one; nor the reverse of these; all are equally pensioners of God.

5 The being of God is *love;* how, oh man! canst thou define it? The rays of hope shine even in hell. O, the infinite love of God!

6 When love reigns in the heart of a man, it furnishes him with strength requisite for all noble and generous actions.

7 Two closely united hearts are like a flower with double blossoms on the same stalk.

8 The science of the ancients was a complete work; it embraced causes and effects; it treated of the rapport of the world of spirits with the world of bodies; while our academies reduce all to the meanest and most narrow limits—*to matter alone.*

9 Modern learned men [who are under the sway of the selfish intellect] have rejected from the sanctuary of the sciences its most beauteous bud—the study of the soul, and of the world of supernatural and invisible causes.

10 Magnetism is the *aurora* of science; Spiritualism *its rising sun.*

11 Materialism reigns in our day as absolute sovereign on earth: we make it a duty to doubt all that is not material, nor susceptible of *chemical analysis.*

12 The merit of our *strong-minded* consists *in knowing nothing* and in *doubting of all*—of God, of present happiness, and of a future life.

13 Our *learned* men do not see that the *truly strong* mind rests not in the small sphere of credible things, but transports itself through the regions of immaterial beings, to study in that region any thing but *imaginary* and truly *substantial*, the nature and the power of the beings who dwell therein.

14 Incredulity has, become, in *our day*, more profoundly rooted than in ancient times. Even the corrupt era of the Cæsars never so entirely lost religious faith.

15 Spiritualism in our day is a faint echo of the sweet melodies from the joyous phalanx of angels, who are preparing to chant the awakening of humanity.

16 The rivers of divine grace, from eternity to eternity, are never dried up.

17 The angels of the holy plain of Mamre are on the banks of the Eurotas transformed into gods.

18 The revelation of Providence is universal. There are no chosen people. That Thou hast given to one of thy children, shalt Thou not give to all?

19 Oh, weak and foolish man! that thou reverest in one nation thou abhorrest in another; that which thou adorest in the town of Salem thou rejectest in the vale of Ida.

20 To see the face of the Eternal is to lead a life of contemplation in His presence.

21 Spiritual manifestations rend the vail between death and life. Death is the entering into another and better life; the celestial aurora from which frequently illumines the face of the dying.

22 Demonophobia and demonolatry are the arms of Satan [Super-

stition?]; the rod of iron he has held suspended for centuries over the church and her bigots.

23 The germs of spirits dwell in the Divinity, whose will detaches them from his essence. When once separated, each germ acquires an independent individuality, which cannot perish; for God cannot and will not unmake that he has made.

24 The unity of all spirit is possible, because all intelligences are conceived and brought forth by the one great Intelligence. Spirits are merely the forms, multiplied and individualized, of one great Spirit.

25 When the shades of death close the eyes of the just in peaceful sleep, his guardian angel opens to him the gates of the isles of the blessed.

26 There is One only who is the alpha and omega—one universal Being, the beginning and the end of all things.

THE GOSPEL ACCORDING TO

ST. JAMES.

CHAPTER I.

James is the given name of one of the pilgrim teachers of the living Gospel. The following is from many of his utterances:

LIFE and death, like the positive and negative forces, are twin brothers; and, with all the Divine arrangements, equally desirable in their time.

2 Winter dies in northern latitudes, that Spring, wreathed in buds and flowers, may come.

3 The worm assumes the chrysalis form, that it may become a winged insect in the mellowed air of morn; and man, that the spirit, released from the physical, may reach, through aspiration and effort, the angelic existence.

4 The Divine principle of life knows no destruction, no waste, considered in relation to the whole.

5 Every thing that dies, dies upward. It is bettered by the process, and prepared to subserve some higher end in the circuitous cycles of being.

6 Change is a fixed law, but nothing is lost. The storms that howl so fiercely, purify the atmosphere; showers that rust grains revive grasses; stars, like the pleiades, that fade from our eyes, illumine remoter parts of the universe.

7 The pearly dew-drops, that from millions of plants hang in glittering crystallizations, to be taken away by the rising sun, are *not lost*, but in aërial regions they become transformed into clouds, from which showers descend, gladdening the earth.

8 Some philosophers teach not only that "kind words can never die," but that every musical sound is immortal—traveling a wandering minstrel, cheering and charming some one forever.

9 And every man's works follow him; they also precede him to the

Spirit Land. Eternity can only measure the effects of one kind deed. The work lives, though the workman dies.

10 Man is a living, thinking, aspiring, and progressive being, looking for the truths and glories of the skies. Yea, more, he is a stream fed from the Infinite fountain—God!

11 The eternity of man's existence is sealed in Infinity, and revealed through the ministry of angels.

12 The desire for immortality is as universal as the races of men.

13 In the beautiful drama of *Ion*, the intuition of immortality finds a deep response in every thoughtful soul. When about to yield his young existence as a sacrifice to fate, his beloved Clemanthe asks if they shall not meet again, to which he replies: "I have asked that dreadful question of the hills, that look eternal—of the clear streams, that flow forever—of the stars, among whose fields of azure my raised spirit hath walked in glory. All were dumb. But when I gazed upon thy living face, I *feel* that there is something in the love that mantles through its beauty that cannot wholly perish. *We shall meet again*, Clemanthe."

14 The human spirit that ever was, is, and eternally will be, was incarnated for the purpose of receiving lessons and experiences, that through struggles, sufferings, and defeats, it might achieve grander victories, and be ultimately intromitted into a higher, diviner consciousness.

15 Do not forget the old painter, who, when some one wondered at his spending an hour on the shading of a finger's point, replied: "*Pingo in æternitatem*—I paint for eternity!" Verily, *we* are all living, acting, painting for eternity.

THE GOSPEL ACCORDING TO

ST. GERRIT.

CHAPTER I.

He proclaimeth against superstition, rebuketh wickedness in high places, and calleth upon all men to render God a reasonable service.

THE priests, be it those of China, Hindostan, Arabia, Persia, Europe, America, or elsewhere, and be they however honest, are the worst enemies of mankind.

2 For it is they pre-eminently who keep mankind down in false states, and upon those low planes, where ignorance and superstition nourish and give scope to all great evils.

3 The people who are most given to these mysteries and superstitions crave the most priests. Where Americans are content with one priest, Spaniards want many.

4 In all ages the priesthood has been deluded as well as deluding.

5 Why do I hold the priesthood to be so largely responsible for the

wrongs and wretchedness of the world? Because, that these come chiefly of the lack of religion, and that this lack comes chiefly of the priesthood.

6 Fear and wonder are the chief elements of superstition. These are supplied by ignorance. Courage and composure come of knowledge, and grow with it.

7 The way to get rid of the priesthood is to *educate* the people to require evidences of what they believe, and to form habits of mind which shall make them as inquisitive as the followers of priests are credulous. Skepticism is the first step in the world's progress from a blind and false to an intelligent and true faith.

8 The study of the natural sciences —including, as it does, the habit of requiring strict proof—constantly diminishes that credulity through which superstition enters, and on which it feeds.

9 Reason and knowledge are conscious of their fallible workings; and therefore do they tolerate differences of opinion. They inspire diffidence as much as ignorance does positiveness.

10 Natural science has already done much to weaken and dispel superstition. It has put astronomy in the place of astrology, and made alchemy and the hunt tor the "Philosopher's Stone" and for the "Universal Solvent" give place to Chemistry. It has liberated millions from their degrading bondage to the authority of sacred books, and left their reason as free to play upon the pages of the Bible as upon the pages of any other book.

11 While the mass of men construct their God out of their dreams and delusions, they who study the natural sciences are carried up through certainties to the certain God. The one imagine, and the other prove, the existence and character of God.

12 Oh, no, religion needs not a priesthood! It is as simple and instinctive as is eating or drinking. It is as much born with us as is our foot or hand. From ancestral faults or other causes our moral affections may be born imperfect. So, too, may our foot or hand be; but in neither case is our interior nature responsible for the imperfection.

13 Verily, man is a religious being. He is made to appreciate the claims of God and man upon him, and to love his great Father and equal brother.

14 The religion of human nature is harmony, not only with human nature, but with all Nature and with God. For every part of Nature is harmonious with every other part of it, and all Nature is in harmony with the Author of all Nature.

15 When the matchless inspirations and sublimities of the Bible stand no longer in authority and superstition, but in reason and in truth only, then they will no longer be made of but the same account with the false and foolish things mixed up in the same pages with them.

16 Now, as they have been falsely educated, good men feel that they would lose the whole Bible, were they to lose their confidence in the least part of it.

17 And what will become of the Bible when men shall cease to take it as an authority, and to worship it as a fetish, and to possess and prize it as a charm or an amulet?

18 Rather ask, what will become of it in the *mean time*, and during the superstitious regard for it. For there is no little danger that an

age of growing intelligence, disgusted with the exaggerated claims for the Bible, will reject it. But when this book shall, like any other book, be submitted to human judgment, and men shall feel at liberty to discriminate between the merits of its different parts—as, for instance, between the incredible story of Jonah and the whale, and the felt truth of the sermon on the Mount—then will it be a new and inestimable blessing.

19 Will there, when the priests are gone, be still a demand for preachers? Yes, greater than ever! What will they preach? Will they, like the priests, spend the time in telling their hearers what religion is? Oh, no; a minute a month will suffice for that! In a dozen words they can say that loving God supremely and the neighbor as ourself; or more briefly, that being true to ourself is religion; or still more briefly, that being ourself *is* religion. But the question remains, What will they preach? They will preach duties; will tell their hearers what religion calls for in the heart and life.

20 And what shall we do for churches when the present ones shall have died out with the priests? We shall have infinitely better; for we shall then have temples in which reason will do as much to enlighten and elevate, as superstition does in the present churches to darken and degrade.

21 Let it not be inferred from what I have said that I do not believe in prayer. I must cease to believe in human nature ere I can cease to believe in prayer. There is not on earth a more unnatural man than the prayerless man. Want, fear, and love urge men as naturally to the Heavenly Parent as they do children to the earthly parent. Beautifully natural was Cornelius, who "prayed to God always." There is nothing, in the bringing about of which men have, or can have, an agency, for which they should not at all times be ready to pray. Prayer for the crop is rational. But prayer for or against rain is as irrational as would be prayer for or against an eclipse. Prayer for a safe voyage is rational. It is, among other things, a prayer for self-possession, wisdom, skill on the part of the navigator. But prayer for this or that wind is irrational.

22 I affirm the supreme importance of religion. The next life is but the continuation of this; and we begin there just where we leave off here. If we are upon low planes here, we shall enter upon low planes there. If here we sustain high relations to wisdom and goodness, we shall there also.

THE GOSPEL ACCORDING TO

ST. THEODORE.

CHAPTER I.

Theodore Parker, born August 21, 1810, at Lexington, Mass., was the grandson of the man who formed the first line of defense and drew the first sword in the war of American Independence. The inspirations of this great and good preacher are full of divine fire. Only a few sentences, among thousands equally inspired, are given below.

GOD has all the qualities of complete and perfect being; He has Infinite Power to *do*, Infinite Mind to *know*, Infinite Conscience to *will*, Infinite Affection to *love*, Infinite Holiness to be *faithful* to his affections, conscience, mind, power.

2 He has Being without limitation—Absolute Being; he is present in all space, at all times; everywhere always, as much as sometimes anywhere.

3 He fills all spirit, not less than all matter; yet is not limited by either, transcending both; being alike the materiality of matter, and the spirituality of spirit—that is, the substantiality which is the ground of each, and which surpasses and comprehends all.

4 The evidence of this God is, first, in man's Consciousness; and, second, in the World of Matter outside of him.

5 In philosophic men the reflective element prevails; but I do not think they often have much intuitive power to perceive religious truths directly, nor do I think that they in the wisest way observe the innermost activities of the human soul.

6 The history of man is the calculated consequence of the faculties God put in man, known beforehand to the Infinite Cause, provided by the Infinite Providence.

7 My consciousness of God colors all the other facts of consciousness; my world of matter and my world of man take their complexion from my world of God.

8 The *feeling* of God implies the idea of Him as lovely, and leads unavoidably to the resolution to serve Him by the means that He has provided.

9 God did not make man with something redundant to be cut off, or lacking something to be sought elsewhere and tied on; he gave us such faculties as are fit for our work.

10 But by the true and philosophic or natural idea of God, all the Evil of the world is something incident to man's development, and no more permanent than the stumbling of a child who learns to walk, or his scrawling letters when he first essays to write. *It will be outgrown*, and not a particle of it or its consequences shall cleave permanent to mankind.

11 The very pain the error gives is remedial, not revengeful; it is medicine to cure and save and bless, not poison to kill and torture with eternal smart.

12 Discipline there is, and must be, but only as means to the noblest and most joyous end. This I say I am sure of, for it follows logically from the very idea of the Infinite Perfect God. Nay, the religious instinct anticipates induction, and declares this with the spontaneous womanly logic of human nature itself.

13 God includes all, the heathen, the Hebrew, the Mahometan, the Atheist, and the Christian; nay, Cain, Iscariot, the kidnapper, are *all folded in the arms of the Infinite Mother*, who will not suffer absolute evil to come to the least or the worst of these, but so tempers the mechanism of humanity that all shall come to the table of blessedness at last! Death itself is no limit. God's love is eternal also, providing retribution for all I do; but pain is medicine. What is not delight is discipline, the avenue to nobler joy.

CHAPTER II.

The preacher declareth the glory of God, and manifesteth his great love for

Him. He glorieth in the Works and Providence of God. He denounceth the wickedness of shutting one's eyes to the beauty and holiness of the Father, and exhorteth all men to walk with God, and enjoy His presence forever in life and its relations.

MY delight in God increases each special joy in the things of matter or in the persons of men.

2 I love the world the more, because I know it is God's world, even as a dry leaf, given by a lover, is dearer than all pearls from whoso loves us not!

3 I remember to have heard a man, of a good deal of power too, declare than a man's love for his garden, his house, his ox, his horse, his wife, and his children, was all nonsense and absurdity; nay, "a sin" in the eyes of God, and just as he loved these things the more, he loved God the less; and if he loved Him supremly, he would care for nothing but God!

4 Every sense has its function, and that function is attended with pleasure, with joy. All these natural and normal delights ought to be enjoyed by every man; it is a sullenness toward God not to rejoice and thus appreciate his beautiful world when we can.

5 St. Bernard walked all day, six or seven hundred years ago, by the shores of the Lake of Geneva, with one of the most glorious prospects in the whole world before him—mountain, lake, river, clouds, gardens, every thing to bless the eye—and that monk never saw a thing all day long. He was thinking about the Trinity!

6 God made the world of matter exceeding beautiful, and meant it should be rejoiced in by these senses of ours: at these five doors what a world of loveliness comes in and brushes against the sides with its garment, and leaves the sign of God's presence on our door-posts and lintels.

7 Think you God made the world so fair, every flower a sister to a star, and did not mean men's eyes to see, and men's hearts to take a sacrament thereat.

8 Our daily bread is a delight which begins in babyhood, and only ends when the Infinite Mother folds us to her arms and gives us the bread which does not perish in the using.

9 In the sunshine of life, every human joy is made more joyous by this delight in God. When these fail, when health is gone, when my eye is dim, when my estate slips through my hands, and my good name becomes a dishonor, when death takes the nearest and dearest of my friends, then my consciousness of God comes out, a great light in my darkness, and a very present help in my time of trouble.

10 I am tormented by the loss of friends—father, mother, wife, child; my dearest of the nearest are gone; but the Infinite Mother folds me to her bosom, and her tenderness wipes the tears from my eyes.

11 God made man to live with matter, and made them both so that there should be good neighborhood between the two, and man should get delight from the contact.

12 God made men so that they might live with each other, and get deeper, dearer, and truer delight from that intimacy.

13 Beauty is made up of these four things—completeness as a whole, perfection of the parts, fitness of each part for its function, and correspondence with the faculties of man. These four things make up the statics and dynamics of beauty.

14 Now, looked at with the intellectual and æsthetic part of human consciousness, *God is absolute beauty!* He is the beauty of being—self-existence; the beauty of power—almightiness; of intellect—all-knowingness; of conscience—all-righteousness; of affection—all-lovingness; of the soul—all-holiness; in a word, He is the Absolute, the altogether Beautiful!

CHAPTER III.

The preacher explaineth the delightful relations existing between God and His creatures. He declareth against superstitions and slothfulness toward God, and revealeth the true idea of the perfections of the infinite Wisdom and love.

WE are all connected with the World of Matter; with the World of Man; and with the World of God. In each of these spheres we have duties to do, and rights to enjoy, which are consequent on the duties done.

2 We may derive our habitual delight from any *one* of these three sources—the *material*, the *human*, and the *Divine*; or, we may draw from all of these.

3 We may content ourselves with the lowest quality of human delights, or we may reach up and get the highest and dearest quality thereof.

4 Complete and perfect piety unites all three,—the great Thought—of the Infinity of God; the great Feeling—of absolute love for Him; and the great Will—the resolution to serve Him.

5 The superstitious man thinks that God must be feared first of all; and the internal worship of God is accordingly, with that man, Fear, and nothing but fear.

6 Fanaticism is Hate before God; as Superstition is Fear before him. Fanaticism is a far greater evil than Superstition; but in our day it is far less common.

7 Mysticism is sloth before God, as Superstition is Fear, and Fanaticism is Hate before God. It exists still in some of the Churches, which cultivate only emotions of reverence, of trust, of love, and the like, but never let the love of God come out of the heart in the shape of the love of man.

8 But the true Idea of God, and the Religion which is to come of it—which is love of that God and keeping all his commandments—will work such a revolution in man's affairs as Luther, nor Moses, nor yet mightiest Jesus ever wrought.

9 God in Genesis represents the conception of the babyhood of humanity. But manhood demands a different conception.

10 All round us lies the World of Matter, this vast world above us and about us and beneath; it proclaims the God of Nature; flower speaking unto flower, star quiring unto star; a God who is resident therein, his law never broke.

11 In us is a World of *Consciousness*, and as that mirror is made clearer by civilization, I look down and behold the Natural Idea of God, Infinite Cause and Providence, Father and Mother to all that are.

12 Into our reverent souls God will come as the morning light into the bosom of the opening rose.

13 Just in proportion as we are faithful, we shall be inspired therewith, and shall frame "conceptions equal to the soul's desires;" and then, in our practice, keep those "heights which the soul is competent to win."

THE GOSPEL ACCORDING TO

ST. OCTAVIUS.

CHAPTER I.

[*Octavius is the given name of an inspired preacher in the great Atlantic city. He proclaimeth the truths of the living God, and giveth special testimony of the Spirit to the people of this generation.*]

IT was said by one of old that God thought the world into existence. The universe is a visible Thought—a mass of divine Ideas.

2 Is not each man, too, a thought? And each woman?—each child? Does not each living creature report some idea of God, which no other creature reports?

3 Verily, we are all thoughts of God—thoughts dark, mysterious, inexplicable, unreadable, unintelligible, possibly—thoughts so small, so delicate, so evanescent, so recondite, that they escape our notice—thoughts so confusing and distracting that they confound our wits; nevertheless, thoughts we are: *divine* thoughts—necessary, in some way, to fill up the sum of the divine thinking, and complete the sensorium of Deity.

4 God's greater thoughts we see as the ages and generations express them. The thought of an epoch is plain. It is a dull mind that cannot discern the idea enfolded in a crisis, or thrown out by a conspicuous event, in history.

5 It seems, sometimes, as if God dropped his thoughts one by one into the mind of mankind—a thought to a century; a thought to an age; a thought to a generation; a thought to a year; a thought to a nation, a community, a tribe—as if to insure its being well comprehended and assimilated by the minds of men. Thus we hear often of men of one idea.

6 Take the most familiar example: the Jews had, so far as appears, but a single object in existence—a single motive for being—that was, to firmly fix and live into the world the doctrine of "one God."

7 The Semitic race was an anvil on which the hammer of God's providence shaped this idea. The Hebrews contributed this, and this only; and it was a contribution that was worth all it cost in time and life.

CHAPTER II.

He showeth the thought of God in this century. He discovereth that the life of a nation, as that of a person, is one with the Father.

EVERY century has its ruling thought; and this thought is always *a thought of God.* It is always a religious, a *divine* thought; it is a thought always involving the moral and spiritual part of man—his belief, his aspiration, his hope.

2 In one age it is the thought of God himself; in the other age it is the thought of God in his providence; in a third it is a thought of God in his moral purposes; in a fourth it is a thought of God in His spiritual manifestation. But always it is a thought of God.

3 The Thought of God, then, which is with us *whenever we* awake to the meaning of our modern life, is this: *The Natural Capacity of Man*—Man, the individual man, as God's child; Man as the organ, the instrument, the recipient of God's influence; Man the worker and co-worker with God.

4 Our America was born first of Puritanism; it was born a second time of Rationalism; its third and more perfect birth will be of Spiritualism.

5 Men are knit to God closer than they suspect. His thoughts are not as our thoughts; but only as they are so much *above* ours in reach and scope—so immeasurably *beyond* ours in their outgoings; but *our* thoughts are *his* thoughts when they are deepest, and richest, and most inspiring.

6 The thought that thrills and burns in our generation is, *that* IN *man is all capacity for receiving divine influence;* that *through* man is all working of the divine operation; that man is the recipient and the organ of that which we call "divine power."

7 To every human being, however mean and degraded, however cheap and vile in the eyes of his fellows, there remains a great consciousness; that of being *designed* for something; that of *signifying* something; that of counting for something, somewhere, if only as the leaves count for something, which enrich the earth by their fall.

8 All things in him are manifest. Ay, all *divine* things. They display themselves in him, and instead of changing him into another being, only make him more perfect in what he is. They are so native to his constitution, they agree so well with him, they feed him so naturally, they mingle so easily and graciously with his elements, that you cannot distinguish them from his natural properties.

9 The philanthropies of our time keep pace exactly with the progress of this glorious thought. The reforms of our age, however crude and coarse in form, express it. The noble charities bear witness to it, bringing opposite classes together for mutual relief.

10 Who fails to see what immeasurable hope is contained in this Thought? Our age is distinguished by its hopefulness. We are the hopeful people of the world.

11 Boundless is our faith in the recuperative power of things. Give time enough, and all will come out right. The body will heal its hurts; the mind will overgrow its doubts; the heart will conquer fear and sorrow, and will rise victorious over the dolors of death. Disbeliefs are but the teething of the soul. Progress, progress, progress is the magical panacea for all ills.

CHAPTER III.

The quality of Man's spirit is revealed by his ideal in religion. The preacher beholdeth a new dispensation; and prophesieth a new interpretation of Christianity, and a new reading of the Scriptures.

THE fact that modern Europe has adored Jesus [as an Ideal] attests the presence of some vailed grandeur in the hearts of the adorers. The nearer one sits to the feet of such an ideal, the nearer is his spirit to the eternal. To sit at the *feet* of a nangel is to be *one's self* an angel.

2 Suffering, vice, degradation, imbecility, limitation, were not so touching in the pagan world as they are in ours; for they were not thought of as affecting so noble a creature. Byron makes us drop a

tear for the Roman gladiator, but the Romans dropped no tear for him—he was only a savage.

3 The cure for every ill is the force that continues us till to-morrow. It is very beautiful, it is very comforting, it is very supporting. Traveling through the valley of Baca it makes the barren place a well, the water filling the pools. To be hopeless is to be unbelieving. To despond is to discard the Thought of the age.

4 It is said that our people have lost the faculty of *praying*. It is true that they do not, as they did, resort to stated and formal exercises of devotion: they do not kneel as they used to do, and offer special petitions for special gifts, expecting special answers. But of PRAYING, in the deep and genuine sense, there was never so much as there is now. There was never so much *looking out toward the Infinite*—never so much craving for light, and life, and immortality.

5 A new form of religious faith is folded up in this Thought of our century. It is the soul of a new interpretation of Christianity; the spirit of a new dispensation. Man is not to be molded by spirituality, but to be developed by it. Religion the highest *expression of* man; not the profoundest *impression upon* him. Religion that thing which reveals to man his greatness, not that thing which charges him with his littleness; a religion which reveals his *angelic* nature, not which insists on the *demonic.*

6 The Bible is a sacred record of man's holiest and tenderest experiences heavenward and Godward—the Book of Books, because the Soul's Book—*inspired as all the Soul's Books are.*

MEDITATIONS OF SAMUEL

IN THE TEMPLE.

S. B. Brittan, the preacher, editor, and author, was among the first and most effective pioneers in the new vineyard. After many years of incessant devotion to the work, he said: "He who plants himself on the foundations of popular Materialism will find that he stands on a SAND-BAR *that is shifting about with every motion of the tides in the affairs of men, while Spiritualism, like an enduring rock, rises up amid the conflicting elements of ignorance and passion—a rock which the surges of Time and Change can never shake—on whose Heaven-lighted pinnacle the Angels build their altars, and kindle beacon-lights to illuminate the world!" He goeth out on the Sabbath and lifteth up his voice to heaven in wonder and praise. He proclaimeth the gospel of Life to the children of men.*

IT is Morning. The sun shines gloriously over mountain, plain, and river.

2 Nature calls me with many voices to worship in her Temple. The willing spirit answers, and I go forth into the great Fane that is consecrated by the Divine presence.

3 No sexton stands at the open portals to point me to the lowest place; and accordingly I will go up and stand on the pinnacle.

4 The chime of the waters, as they gush from the sides of the hill, is like the music of silver bells, as from some lofty spire the notes descend through the still air, to track the silent calls of sense.

5 It is the Sabbath! yet all Nature violates the statute, and works without interruption. She is weaving virgin robes for the renovated earth to wear.

6 The village, reposing beneath, at the foot of the hill, looks like a silent worshiper, on bended knee, before the high altar whereon we will offer the incense of our grateful joy.

7 Spring is here! I feel her balmy breath on this brow, and her pulses in these veins.

8 Nature's great heart beats under my feet and over my head.

9 Electric currents run through every nerve of her mighty frame, and every fiber moves. They play over the delicate pinions of the swallow, and he cuts the air with arrow-like swiftness; they dance in the throat of the robin and the bluebird, and they come to me in music on every breath of the morning.

10 The currents of the all-pervading Life flow into every form of the natural world, and therefore all forms partake of the Divine energy.

11 They are beautiful, because in and through them we perceive the *light* and *life* of the Omnipresent One.

12 These green aisles, O Nature! are hallowed by the footsteps of Deity.

13 GOD IS HERE, and the quick soul feels his presence in the midst of his Temple.

24 The great dome is radiant with his light, and these emerald halls were fashioned and garnished by his hand.

15 He touches the majestic mountains, and they are arrayed in soft robes of living beauty.

16 He smiles on the valleys, and they blossom and offer grateful incense.

17 Surrounded by all this beauty and harmony, I look, and listen, and am silent—speechless with admiration, with the fullness of joy that finds no earthly expression.

18 Let me muse a while by this grove of young pines. This is consecrated ground. The forms of the departed repose beneath these shades.

19 Here and there, through the evergreen boughs, the white stones are visible, pale emblems by which affection marks the places where its treasures lie buried.

20 Ah, how many have a vague and terrible apprehension that their friends thus sleep in the realms of dark forgetfulness, and how few realize that the departed, even now, *possess* the boon of conscious and happy existence.

21 These pines wave with a graceful and reverent emotion, as the aërial currents from the adjacent hills flow through the numberless branches.

22 Nature's airy halls are filled with weird strains of sweet and solemn music.

23 By that white slab kneels a pale mourner; with her tears she moistens the grave of her buried hopes, while her subdued moan blends with the low cadences of the murmuring woods.

24 But my spirit rejoices even here and now; for I know that all that is vital in man still lives, and must live forever.

25 All life, as it is presented for human contemplation, is the Divine presence made visible in outward forms.

26 The great Spirit is the primal source of life: God is self-existent and eternal; therefore, all life is of necessity immortal.

27 This doctrine is taught here, above these graves.

28 Every tree that spreads its branches over the earth; every leaf that unfolds itself to the sunshine; every flower that exhales its perfume on the air, and every spire of grass that points toward the Heavens, is an eloquent and instructive minister, ordained of God to preach the Resurrection and the Life!

THE GOSPEL ACCORDING TO

ST. ELIZA.

CHAPTER I.

Of the spiritual nature of Woman.

WOMAN is feminine, or a true woman, in proportion as she is spiritual. An unspiritual woman is masculine, and is therefore repulsive.

2 The Masculine is the minister of the Material, and of Force, whether intellectual or corporeal; and the Feminine of the Spiritual, and of Power in its finer and higher relations of Divine use.

3 The spiritual is the Creative power in the soul of Man or Woman. It is so by virtue of its *oneness* with the Great Artist and Creator. It never lacks resource — is not daunted by any array of circumstances, for is not the Infinite its all-suffering support? It knows no despair, sees no failure; knows that failure is impossible, because its aims are one with the Divine aims, which cannot fail.

4 But the aim of the spiritual nature is expansion, and the simplest form of pure, earnest desire secures that. "Ask, and it *shall* be given; seek, and ye *shall* find; knock, and it *shall* be opened unto you."

5 When the spirit acts sovereignly, it employs the whole nature harmoniously. Sense, passion, affection, intellect, have all and each their sufficient work; when the spirit is satisfied, they too are filled and content. Its perfect sovereignty is—not in their extinction; for spirit is cherishing, never destructive, toward any thing that exists—but in their cheerful abdication in its favor. They forget themselves.

6 There is a great inner fullness, which comes not of bread and meat; an inner warmth, that is not of fireside or ermine; an inner radiance, which the material sun can little affect; an unfailing abundance, which no tide in outward affairs can turn to scarcity.

7 For life is not devised to disappoint the human soul, but to afford it the fullest measure of satisfaction. If the satisfaction is not instant, it is because it could not, in the nature of things, be *both instant*

and ultimate; for Nature, of which spirit is the essential, works for ultimates.

8 Spiritual power is self-renewing; it increases by diffusion. Give it away if you would enrich yourself in it. Empty your soul every evening of all that you can impart, if you would find it overflowing in the morning.

9 O heavenly state! O divine victory, which defeat can never dim! Calamity may do its worst. Poverty may come, desertion, coldness of friends, bitterness of enemies, scorn of the world. They only kindle a diviner strength or pity, and throw the soul more completely into the arms of the Infinite.

CHAPTER II.

Of the spirit's office in maternity.

IT is the spiritual which is the creative element of the human mother-nature, as of Mother Nature in the universal sense. Matter does not create.

2 In the mother, spirituality is that deepest possible unfolding of the life of which only the consciousness can take cognizance. It is the opening of the heart of the rose, whence the tiny, subtle humming-bird may extract the nectar that sustains him.

3 Spirituality is the characteristic of the maiden compared with the youth, as it is of the Woman compared with the Man; but the years which make him more masculine, should make her more feminine (spiritual); for no other development whatever can give her a true, divine, creative maternity.

4 The Romish Church has acted upon a true instinct in making Mary illustrious among women. Art, a far truer system than Papacy, has done the same thing. She has been one of its grandest and most fruitful Inspirations—the typical mother and child multiplied in various forms for the eyes and souls of all Women, saying to them, "Go thou and do likewise."

5 And the universal human heart, even though blind and cold, pays a certain involuntary homage to the mothers whose children have acted the Christ-part in their generations.

6 Spirituality magnifies maternity, sees its real glory, and rejoices in it, as never other sovereign rejoiced in her earthly crown and scepter. It gives the mother at once pride and humility—pride, in her great office, though a manger be its cradle—humility, in herself as an instrument in the Divine hand for its accomplishment. "Behold the handmaid of the Lord; be it unto me according to thy law. My soul doth magnify the Lord, and my spirit hath rejoiced in God, my Saviour. For he hath regarded the low estate of his handmaiden; for, behold, from henceforth all generations shall call me blessed. For he that is mighty hath done to me great things; and holy is his name." This is the language of every true spiritual mother.

7 We acknowledge with more unstinted speech and feeling, the fullness of the Holy Spirit in the mother; and have a worshipful feeling toward her, as its pure, responsive recipient; a feeling which all mothers command in the degree that they are pure, divine, and aspiring in maternity; and will more and more command in proportion as they liken themselves to the typical Mary in becoming *susceptible to spiritual aids therein;* of which susceptibility a profound humility as to herself, and gratitude for the greatness of her privileges, are always among the clearest evidences.

THE GOSPEL ACCORDING TO

ST. EMMA.

CHAPTER I.

Emma Hardinge was born in London, England. She came to America in 1855. She was then opposed to the idea of communion with the arisen. At length she became entranced. Then came the word of power: "Emma! you must go out and speak to the world." After a time, with much reluctance, she obeyed the voice from heaven, and her words were good and many, and her fame went before her. The following are selections from her sermons to the people.

THE aim of the people is, liberty. In every corner of the known earth, at this day, the cry is "liberty." Liberty for the body; liberty for the soul.

2 It is not alone the masses; but individuals are struggling for liberty. The cry has gone forth. That thought stimulates every brain and every heart. Hence, from before every pulpit, around the desk of every writer, the cry comes, "Liberty for the soul."

3 Oh, Mystery! thou art indeed the mother of the abominations of the earth.

4 Oh, mystery! can there be truth and mystery together? Is it a possibility that God's works, if he be our Father, shall be a mystery to us, his children?

5 There is no mystery save your own ignorance, and your submission or tyranny one to another. All the wonders of the Almighty's gospel have unrolled themselves in the light of knowledge, or are now becoming manifest to the investigating spirit of man.

6 The vail of mystery being lifted discloses the fact that the Almighty is the God of the living, not the God of the dead; that the living are his ministering spirits; that they can and do come to earth; that they are the ministers of light and knowledge, who, in all ages of the world, have gone forth to minister to the heirs of salvation.

7 Yes, the last great vail of mystery is breaking fast. The great seventh seal, that so long has hidden the word of God, is broken, and the destiny of man and the knowledge of God are being revealed. The vail is rent in twain!

8 Progress is a portion of the eternal gospel of nature, which the ages tell; which the history of all nations teaches; which the advance of every art and every science indicates; which the history of planets, suns, and stars proclaims; which man himself spells out from the cradle to the grave, in a perpetual series of progressive experiments, each one leading to the culminating point when his spirit is set free, to put in practice the results of the follies, the trespasses, the hopes, the wishes, the aspirations which he has gained in his earthly career.

CHAPTER II.

She teacheth the gospel of God's providence in his laws and works. She upbraideth the people for lukewarmness, and counseleth all to live truly and die like the ancient one.

OH! we need not go and listen to the boom of the mighty ocean; we need not wait for the thunder of the skies or the flash of the lightning; we need not gaze into the immensity of space to find out God. Every forest tree and every blade of grass will tell the tale—will show wisdom, design, calculation.

2 All things in nature reach their perfection here, except the spirit.

3 We find that there is in the spirit a constant progress; from the cradle to the grave, the spirit manifests growth, but never change. Whatever is impressed upon the consciousness of the babe, remains with the old man.

4 Yea, the destiny of the spirit is eternal progress! Stand upon the highest point to which your imagination can climb, amid all the glories of sunlit skies and rainbow arches, pointing up to higher and yet higher worlds of light and splendor; and doth not thy spirit aspire to it all?

5 Who among ye white-haired old men, as ye plant your trembling feet on the verge of the grave, can say: "My soul is full; I ask for no more; my soul is the perfect flower of my existence; there is no more to be added?" The cry is still for to-morrow; the cry is still for light; and the dim eye opens like a window of the soul looking through upon eternity, and still searching for and feeling after the endless vistas of a perpetually returning to-morrow. These are the evidences of immortality.

6 In every condition of life this immortality would be a lamp for your feet. Ye build houses for to-morrow; why are none building mansions for eternity? Alas! alas! either ye do not believe what your religionists teach ye, or ye fail in your life-practice.

7 Neither believe ye in the immortality of the soul, or if ye do, ye do not manifest it. Ye write on tombstones: "Here lies," "Here remains," "Here sleeps;" and ye do this in view of that word which tells you of the God of the living.

8 O, Man! behold what thy spirit is; take heed of its destiny, observe its origin; know that knowledge is power; as thou dost know thyself, so wilt thou die as the wise and virtuous Socrates died.

9 Give us our daily bread for the body, is the cry of the materialist; but wherefore do you *not* ask daily bread for the soul? We will tell you why ye do not ask it—because it has been poured upon you; because the measure has been pressed down and running over; because the light has shone in the darkness, though the darkness comprehended it not.

CHAPTER III.

She glorieth in the processes of death as the steps of life. The finality of Sin is prophesied. God's light shineth in man's darkness.

ROME, on her seven hills of pride, with her noble Coliseum, her towers, her mighty palaces, her men of wisdom, her legislation, her warrior strength and martial freedom, was enough for her day.

2 Corinth and Athens were enough for their time, but not enough for after time.

3 They had no great factories, no steam-engines, no telegraphs, no railroads, no labor-saving machinery, no printing-press, nothing of all that beautiful new life that has grown up out of the ashes of the old world. She has perished in the night of death for her imperfection.

4 All hail, then, to that which ye term "death." Trace its action, and ye find it touches nothing

but sin; that it leaves the good—that which is the gift of God it leaves to the inheritance of eternal life.

5 Nothing which has been, which was beautiful or true in the past, has ever died.

6 Man's' sin is finite; must not his punishment be so also?

7 Oh! ye who advocate the eternity of punishment for a finite sin, open the page of your Bible and read that the wages is paid with death.

8 When sin is accomplished, the inharmony produced is life; the misery that follows is death.

9 The world revolts against sin, and pronounces judgment upon it. "It shall not be," is the cry of the world.

10 Nature grants to every thing a stereotyped form, for the purpose of incarnating the life, and giving the spirit expression.

11 Hence, premature or violent death is a misfortune, for it is an infraction of the order of nature.

21 But God is good, and bringeth light out of man's darkness.

THE GOSPEL ACCORDING TO

ST. RALPH.

CHAPTER I.

Ralph Waldo Emerson, one of the inspired Scripturalists of this century, uttereth the living axioms of God to the multitude. From his many revelations the following passages are taken.

TO the poet, to the philosopher, to the saint, all things are friendly and sacred, all events profitable, all days holy, all men divine.

2 A man should learn to detect and watch that gleam of light which flashes across his mind from within, more than the luster of the firmament of bards and sages.

3 We lie in the lap of immense intelligence, which makes us receivers of its truth and organs of its activity.

4 The relations of the soul to the Divine Spirit are so pure, that it is profane to seek to interpose helps.

5 Whenever a mind is simple, and receives a divine wisdom, old things pass away,—means, teachers, texts, temples, fall; it lives now, and absorbs past and future into the present hour. All things are made sacred by relation to it.

6 When a man lives with God, his voice shall be as sweet as the murmur of the brook and the rustle of the corn.

7 The soul raised over passion beholds identity and eternal causation, perceives the self-existence of Truth and Right, and calms itself with knowing that all things go well.

8 Nothing can bring you peace but yourself. Nothing can bring you peace but the triumph of principles.

9 Proverbs, like the sacred books of each nation, are the sanctuary of the intuitions.

10 The soul will not know either deformity or pain.

11 For it is only the finite that has wrought and suffered; the infinite lies stretched in smiling repose.

12 O my brothers, God exists. There is a soul at the center of Nature, and over the will of every man, so that none of us can wrong the universe.

13 The way to speak and write what shall not go out of fashion is, to speak and write sincerely.

14 A man passes for what he is worth. Very idle is all curiosity concerning other people's estimate of us, and all fear of remaining unknown is not less so.

15 Never was a sincere word utterly lost. Never a magnanimity fell to the ground, but there is some heart to greet and accept it unexpectedly.

16 Let us, if we must have great actions, make our own so.

17 This over-estimate of the possibilities of Paul and Pericles, this under-estimate of our own, comes from a neglect of the fact of an identical nature.

CHAPTER II.

He revealeth the origin of friendship, and the relations of man to the words and commandments of truth he describeth. And he introduceth the spirit of man to the divine original.

THE essence of friendship is entireness, a total magnanimity and trust.

2 You demonstrate yourself, so as to put yourself out of the reach of false relations, and you draw to you the firstborn of the world.

3 Every violation of truth is not only a sort of suicide in the liar, but is a stab at the health of human society.

4 Trust men and they will be true to you; treat them greatly, and they will show themselves great, though they make an exception in your favor to all their rules of trade.

5 I see not any road of perfect peace which a man can walk, but after the counsel of his own bosom.

6 We live in succession, in division, in parts, in particles. Meantime within man is the soul of the whole; the wise silence; the universal beauty, to which every part and particle is equally related; the eternal ONE.

7 Every man's words, who speaks from that life, must sound vain to those who do not dwell in the same thought on their own part.

8 Only itself can inspire whom it will, and behold! their speech shall be lyrical, and sweet, and universal as the rising of the wind.

9 As there is no screen or ceiling between our heads and the infinite heavens, so is there no bar or wall in the soul where man, the effect, ceases, and God, the cause, begins.

10 We lie open on one side to the deeps of spiritual nature, to the attributes of God.

11 Some thoughts always find us young, and keep us so. Such a thought is the love of the universal and eternal beauty.

12 With each divine impulse the mind rends the thin rinds of the visible and finite, and comes out into eternity, and inspires and expires its air.

13 The heart which abandons itself to the Supreme Mind finds itself related to all its works, and will travel a royal road to particular knowledges and powers.

14 Ineffable is the union of man and God in every act of the soul.

15 The simplest person, who in his integrity worships God, becomes God; yet forever and ever the influx of this better and univer-

sal self is new and unsearchable.

16 How dear, how soothing to man, arises the idea of God, peopling the lonely place, effacing the scars of our mistakes and disappointments!

17 The soul gives itself, alone, original and pure, to the Lonely, Original, and Pure, who, on that condition, gladly inhabits, leads, and speaks through it.

18 Behold, it saith, I am born into the great, the universal mind.

19 More and more the surges of everlasting nature enter into me, and I become public and human in my regards and actions.

20 Through the years and the centuries, through evil agents, through toys and atoms, a great and beneficent tendency irresistibly streams.

THE GOSPEL ACCORDING TO

ST. ASAPH.

CHAPTER I.

He sheweth the right of every man to know his maker. The impersonality of God's spirit is taught, and the blessing of God's presence is promised even to sinners. He defendeth human nature.

BIRTH, death, and every act that lies between, are physical effects of metaphysical causes.

2 How little man yet knows of the demands of his spiritual nature.

3 It is the right of man to know the Power, to recognize the Hand, that gives him all he has, that guides him, that leads him, that blesses him.

4 Who made the soul, with its conditions? and who made the laws that govern it? God did these things.

5 It will be by all men acknowledged, that God is in all presence, in all intelligence, in all power, in all love; for the recognition of God's infinitude commands this acknowledgment.

6 Therefore the ways of nature are divine, and the purposes of nature cannot be hindered.

7 Every sinner is a lawful heir to God's love and goodness.

8 The soul of one man is not superior to the soul of another man; for if one possesses the properties of eternal life and unending progress, the other also does.

9 My soul is my Bible, in which I read the truths of eternal life; its longings and its desires are the utterances of my Bible.

10 Every precept that Christ [Arabula?] has given to the world is an invitation of love; the law that resists not evil—a law of attraction.

11 Human nature may be invited, led, directed; but *never* driven.

CHAPTER II.

He proclaimeth the positive advent of Arabula in those who work good deeds, and not in those who only pray and profess. He denounceth selfishness and terrestrial greatness, and explaineth the causes of man's indifference to spiritual things.

CHRIST has come again with many messengers; not to those who profess, but to those who practise without profession.

2 The true religion of God is in the bosom of the sinner, no less than it is in the saint.

3 Religion is not to be confined to temples made of wood and stone, to rites and ceremonies, to any outside show of righteousness or rectitude.

4 Bishops, priests, and deacons are just as blind and just as sinful as the sinners they preach to and pray for.

5 The acts and utterances of Christ that caused his crucifixion, the Jews called sinful; and who, in all the Christian world, does not call the *act* that crucified Christ an awful sin?

6 In the fullness of selfishness man cannot see God, save in what is good for himself; all else is the devil.

7 In the fullness of selfishness man cannot see angels, save in flesh and blood; all else is fiction.

8 Greatness among men is alone a property of the sensuous world; it does not belong to the world of spirits.

9 Man has no love for spiritual life and immortality, until sin breaks to pieces the earthly things on which his affections are fastened.

CHAPTER III.

He preacheth the sorrows of Gethsemane. Heaven is described, and hell also. He sendeth to hell every saint and every sinner; none shall escape, no not one. He foretelleth an era of universal love, and promiseth abundance to those who shall live in that day.

THE agonies of the Garden of Gethsemane must be passed by man before he comes to the development of his manhood.

2 Heaven is rest of the soul. All that is peace, harmony, joy, happiness, is heaven. Wisdom, order, design, are emanations of the atmosphere of heaven.

3 The sin and suffering incident to the school of man's earthly progress is hell.

4 Hell is a soul-conflict, which is the effect of soul-growth; it is a struggle between the material and the spiritual.

5 There is no task in the school of earthly experiences that is not initiatory to the vast existence hereafter.

6 Sooner or later, the unhappiness of one will be the recognized unhappiness of all; and the happiness of one will be the recognized happiness of all.

7 Every cruel man and every cruel nation has yet to suffer cruelty at the hand of nature's unyielding justice.

8 When man begins to love his neighbor as himself, he begins to give the same blessings to his neighbor that, in the school of selfishness, he has taken to himself.

9 The mighty power of self-love will grow weak and weaker, and cease to be; and the love of one for another will come in its place; and then the productions of nature, given for all alike, will be free for one common household.

CHAPTER IV.

He beginneth his lesson by declaring the eternity of good, and the final destruction of evil. Exhorteth to suffer evil, rather than resist it; and calleth all men blessed because of the new road that leadeth to the Promised Land.

GOOD is eternal! evil is a phantom of time. Good is real and indestructible; evil is unreal, and exists only as a shadow made by the sunlight of Infinite Wisdom.

2 Each man follows his inclinations, though he may think he thwarts them; these are his pursuits of happiness.

3 Hope is pleasure. Fear is pain; and pain is the task, and pleasure the respite, in the school of life.

4 Merit and demerit (in morality and in religion) will have no foundation to rest upon, when it is discovered that the will of man does not control his love.

5 It hath been said, "How beautiful are the feet of them that preach the gospel of peace, and bring glad tidings of good things!"

6 *To resist not evil*, is to gather the flowers of life; to resist evil, is to war with the thorns that grow upon the same tree with the flowers.

7 How finite are the mightiest conceptions of the soul's vision now, when compared with the illimitable grandeur of its undefined, eternal progression in truth and light.

8 Blessed are ye, for a new era is beginning; a new religion is coming; a new day of morals is dawning; a new road for human progress is making.

9 This is that road which the toiling hands and sacrifices of millions have graded, over lowlands and through highlands, over the swamps of humility and through the mountains of pride. It is a straight, a level, and a grand highway for *all* humanity; it leads onward forever.

THE GOSPEL ACCORDING TO

ST. MARY.

CHAPTER I.

Mary's spirit-eyes were opened as in a dream; and she hath a vision of heaven. She beholdeth a great sea, and standeth by the side thereof. She entereth the grove of her father, and from thence beheld the unfolding of a new heaven and a new earth.

ONE morning, as I lay between sleeping and waking, in a state of semi-unconsciousness, I was accosted by a familiar friend, who was at that time separated from me by many leagues of ocean.

2 And the sea on which she had embarked was at our feet, and stretched away into the distance.

3 And I was aware, as we gazed upon it, that it was actually between us, and yet we clasped hands and exchanged affectionate words, and agreed to remember that on *that* day and hour we met there, though bodily she was two thousand miles away.

4 And then I ceased to be cognizant of my friend's presence.

5 But still I looked out upon the sea, which became irradiated with a strange beauty, which appearance I saw, on looking up and around me, was worn by sky and earth as well as ocean.

6 And I was in the midst of a new scene. The waves before me were tinged with the softest, mellowest tints—rich, warm, and radiant; and in their midst I saw islands which looked like enchanted regions, clothed in a mantle of supernal beauty.

7 The scene now faded, and in the twinkling of an eye I seemed to be upon a spot to which my feet had often strayed in childhood and youth—the summit of a hillside, on which my father had planted and brought to rare perfection an apple grove.

8 And as I leaned against the bars, at the upper limit of the grove, for support, I became aware of the presence of two young girls.

9 Then a blindness fell upon my outer vision, and my eyes closed heavily, but with an effort I lifted the lids again.

10 When lo! I saw, as with a wondrous, deeper vision, a New Heaven and a New Earth.

11 And I no longer realized any mortal presence—I was alone with the BEAUTIFUL.

12 And behold, the same glow of unearthly loveliness irradiated all things, such as I had seen envelop-ing the sea and its island gems.

13 And the sky was warm and golden, and encompassed the radi-iant earth like overshadowing wings of love.

14 The forest, clothed with rich and varied foliage, waved and glis-tened in the resplendent sunlight and odorous breeze.

15 And the azure-hued and purple mountains lay sleeping upon the distant horizon; and the far-spreading plains drank in the balmy, life-giving, pellucid atmo-sphere, and reflected the subdued luster of its wondrous beauty.

CHAPTER II.

Her vision continueth, and she saw skies and landscapes not possible to describe. She beheld the golden glories of the Summer Land, the same that was called by the Apostle "the third heaven."

UNWILLINGLY, I closed my eyes upon this holy scene.

2 But after a moment's rest raised the lids of my eyes again with much effort, fearful that I should fail to get another glimpse of the surpassing beauty which enraptur-ed my spirit.

3 And behold, the cloud-like dim-ness cleared away, and again there grew upon my inner sight the golden, opalescent sky, loving-ly overarching the responsive earth.

4 And lo! nothing that my bodily eyes ever beheld, or that poets have pictured to my imagination, equals the beauty which my en-franchised vision now drank in from the vast landscape surround-ing me.

5 Yea, to describe it, my speech should be "lyrical, and sweet, and universal, as the rising of the wind."

6 On my right, a scene like an "Indian Summer," but far surpass-ing it in tender, dreamy, divine repose, first claimed and chained my attention.

7 The foreground rolled back by gentle undulations, till it blended with a luxurious grove, whose branches swayed with a melodious motion, like a surging sea of myriad gems.

8 In that foreground and in that forest the colors were so intricately blended, so changing, so vastly more charming than colors called the same when seen by bodily eyes, that language comes far, far short of giving the picture an ade-quate representation.

9 Amber, and violet, and green, the ruby's burning red, the purple of the amaranth, the golden glory of the orange blossom, there blend-ed in transfigured and ethereal loveliness.

10 And the undulating, iridescent sky drooped low to touch the tree-tops, and the sweet calm surface

of the swelling and retreating landscape with its splendor.

CHAPTER III.

On opening her spirit eyes for the third time, she witnesseth the great trees of life, and the lakes, and the grouped habitations of the angels. She beholdeth the central dwelling of a great Brotherhood.

ONCE more my eyes closed unwillingly, but I quickly forced them open lest I should lose the sacred enjoyment of this heavenly scene.

2 And now looking to the left I saw, seemingly very near me, a grove of tall trees, which were in form and structure like our aspen or poplar trees, but far surpassing them in height, luxuriance, and luster.

3 And with a basis of deep green, the glossy leaves, as they trembled in that blessed sunlight, reflected "the rich hues of all glorious things," rapidly changing meanwhile like the colors of the kaleidoscope.

4 And behold, these trees rose to an immense height, and were grand in assemblage, forming a fit temple for the heart's joyous adoration.

5 And, directly in front, an open landscape stretched away into the distance, in which I could discern a lake with its silver tide of softly flowing waters.

6 And beyond this lake I beheld castellated dwellings, with crystal domes, nestled amid surrounding hills.

7 And between me and the lake the green-sward rolled gently down to the margin of the water; and I could see the taller grasses near the lake glisten in their wavy motion, as if each leaf were a transparent emerald, diamond-crowned.

8 And behold, the dwellings beyond the lake were very far off, but I could see that they were all grouped about a Central Building, large, dome-crowned, beautiful and graceful in outline and proportion;

9 And so harmoniously arranged were the adjacent homes, with regard to this central building, that all seemed like one vast edifice with numberless architectural and artistic variations.

10 Yea, most ethereal and delicately beautiful seemed this castellated group—these palaces of a Brotherhood; and over them hovered the atmosphere of eternal peace.

11 And the lake was large; at the left I could not trace its whole extent.

12 But how pure and sweet were its waters; how peaceful and melodious their flow; and how marvelous the beauty of their sky-reflecting depths.

13 In one place something caused an eddy, and a slight tossing of spray. And lo, how lustrous the sheen of those limpid waves; how resplendent the feathery crescent which leaped from their depths and fell again like a shower of liquid light.

14 Fain would I have lingered and gazed forever on this sacred realm of immortal beauty;

15 But, now, darkness gathered upon my senses like a pall; my eyelids drooped wearily; a sound like the rumbling of chariot wheels rang in my ears; and, with a shudder, I returned to my bodily consciousness.

THE GOSPEL ACCORDING TO

ST. SELDEN.

CHAPTER I.

Selden Johnson Finney is an inspired philosopher and preacher of this century. The Arabula moveth his tongue to marvelous eloquence, and filleth his mind with prophecies and far-reaching revelations of truth. From his numerous utterances the following passages are selected.

I SOMETIMES tremble when I contemplate the vastness of the possibilities of mankind; tethered as they are to the world that was, to the world that is, and to the endless future.

2 Man is a myriad-stringed instrument facing every point of the infinite radius, and able to receive and repeat all the harmonies of the universe. His bosom contains the germs of all conceivable grace, personal perfection, and spiritual beauty. The glory of sun and star is eclipsed by the glory of that reason, of that soul that can weigh and measure sun and star.

3 The way of life is wonderful; it proceeds by abandonment to the currents of eternal power. Tendencies are streams of power setting into us from the eternal deeps of Spiritual Being, and indicate at once the duties and destinies of the times.

4 I would fain turn away my mind for a few brief moments from the glittering revel of this phenomenal world, and in spirit stand uncovered and serene beneath the boundless expanse of absolute liberty, justice, love, law, light, and beauty.

5 Man is found to be the divinest creation on the planet. The idea of man is rising. He is no longer to be controlled by institutions. They are made for him, not he for them. It is the age of spiritual and political liberty, because it is the age of spiritual inspiration.

6 Let us no longer distrust our spiritual powers. Let us no longer be enslaved with these external things; let us use them, and not let them use us; and remember it is only when in the higher moments of our interior life we do consciously feel the surges of the everlasting nature, that we can realize the sweet and holy significance of immortal life.

7 The rays of man's selfish intellectuality fall on the soul like moonbeams reflected from an iceberg; only to freeze the germs of our spiritual affections, which yearn to be ingulfed in divine love and beauty.

8 Divine truth proves the unity of Nature, and shows that our hells are kindled here by our own hands, in our own breasts.

9 All substance and power is ONE, or no universe could arise out of them. Hence man is the autocrat of creation. He carries, sheathed within his flesh, the potent secret of all things.

10 Man fronts two worlds at once; with something of the animal and something of the angel in him. He belongs to substance, yet lives amid the shadows; he lives in the world of forms, while the eternal perfections of which these forms are

symbols live in him; he sees the symbols with his eyes, but he *feels* the divine verities signified, with his spirit.

11 Not only is man the culmination of all the kingdoms that have preceded him as phenomena, but he is more—he is causation itself in both law and substance.

12 All the powers of dead generations are transmuted into the fresh activities of the present. Even the experience of all ages is living in the brains and blood of this generation.

13 The ganglionic centers of the race have received and will yield all that is lasting of the very life of the thought of the dead; so that if all books of history and all art and all law were destroyed to-day, we could rebuild to-morrow the age, and improve upon it, too. For the world is alive.

14 But there is no permanent element of wealth but truth, justice, love, wisdom—the eternal verities of the soul and of God.

15 The records of eternity fled, are wrought into the structure of his spirit, so the great function of his immortal life is, to *remember*—to bethink himself. And this shall be our worship, far above the "starry floor of heaven." And this is the unutterable prayer: Let us possess ourselves.

16 It is not what we *do*, it is not our *history*, that makes us divine—it is what we *are*, and what *we are to be forever.*

CHAPTER II.

A great multitude gathered under the trees for amusement; but Selden being among them, and seeing the throng, openeth his mouth and taught them concerning the divinity of man. He extolleth the sublime capacities and deathless relationships of the human soul.

THERE is no middle ground between natural religious inspiration and the great spiritual idea. The farthest star sends its beams down into our world, and celestial chemistry picks them to pieces, and ascertains thereby the constituents of distant suns. So with the light of immortal life. Its idea, an intuition in us, is the eternal recognition of the far-fallen beams of celestial being—of Spiritual life.

2 Intuition of the spiritual and divine is the spontaneous spiritual chemistry of the soul. There are no "discreet degrees" in nature between "matter" and "spirit;" there is no qualitative chasm or vacuum over which, from either side, influences cannot pass.

3 The same energies of Nature which hardened the Azoic rocks, which grew the vegetation of the carboniferous era, and which has crowded whole epochs of wonderful life into the crust of the world, are to-day operating on the surface or within its depths.

4 The expanded earth and unfolded heavens are manifestations of an Eternal Spirit. The rocks, hills, valleys, rivers, ocean, and stars gleam with the white splendors of the Divine Reason.

5 The Spiritual idea of substance is arising from science. All bodies are now proved to be only petrified forms of force; all forces are proved, by their mutual transformability, to be only modes of the action of some common, simple, homogeneous, invisible or spiritual Power; and all power is eternal, infinite and divine.

6 For how could man receive life, power, substance, light, heat, gravitation, electricity, beauty, and wisdom, if he were not composed at bottom of substance, and power, and law, one and identical with these?

7 If man did not stand connected in this sympathetic and actual relationship with molten fires in the

bosom of the globe, which shoot out in volcanoes, and crack the solid continents, man never would have had a revolution.

8 If the solid rocks we tread had not, by the laws of disintegration and organization, ascended into the composition of the human structure, geology would be a sealed book, an impossible study to man.

9 If the star-beam had never been wrought up into the composition of your baby in the cradle, he would never in his manhood see these glimmers through the midnight air. If the sunlight had never kissed itself into the structural intelligence of your boy, he never would know of its existence, or feel its warmth, or recognize its beauty and power.

10 How can that which is spirit, if it be totally different from matter, as some have supposed, be connected with matter? What law exists between two unlike and opposite substances, which, as a chain, can unite those two extremes?

11 It is utterly impossible for God to make an eye unless he has the medium to do it through, and that medium is light.

12 Suppose light is one kind of stuff, governed by one kind of laws, and the eye another kind of stuff, governed by another law, totally different from the light, can you get them together? There could be no sympathy between them. The eye would never know that there was any light, nor would the light make reflections on the eye.

13 So I say of the eye, it is light gone into structure, on its road to consciousness; that is to say, it is the function of light worked up into structure, in such a shape that the next step inward is consciousness itself.

14 Therefore I say unto you, the substance *of* the world is the intelligence *in* the world; and that intelligence is revealed primarily, not *to*, but *in* man. Wherefore revelation is of two kinds—objective and subjective; or external and phenomenal, and interior, and substantial.

15 Now what is inspiration? Is it not the cognition by the personal soul of the existence and flow of the Eternal? It cometh from the relation of the personal to the impersonal, of the relative to the absolute, of the dependent to the independent, of the shadow to the substance.

16 The painting on the canvas, or the musical composition, is man's effort to reduce his intuitions of perfect beauty and of perfect harmony to expression.

17 Is not consciousness itself self-cognition by substance? What is pure intelligence but simple self-apprehension by substance? Existence is not being—being is existence, apprehending the fact of existence, as also the qualities of such existence. Pure intelligence is pure substance, knowing itself in *esse.*

CHAPTER III.

He continueth his discourse to the multitude in the grove. The history of man's spirit is the history of God becoming incarnated. No essential difference between phenomena and their causative principles.

NO man can conceive two distinct and eternally different substances—spirit and matter—and get a live universe out of their union. For how can two eternally distinct and essentially different substances be brought together?

2 "Deity" is infinite, according to popular theology. The Divine Attributes—"Ideas"—are everywhere present. Thus Love, Will, Wisdom, Justice, Harmony, Holiness,

Beauty, and Perfection, are everywhere present. They are *in* Nature. For what is so natural as that which is eternal—the uncreated?

3 The aim of science should be to fathom those hidden, secret, invisible spiritual forces of which the suns and stars are the merest precipitations and residue. If there be a God, then "matter" is but spiritual sediment; "suns" are only shadows of eternal Reason; so that the spirit *in* Nature and *in* man is the only permanent, solid, and enduring substance.

4 Nature gives us no beginning of love, law, light, or wisdom; nor do we see, or perceive, either in the world of forms or in the world of Ideas--of Reason—any actual starting-point in the absolute order of things. True, special individualities seem to appear from a certain point of local career; and, indeed, the present forms of such appearance do begin; but when we look for the connections and relations of these special forms, *we at once get swept into the vast cycles of universal career*, and by induction remount upward through geological and sidereal epochs, until we find ourselves contemplating the eternity of Spirit, of pure Reason, and the logical order of Ideas.

5 The fraternity of souls and the paternity of God rests at last on the *identity* of the original substance of each being. If human spirits are the children of God—if the idea of the fatherhood of God be not a delusion—then the substance of the Creator is the foundation of each soul. Yea, the *identity* of the primordial essence of the human and the Divine Spirit, is the only logical basis; and it is on this foundation alone that religion itself is possible.

6 Infinite Spirit cannot be bounded or limited. It cannot take cognizance, therefore, of any thing different from itself, for it is "all in all." It cannot be a personality, because *infinite individual* is a contradiction in terms.

7 For if God be Spirit and Infinite there is no room for any other substance than spirit. Spirit is the primordial Power at the center, and the original substance at the foundation of the world.

8 Personality, therefore, cannot be predicated of a Boundless Being, of the Infinite Beneficence.

9 Individuality is, necessarily, relative and dependent, and pre-supposes the absolute and independent, which is Infinite Spirit, eternal law. But Infinite Spirit is absolute, not relative; is independent, not limited.

CHAPTER IV.

After his preaching, he sendeth an epistle to the people; and by it some were persuaded, and some believed not. He openeth his subject to the wise men and chief priests; but they hear him not, neither answer they him. He rebuketh the foolishness of false philosophy. He denounceth superstition, and openeth eternity to man's mind.

THE first effort in the history of man is to unite science, philosophy, and religion into organic form, under the auspices of associative action, such that all great reforms growing out of them, and out of the needs of man, can be united together into one body and method, animated by one spirit, and aiming at one end—the whole good of man.

2 Science cannot exhaust us; objects cannot, therefore, exhaust us. We have within us still the unsung powers of this Infinite Perfection, which will make us live and grow through all the rolling centuries of the great hereafter.

3 Like Nature, our philosophy is

two-sided. It has facts by the million—facts which appeal to every possible condition of mind, from the most sensuous to the most spiritual-minded; while for the deep and intuitive thinker it has the most transcendent and spiritual ideas. The unlettered can be surprised by the movement of a table without contact of visible power; while under the inspiration of the gifted seer and poet, the great fields of eternal day break on our rapt vision. It opens on the one hand the great questions of physiological psychology, and, on the other, the profound questions of transcendental theology. Hence it promises to reach all the world and every soul thereof. It is the democracy of religion and of philosophy combined. *It is the Catholicism of Rationalism*, with a fact, an idea, a reason, and a symbol, for every possible mood of man. In bridging over the grave, it connects the poorest barefooted, ragged child of earth—whose kindred watch him from the homes of the pure and the free, weeping when he strays, and rejoicing when he returns to the true path—with the highest archangel of the Summer Land.

4 The first act of the Divine Intelligence, as it appears in man's personality, is a vast synthetic intuition, involving a revelation of two worlds —the world of manifestations and the world of inter-conscious Ideas. The fact of sensation pre-supposes the reality of these coequal worlds. Hence the folly of the war of the "Idealists" and "Sensualists" of modern Europe.

5 Nothing can precede eternal dynamics. Nothing can antedate everlasting Ideas, which are archetypes of worlds.

6 The idealism of Berkeley, which reduced all the external world to a mere phantasm of sensation; to a mere picture on the nerves of the body, whose cause was forever shut away from our reach; and the Pantheism of Spinoza, or more especially of his one-sided disciples, here find their grave, in common with that subjective Idealism of Spencer, Sir William Hamilton, and Mr. Mansel, which is of late so much in vogue. Sensationalism has a half truth; Idealism has a half truth; Pantheism has another half truth: but so long as each claimed to be the only truth, all were false in a double sense, and blind. The truth in each of these schools is revived, emancipated, and united in the Hramonial Philosophy.

7 Demonstrate the naturalness of spiritual forces and laws, and the realm of the divine is brought within reach of science. Science may then push its discoveries up into the immortal world; may—must—link the two worlds together in the bonds of a *scientific* as well as sacred fellowship, and so banish all hobgoblins, all ghosts, all superstitions, and all senseless religious fanaticism from the world.

8 Worlds come from suns, suns from vaster suns, and all, at first, from that burning vortex of eternal light in which converge the infinite laws of Pure Intelligence. This focus is the vortex through which the Ideas of Pure Reason rush forth into cosmic chronology, just as the human spirit is the other vortex of life through which these worlds rush upward into love, will, wisdom, philosophy.

9 I deny that a rock is a substance; I deny that a tree is a substance. Yet, on the other hand, I affirm the outward world to be *real*. I am not a Berkeleian, because I affirm the external world to be a

real world. But it is a real phenomenon only.

10 I never realized more thoroughly than at this hour, that the world that men regard as so substantial, is only a world of shadow. These outside forms and facts are nothing but phenomena.

11 When we perceive the unity of nature; when we regard the mutual transformability of bodies, and of all forces; when we discover in the analyzed sunbeam and starbeam the elements which have been precipitated and hardened into rocks, and coal, and iron, and other metals; when we behold everywhere the reign of the same invisible power, ever changing in form, but ever the same in *esse*—the soul is carried on and on in the tide of inspiration, up to the same great central conception that spirit "is all, and in all."

12 Substance is necessarily eternal; phenomena necessarily limited in time and space.

13 Induction deals only with shadows; deals only with form, not substance; deals only with phenomenalities.

14 The universe swings between these two vortices: First, downward and outward, into forms of appearance; second, upward and inward—into thought, into consciousness, into eternal Light.

15 Does any one suppose that men first inferred that there was such a thing as love by induction? No! the human heart loves as spontaneously as the bird sings, because it cannot help it.

16 By induction we learn, from the present state of the rocks, that, though now so solid, they were once fluid. Then we find that the whole earth was a fire-mist; and, following the same inductive lead, where can we stop?

CHAPTER V.

Selden preacheth in the great cities, and pleadeth the cause of ministering spirits, and encourageth all men to seek the truth for its own sake. He declareth the aims of spiritualism, and calleth upon all men to behold the light.

NATURE is a unity—an undivided empire; and to him who affirms the God in it, there is no escape from the spiritual fraternity of all things, and of all spheres of being. SPIRITUAL COMMUNION *is the glorious flower of all religious experience;* the answer to all prayer; the ultimate of all study, the goal of all science and scholarship.

2 Spirit is the foundation of all things; continued inspiration from God the one condition of all life, high and low, and hence communion with Nature, universal. There is no world too fine for the spirit in man; no angel too pure to work for us earthlings; and no spiritual aristocracy allowable in this God's world.

3 "Man lives in two worlds at once," said an ancient seer. "Forms are but images of ideas," said an immortal soul, fresh from the spirit land.

4 The only real substance in man is that divine intelligence which, operating from within through the senses, fills the body with light, compared to which the light of suns and stars is dim indeed. It is that light of wisdom which illumines the pathway of planets and holds worlds in order and orbit.

5 Believe me, brethren, there is a grander world than that in which these shadows dance across the sensible horizon; there is a diviner life, a serener consciousness, a more golden condition, than that of the body and its relations to the world.

6 Spiritualism is the only resort of all Christian progressives, who hold on to the idea of God, and in the possibility of a natural divine life; and Atheism is the only resort of all those who cannot so hold on.

7 Just where Spiritualism differs from Theology it agrees with the religion of Jesus. It is alive, fresh, spontaneous, progressive.

8 But what is the genius, spirit, scope of the great Spiritual Movement? What are its ideas, methods, sources of power, and aims? Is it all confined to the fact of intercourse between the two worlds? Nay, far from it.

9 He who accepts the fact of spiritual intercourse, must take all that goes logically with that fact as part of the truth of the whole Movement.

10 Spiritualism shows how the career of a soul in this life affects its condition in the next. Is it not proper, then, for it to deal with the conditions of this life?

11 We felt that the ministering angels of the spiritual world inspired and pushed us on to the work, as well as the deep voice of our inmost spiritual nature.

12 Our aim is the attainment of that "perfection and truthfulness of mind which is the secret intention of Nature." Verily, our aim is too large to admit a creed or sect.

13 We hold that the "chief end of man" is the highest and most harmonious development of all the powers of life to a complete and consistent whole.

14 We do not wish to get "settled" or "fixed." There is no more hope of a society than of a person when it becomes "fixed."

15 We have not sought to found a sect or to establish a creed. We seek no coerced uniformity of opinion; we draw no lines of limitation around the empire of independent thought; we dictate no terms of belief; we establish no religious or ecclesiastical Sanhedrim.

16 Every argument that can be brought to sustain the popular religion, is stronger when applied to the great spiritual religion. It is said Jesus was inspired, communed with angels, was strengthened by them, healed the sick by the laying on of hands, read the hearts of men, opened the eyes of the blind, and hence that his religion is divinely revealed? We reply, So do hundreds of spiritual mediums. Did the disciples speak in unknown tongues? So do spiritual mediums —by the thousand. Was Jesus and the disciples persecuted? So are mediums. Are spiritual mediums accused of every wickedness? So were the disciples.

17 The breadth of our purpose is parallel to the very purpose of the providence of God, as displayed in the history of the human race; for, what else than the complete education of man can be considered as an adequate aim for the providence of history?

CHAPTER VI.

Again he preacheth to a great multitude beyond the Alleghanies. The Spirit of prophecy possesseth him, and he lifteth up his voice against the Babylon of Supernaturalism. He speaketh in plain tongues. He succeedeth in afflicting all the disciples of "Peace" who heard him. But he strengtheneth the young men, and counseleth eternal resistance to the imps of tyranny.

RELIGION and Philosophy are both possible to man only because he *is* whatever God and truth are. Light and love could not pour into us, unless we were built of both light and love, and so could draw both from the deeps of the universe by native attraction. As the solid earth is but precipitated sunbeams so the nature of man is organized spirit. The body is but the secreted shell of the soul. Our proper self is pure spirit—pure as God. To feel and to realize our native divinity, is the only true method of salvation, and the aim of philosophy.

2 Brethren, our word to you is, "Come up higher;" leave for a little time your dusty libraries, step out under the stars and open your eyes, and you will then find that no *ism* can command the soul of this rising world.

3 When souls awake, thrones and oligarchies crumble in ruin; Liberty, Equality, and Education become the watchwords of the race. From the rising consciousness of the democracy of souls comes the demand for "equality of all before the law," and the consequent enfranchisement of woman, of labor, and of the negro. Society is being remolded; creeds are falling to ruins; *principles* lead the march of nations. And all this because the era of spiritual fraternity has dawned in society, and unfolded a Spiritual Philosophy of religion.

4 The gospel of this epoch is for progress—for the enfranchisement of woman, and her admission, on terms of equality with man, to all the rights, privileges, and immunities of life. It demands justice to all classes of citizens. It calls on government to make all equal before the law. It opens itself to science and philosophy, and all truth, from every quarter of the globe.

5 While in religion, the advent of the Spiritual Dispensation, emancipating millions in our own land as well as in Europe; the decay of the Papal hierarchy, and revival of the spirit of art, and its consecration to Nature, attests the immense activity and spiritual energy of this century. All these facts are the sure signs of coming benefits.

6 The greatness of antiquity stands eclipsed before the prowess of this time! The control of steam and of lightning, the laying of the Atlantic Cable, the emancipation of the American Republic, the downfall of Russian serfdom, and the political resurrection of Italy, are among the marvels of but a few years in this century.

7 Supernaturalism is now rapidly sinking into hopeless decrepitude and remediless decay. Under the influence of liberal scholarship, free thought, fearless criticism, and the great Spiritual Movement, joined with the late discoveries in science, popular theology is being actually destroyed.

8 And yet this same Supernaturalism, with its tyrant God, its despair of man, its chronic distrust of human nature, its curses on the human heart, its worn-out creed and ritual, its "infallible Bible," its priestly aristocracy, "chanting damnation hymns over dead babies," with its subjugation of slaves to masters and of women to their husbands, its Jesuitism, and its horrid lust after political power and authority, *is aiming to become the religion of the Republic!*

9 The time has arrived, say the popular "evangelical" divines, when the affairs of government are to be taken out of the hands of the "ungodly," and to be administered by "the saints"—*i. e.*, by themselves, or by their supporters.

10 Behold, the seventh great religious revolution of the world is upon us. Brahminism, Buddhism, Judaism, Classicalism, Mohammedanism, and even modern Christianity, are, regarding their claims, only failures. All have failed to save man from ignorance, crime, war,

slavery, and woe. Now, the race advances either to Atheism or to a universal Spiritualism.

11 Millions of men and women have believed these things with all their might, and yet their lives have been the purest of the pure, the truest of the true, and, like fair trees, have blossomed sweetly forth on every side with fair humanities, and bent beneath a golden weight of love. But were they so *because of* their belief? No, but *in spite of it.*

12 We do not forget the history of sects, creeds, and ecclesiastical despotisms on the one side; neither do we neglect to note the anarchy and isolation of absolute individualism on the other.

13 Religious anarchy has nearly come again. It was not till the old world was reduced to a similar chaos, that the Divine voice said, "Let there be light."

14 The spirit of nature is always fixing and unfixing things, molding and remolding over and over her forms of inanimate and animate being; continual flux and reflux keeps ocean, air, and stars pure, lifegiving, and beneficent.

15 The wrecks of the old institutions floating around us, attest that the currents of Spiritual power have risen to high-water mark, and will, out of their sediment, create a fairer world.

16 That holy "Providence" which guides justice and liberty to victory is the "Providence" of armies of angels, inspired and sent down to us by the eternal decrees of the Infinite Reason.

17 At last the whole human race shall break away from idolatries, bibliolatrous creeds, and church craft, and, uniting, build the temple of a World-Religion out of blocks of solid Light, quarried from the zenith of Eternal Love, Liberty, and Law.

18 A day will come to every soul, when into the channels of its purified being will pour the Love, the Truth, and the Beauty of the world.

19 To be passive to the spirit of Nature is the secret of genius, and the path of salvation.

THE GOSPEL ACCORDING TO

ST. LOTTA.

CHAPTER I.

Lotta, the prophetess, leaveth her home for a time, and, under the inspirations of Arabula, carrieth the tidings of angels to multitudes. She presenteth the wonders of Beauty, and sheweth that it is prophetic.

ALL are lovers of Beauty, according to their several powers of appropriating that delicate emanation from the all-forming Spirit.

2 The plowboy, as he follows, all day long, the dull motions of the laboring ox, has in his mind some fairer image than his eye beholds, in which his thoughts find a con-

tinual joy, or toward which his memory recurs with a renewed delight.

3 The youth who climbs the laborious steeps of knowledge, or walks the lowly paths of ordinary toil, has yet an eye for finer vision than appears. Some grace not obvious shines in the dull drilled lessons—some beautiful form of the fancy floats in his day-dreams, and hovers still more palpably in the hushed slumbers of the night.

4 The rude, frank-hearted sailor, fighting his defiant way against the storms of heaven and the wild wrath of waters, keeps in his heart an image, fair to him, and so full of controlling beauty that his eye sees her, calm and unrippled as the sleeping Halcyon, between the groaning planks and the roaring deep. She flutters through his brain, an image of delight, in the calm hours of the solitary watch; and when his eye gloats on the beauty of a favorite ship, its every curve and undulation, through all a perfect model is rounded to some graceful semblance to his heart's idol.

5 This universal attraction toward the Beautiful is perhaps the deepest in our natures, and surely is the strongest element in molding rude, half-fashioned souls to the symmetry of the cultivated spirit.

6 It is the first gleam of "light" in the night of barbaric ages, where the dark-minded savage, in his instinctive desire to please, puts on some shining bauble, and feels less a savage in the contemplation of its glitter.

7 At that moment there gleams upon him, could he but understand it, a true flash from the tremendous portals of all future attainments. That sparkle of clear crystal is a *predictive* beam from the morning star of his immortal day. From that point his course is onward, upward, through the slow ascending grades of an everlasting progress, taking in the whole broad range of civilization and the arts, of mental culture and the soul's tuition.

CHAPTER II.

Her thankfulness for the universal love of Beauty. She witnesseth the Divine Providence even in the heart of savages. The world's bibles are records of man's early glimpses of the heavenly life.

THE prophetic desire for something fairer, *better* than his lot—something with an ideal or extrinsic value—is shown by the savage in his taste for the glittering and gaudy. Jewels are his stepping-stones to heaven.

2 So, too, after all our progress, the highest conceptions of the future heaven have been expressed, and are still symbolized, by the same jewels which the rude barbarian loved.

3 The intimate cord is not broken. The hand of the swarthy savage is clearly visible, reaching up from the rudeness of his undeveloped life to grasp the splendors of his future patrimony.

4 The vitality of these symbols may be justly attributed, in a good degree, to *the intrinsic beauty* of the objects, and their permanent, indestructive nature.

5 Time will not tarnish them; their undecaying luster shines on after many generations, as it shone on the first possessor.

6 The diamonds of Haroun al Raschid glitter on Victoria's diadem. The blood-red garnets of the Indian Krishna—the swart, voluptuous Venus of the East—burn on the bosom of the fair and pure young vestals in the chapels of the Cross.

7 It is fitting that a visible immutability of Beauty should be the symbols of the unseen, eternal glory.

8 But another cause shares the honor with this in giving endurance to the heavenly significance of gems. The first prophets were Orientals, Sons of the Sun, and dwellers on a soil rich with ripe crystallizations of its many-colored light.

9 They were, too, the simple first men, full of the growing sense of a nascent progress, full of the child-like, barbaric taste for jewels, the brilliant and the dazzling.

10 Our bibles are the outpourings of the child-heart of the world, thrilling with *the first insight* of the immeasurable destiny of the soul, and the inexpressible glories which were in store for it.

11 In the deep enthusiasm of that *inflow* of divine life, they called up all the glories of the visible world, their dazzling gems and symbols of royalty, to give some adequate expression to their visions of the invisible and future.

12 First impulses are strongest; first enthusiasm is most unbounded, and deals in glowing hyperboles.

13 Hence, the gorgeousness and dignity of the elder prophecies of the spiritual have scarcely been transcended by the brightest conceptions of the advanced teachers in later years—by none, perhaps, till the dawning of this new spiritual age, so little appreciated and so much discussed.

CHAPTER III.

The prophetess again lifteth up her eyes, and portrayeth the physical glories of the ancient apocalyptic heaven. She discerneth the beautiful within that relic of barbarism. Her eyes were open, and yet she saw not "a mighty strong angel with a book in his hand."

THE deep significance of beauty, and the supreme beauty of "the world to come"—which verily *has* come to thousands yet in the flesh—have not been without their witnesses long before our era.

2 You have heard from a multitude of pulpits the glowing picture of "the heaven" that, through many forms of worship, all hearts aspire to.

3 And all that the most gorgeous imagery could do, to paint and glorify and exalt that picture, has been done in reiterated poetry and eloquence; till the image is crowded with dazzling jewels that blind the gazer, and stiffen the form it would illustrate, like some barbarian princess cumbered with blazing gems that mar her natural grace and beauty.

4 We have seen gifted teachers revel in the eastern splendors of that glorious city of God, the New Jerusalem, whose vast transparent cube shone from the heavens on the rapt eyes of John in his Apocalypse.

5 Glance for a moment at that glorious picture, full of barbaric wealth—the dazzling splendor of the Orient—mixed with the high, wild fancies of a mystic enthusiast.

6 There glow the "twelve foundations" of its jasper walls, the first like the vast wall itself, a solid jasper, mingling its lucid green with the green earth it settled on, and guarding the redeemed, with its strong counter-charms, from the most subtile wiles of the tempter, the fatal sorceries of the enemy.

7 There the clear sapphire sheds its purpling azure, dropping with gold.

8 There glows the scintillant chalcedony, crowned with green emeralds flashing light, like that which shoots to the pale chambers of the ocean.

9 The sardonyx gleams half incarnadine, like fire through pearl and black onyx; the deep tinted sardius sparkles with luminous darkness like a midnight sky, or the unfathomable eyes of houris to the heroes of Islam.

10 The golden chrysolite—transparent gold indeed, mighty to conquer the keen pangs of thirst—blazes like a new sun around the holy place, where souls shall thirst no more.

11 Above it shimmers the faint beryl's sea-green lucidness, deepening upward to the topaz hues, and growing yet more golden in the mingled gold and green of the clear chrysoprasus.

12 And, crowning these, the jacinth flashes with pale violet beams that make earth's lightning-flash a harmless meteor play, and guards the jeweled wearer against pestilence, and lures to quiet slumber—fit jewel for the walls of that bright city, where no more are suffering and death, and where He who rules and watches "giveth his beloved sleep."

13 One living amethyst crowns all with its deep violet, fabled on earth to guard against inebriation—safeguard in heaven against the wine-cup of the wrath of God.

14 The redeemed of the Lord walk in white garments through the golden streets; golden harps are in their hands, palms of victory wave on the vibrating air with the wide pulses of their loud hosannas, golden crowns are on their heads, and a perpetual song is on their tongues: "Glory to God and to the Lamb forever."

15 Such images have survived the very creeds that they glorified—the very gods they were made to glorify; and yet, with *all* their splendor, they *may* be *transcended;* yea, a more lovely heaven, a more true, a more beautiful spirit-realm has been revealed to us of the new dispensation.

CHAPTER IV.

The people admire the wisdom and beauty of her words; a few only gave heed to the power and good of her utterances. She complaineth not. She discourseth on, and sheweth the difference between things and ideas.

VERILY, the white arms of one loving angel—one wingless and warm with human sweetness—twined round a lowlier brother or sister soul, leading it up to more pure delight, and therefore to more purity, *is a far richer picture,* transcending the pearl-gated, gem-walled heavens, as far as human *love* surpasses *wealth* in true worth.

2 All that mechanic glory, the old masonic splendor, dazzles and confounds us. But this human tenderness attracts and warms us.

3 Our new heaven—which the ignorant or perverse characterized as earthly and gross, and unworthy the name of heaven—is spiritual, airy, fragrant, natural, and sweet.

4 Its grace and warmth, its fineness, its naturalness, its freedom and delight, are like a home—lovely for its home nature; whilst the old rectangular, metallic heaven seems so mechanical and artificial, that all its splendid symbolism is lost upon the heart.

5 St. Augustine tells us in vain that the gems of "the twelve foundations are the virtues of the redeemed."

6 Human hearts love human hearts, but jewels they only *admire.*

7 Green valley-paths and bright flowers are akin to our sympathies. They have ardor and beauty at once, and the heart can repose among them as with companions, whose radiant faces are yet more

beautiful with affection. But by the splendor of gems we are only awakened to admiration—still feeling a *want* their glitter reaches not, as if we sat down before a splendid face which lacked the redeeming graces of the soul and heart.

8 Such is the radical difference between symbols, and the *realities* or ideas they symbolize. Truly seen, they are the soul's effort to express to the senses what belongs to its own unutterable experiences and ineffable surroundings.

CHAPTER V.

The light shineth down through her eyes into her soul, making her face to beam with a wondrous radiance. The people marveled greatly. She beheld and described the glory of the New Heaven.

THE beauties of the spiritual, as developed by the higher souls in all ages—whether we accept their words as a literal transcript of distinct existences in proper form, or as types by which the superior spheres are pictured to our understanding—are still divisible into two grand classes. They are, first, the *physical* beauties of the higher sphere; and second, what are properly the *moral*, pertaining to spirit inherently.

2 No one can conceive of a soul without surroundings. It cannot exist unless it exists *somewhere*, with attending circumstances.

3 It may be possible for a fanciful intellect to suppose these circumstances to be *ideas* of the seer, or the scene flung round him as objects, to relieve the mind from the painful sense of vacuity and contradiction, which a solitary existence, an existence existing nowhere—that is, standing in no relation to any other order of beings—would present.

4 Such fancies are too fine-strung and intangible to really satisfy one for a moment.

5 If there is no reality to our terrestrial surroundings, we might understand how the beautiful landscape which surrounds the freed soul might also be unreal.

6 But we shall not give up clay, and iron, and wood, at the challenge of bishop or priest; nor the ethereal groves and plains of the spirit realms, at the summons of any canonical or uncanonical skeptics.

7 Existing in and floating with the atmosphere of worlds, is the true local heaven—or the dwelling of freed souls, whose luminous affinities attract them upward.

8 Over the broad landscape of this other world, there are the most beautiful plains, enameled with flowers of perpetual bloom and fragrance; glorious rivers wind out among the undulating hills, and the murmur of their waters is articulate music and song; clear in the depths below gem-like pebbles glitter, the golden and silver fishes glide; while purest forms of angelic beings bathe in the waters that all around them seem to take a roseate flush from the lucid limbs and glorious forms they embrace.

9 The polish of the many-colored foliage makes the deep woods yield no shadows, but only mellowed light.

10 The birds are of a richer plumage than any upon earth, and all are songsters with diversal melodies, making one vast harmony.

11 There are no noxious insects, beasts, or birds, in all these upper countries. They are confined to the subterranean realm.

12 The songs of birds are translatable into human speech, by souls attuned to the melody they pour.

13 There is nothing of the abrupt

and harsh, precipitous and rude, which mark the grandeur of our landscape; but all is mellowed and softened, without diminishing the majesty of the scene.

14 All is intensely beautiful, undulating, free, and perfect, and transparent to the eye of mortals, nay, to all eyes.

15 But, to the spiritual eye, it is enriched with thousand-colored shadings, which in pure beauty surpass almost infinitely the fairest pencilings of art.

16 Highest poetry has sometimes drawn from this sphere the glimpse-seen glories, to intensify the scenery of its earth-pictures; and a few inspired musicians have caught the actual notes that vibrate in that far tingling air.

17 It seems as if this spirit land might be the divine image or antetype toward which the rude mass of earth ripens in its slow centuries, and that an age may come when the earth and the heavens shall embrace and form one translucent sphere.

18 To many minds these indescribable glories of the bright superphysical surroundings of the enfranchised soul are not objective forms, but mere associate idealities. I behold them to be both.

19 Seers have gone over their beautiful hills and vales, hand in hand, and seen the same bright images; returned unto the same localities after long absence, found such changes as progressive forms must undergo, but with such resemblance as fixed localities would keep.

20 And so might one in dream landscape. So might *two*, possibly, if in perfect magnetic relations to each other.

21 But not so should we find, as we *do* find, an almost universal *likeness of general description*, in endless variety of minor detail, of this wonder-world.

CHAPTER VI.

Her eyes, being full of the light of Arabula, behold the more exalted attractions of heaven. She proclaimeth the prevalence of Charity among the inhabitants of the Summer Land. And denounceth the eternal psalm-singing heaven of crude religionirts.

FROM the physical, I turn to the second class of beauties, which are more widely recognized as "spiritual:" I mean the *moral* traits.

2 It is the privilege of a favored few to *see* those delicate aromal forms of bird, and tree, and flashing river; but any pure soul, any true heart, is open to these *nobler* forms of spiritual existence—may catch some inspiration from their presence, and shape their growing lives by the sublimer types of Beauty which they offer.

3 The moral beauties, like the physical, are common to both spheres, with the same difference of finer development, of more ethereal and pure natures—the same mellowing of the rugged and abrupt, the softening to intenser life of the thunderous elements of this lower world.

4 Many creeds have left "no room in heaven" for the most beautiful features of the human soul—the finest impulses of the sanctified.

5 But we have assurance, sweet as immortality itself, that there is no death for the soul's whole attributes, none for the heart's holy affections.

6 The propensities are all hallowed in purified natures, and have a position assigned them corresponding to their exalted and refined characters; in which they are de-

veloped in harmony with the whole soul, and are gratified as divinely as the inclinations to worship and gratitude.

7 Spirits love with a white and beautiful love, and twine their several elements, purely, warmly, into one wreathed gladness of whole heart and mind.

8 This love is a transparent passion, seeking not the vail of a concealment that it cannot need; and if it flush, it is but the quicker flow of the pure blood to a more vivid delight, with no taint of earthliness.

9 They walk with fair arms intertwined, under the eye of God. And you would only know by the transfigured beauty of their faces, and by the heightened glow of all their radiant forms, that a more deep and hallowed relation existed between the wedded twain than that which binds all lovely souls to all as lovely.

10 I cannot linger now to read to you this mystery of spirit-marriage, or what it is, or how it should be named on earth. I only see a twofold unity that is beautiful—transcendingly and purely beautiful.

11 But the crowning excellence of this celestial sphere, and which distinguishes the souls of the just from the dark spirits below—and marks the difference between our visions of the heavens from all revelations hitherto—is the high, paramount prominence, which is awarded to the great love-element of universal *charity*.

12 Here we find no loud eternity of idle harping and perpetual song; no cruel transports of unpitying delight over the ever-ascending smoke of a brother's torment; no dreamless slumber of an everlasting repose; no drowsy revelings in the lotus-dreams of an eternal voluptuousness; no heaven of beatific sensualism, where, bright and beautiful, ten thousand houris minister to the royal pleasure of a single hero —hero no longer in his luxurious abode; no airy Valhalla, where the ghosts of warriors drink the foaming mead, and clash their resounding arms in day-long wassailing and the fabled tales of heroes; though all these images are humanely acceptable, as types of the ever-acknowledged fact that *souls in heaven are intrinsically and essentially what they are on earth*, only perfecting there the ideal of all excellence here.

CHAPTER VII.

She lifteth up her voice before a great multitude, and pictureth the naturalness of the New heaven; and telleth of the glorious works of love performed by angels for the low and fallen of earth. And in her vision she beheld the Lyceum children in the Summer Land.

MOREOVER, our new heaven infringes not on the domain of any other heaven. Ours is that vast unclaimed—the heart's unexplored realm of *generous work*—of work that blesses others and delights the doer.

2 The inhabitants of that beautiful domain are souls that keep their warm love and the blessed sympathies which made them so beautiful on earth—higher, and deeper, and broader, there, making them still more beautiful.

3 No heart could retain its best and loveliest element in a home of delight from which it knew a fellow heart was excluded; and to be ignorant of a brother's fate were a loss, and, to souls of an high order, an impossibility.

4 I pray that I may not forget erring and wandering souls in the brightest hour that ever dawns upon my spirit.

5 The revelations of these last years show us how to reconcile the beatified soul's completeness with the fact of souls in gloom and misery.

6 In bringing the wanderer back to light, in breathing hope and cheer into hearts yet repining in their clay, in pouring promise down the dark abysses of despair and pain—in this work the souls of the redeemed find their best delight, and deeds of mercy *make* the heaven they people with all renovated lives.

7 Could they who seek the desert sands, and scour Golconda for the types of beauty to adorn their heavens, see for one moment the pure face of a commissioned angel, as he brings glad tidings to the weary heart and hope to the benighted wanderer, they would learn well the meaning of those words, "The Beauty of Holiness."

8 The flashing jewels of a queen's tiara shed no luster on her brow, like that which pure *love* lends the stooping forehead of an angel sister; as the light of her deep eye thrills down the depths of a brother's agony, with healing in its beams.

9 The regal purple of King Solomon in all his glory, stiff with barbaric pearl and gold, arrayed him not in beauty to compare with the pure lilies that bloom white and flushed with tender love on the twin cheeks of my little angel brother.

10 The sunshine quivering through rose petals on a translucent pearl, might faintly image the clear, rich beauty of his tiny hand, pressed on my burning forehead in the hour of pain; but not that blushing pearl, nor the more glorious hand, could lend an image of the inward beauty which inspired that act—his young, pure, everlasting love, whose touch is healing and delight.

11 The dance of happy children in their rosy heaven, as their light feet trip pattering like the rain, and sparkling rain-like in the harmonious air—their twining arms, round, dimpling, clear, and warm—their universally deep bright eyes, that speak more life and happiness than even angel's tongues can utter—and the wreathed melody of motion that winds in and out, around each other in interminable mazes, never broken, never jarring on the joyous cadence of their linked utterances—these make a picture which might once have driven dumb the favored poet who should have caught the vision, and swooned in mute despair of breathing into song its unutterable beauty.

12 Yet all this grace and beauty is but a language in the heaven—speaking in symbolic glories of the ineffable light, and joy, and crowning love of their young lives.

CHAPTER VIII.

The transforming power of love is described, and the prophetess giveth the people a new definition of worship as it is in the heavenly state. She calleth upon the celestial hosts to visit the people of earth. The real living angels have no wings. She exhorteth all mankind to open their eyes to the "light," and to doubt not.

HAVE you not seen how a most beautiful face grows more intensely beautiful with deep thought? How even conquered suffering, and the soul's hard-earned victory over loss, desolation, and woe, can make the calm eye like a spirit's, and the pale cheek radiant with more than earthly physical beauty?

2 With a far more prevailing power, the soul in light shapes the obedient features of its vesture, the spirit-body, which in cumbers it not.

3 Every sweet thought is a line of beauty to the fluctuant form.

4 Every noble impulse shapes the dilated figure to a grander expression of its strength, beauty, and grace.

5 Every beat of the heart of love and holy sympathy flushes the remotest limb with rose-light, and a deeper meaning glows in the lightest face, and burns far back in the deep crystal of the glorious eyes. The worship which goes on forever —in every act—and in every word, and in every thought, and even in the unconscious motions of their lives—gives an all-hallowing sweetness to their every look.

6 This beautiful, natural life, speaks no fear, no crouching vassalage of soul, but a deep, natural, filial love, that so involves and permeates all the being, that existence with them can be nothing less than "worship"—an expression meaning naught else but high aspiration and unceasing praise to the all-loving Father.

7 They do his work on earth, and in the nether spheres; and this is joy—this is life; this, the immortal heaven of souls who have gone up from suffering to delight.

8 And in the joy of their great ransom, knowing how grateful is unexpected kindness, how inexpressibly dear is guardian love, they can never forget from whence they came, nor the pained, struggling souls that lift their eyes to the blank heaven with such hushed agony of mute beseeching, where, thanks to the new light they find the heavens no longer brass over their heads.

9 They come! the beautiful ones! the shining angels, in their love and light.

10 Their wings are only their own swift desires; their crowns the immortal amaranths, that glitter with the dewy spray-drops from the river of life; their harps are but their choiring thoughts that breathe instinctive melody into every motion; and their high mission is to *cheer* and to bless.

11 Oh! beautiful upon the mountains are their feet, as they come laden with glad tidings.

12 The mourner, though he sees not their transparent glory, hears not the mellow music of their love-breathing voices, nor even feels the, quiet presence hallowing the spot, and the tender touch that soothes the throbbing head, yet feels that the hot tear has been swept away —the heart's strained pulses softened to a gentler flow—and blessed glimpses of a clearer faith come stealthily in upon the night of his grief.

13 Look, O ye of the earth, look to these realms of light and love, when care, and pain, and doubt, make life a weariness. Oh! let not dark, deep, and cruel unbelief put away so successfully the promise of "the light" which comes only to bless.

CHAPTER LI.

LET US RETURN THANKS.

We thank thee, O Light, for the inspirations and ministrations of thy new gospels. Thou hast completed the answer to prayers breathed to thee in moments of darkness and doubt. When we were walking in the ways of desolation, without thy truth and love and wisdom, behold, thy presence was felt and seen like the sun shining through and fertilizing the whole domain of life. Thy unslumbering care covered us like a mantle, and thy pure and powerful presence drove pride, and selfishness, and many passions, out of the temple of our being.

We thank thee, O Light, for thy gracious guidance, for the comfort of thy rod and staff, for the ten thousand tokens of thy love and wisdom. Thou hast blest us, for we now know that all the realms of creation are covered with the wings of thy righteousness. The past was not evil, for thy ways were through it all; and to the hearts of the true, thou didst prove thyself an angel from God. In all human life thou hast wrought miracles. Thou hast turned the water of many a poor life into the wine of a life of richest usefulness. Thou hast changed the stones of hatred and passion into the life-bread of tender affections. Thou hast raised from the grave of despair, and given new life and nobler purposes to, many social sympathies and beautiful ties.

And the weakness, and dullness, and darkness, and wickedness of our lives thou hast converted into the prophets and apostles of the Good, the True, and the Beautiful.

We thank thee, O bright angel of the Mother and Father! for carrying us in thine arms even as the sun carries the planets in its warm bosom. In thee we find *rest*—glorious, heavenly, divine repose—out of which *action* flows joyfully even as music flows from the myriad voices of Nature. We beseech thee for nothing, for "thou doest all things well." Every moment thou art calling minds out of the darkness. In thee they find strength, and enlightenment, and sanctification. They love; and they fear not. They walk; and they do not stumble. They look upon thee; and their doubts flee away. We beseech thee for nothing, because thy gracious omniscience comprehendeth the least as well as the greatest; and thy life is in all and through all; and in thee all "live and move and have their being."

O Father! O Mother! O Light! Receive from all thy children everlasting love—the flower of their eternal gratitude to thee.

CHAPTER LII.

THE FINITE AND INFINITE IN MAN.

HUMAN nature is organized and perfectly equipt for progression throughout the everlasting ages, and can, therefore, be neither absolutely happy at any one time nor harmoniously revealed by any one person.

Not only is the individual thus organized for all-sided progression through Eternity, but so also is each particular faculty and quality of his being replete with the same irresistible tendency to grow and unfold in the direction of its endless career. And therefore it happens that, whilst one organ, faculty, or attribute of his nature is profoundly slumbering, or perchance just beginning to dream in a state of semi-unconsciousness between sleeping and waking, its fellow-organ, faculty, or attribute may at the same moment, be "wide awake" not only, but making real and rapid advancement in its own legitimate sphere of usefulness, happiness, and development. Contradictions and painful paradoxes in human character are, to a very considerable extent, referable to these phrenological inequalities of individual development.

The high-born proprietor of the temple is at once a king of the earth and an angel of heaven; but, be it remembered, both himself and his palace were built by feelings and constructive forces which ante-date his consciousness of being; over which feelings and forces, therefore, he could exercise none of the privileges of self-government. And from this fruitful cause—the hereditary possessions of individuals—spring the monstrosities as well as the angels of humanity.

One inherits a noble physical constitution associated with an equally noble brain, adapted to the full manifestation of mind; another inherits a sickly brain and a sicklier body, making intellectual nobleness and beautiful physical development in this life impossible. But, owing to the inherent progressiveness of the human mental attributes, the constitutionally enfeebled one may, in some particular, far surpass the one who was more fortunately organized. The nobler-born, by habitually cultivating his intellect and gratifying his selfish instincts, and equally neglecting the fair and beautiful growth of the higher powers and affections, may become knavish, licentious, ugly, and eventually loathsome. Whilst the unfortunately-born, by contemplation of ennobling and spiritualizing themes, united to industry of perception in reading and studying facts and philosophy, may unfold beautifully like a white lily beneath the bending willows. Both these suppositions are possible. and have been many times realized; but neither parents nor society can safely rely upon foundations so sandy and changeful.

The reliable rule is—that effects and causes invariably correspond. A brutal brain is the mother and cradle of brutal thoughts and brutal practices. A low, coarse nervous system is the cause of low, coarse physical sensations. A small brain is the hovel instead of a palace, in which the eternal king was born; therefore a hovel life, instead of a regal life, will be poured into society. Beautiful sentiments, pulpit ethics, and divine commandments exert no influence upon flat heads, small craniums, and low physical temperaments. Persons of this mold are pre-eminently conscious of bodily wants and physical instincts, and are maddened by social limits and the police restrictions to their gratification.

The animal instincts and characteristics of the lower world, are visible at the basis of human nature. The truly *human* arrives only when the animal is quiet and tame; and the inner *angel* comes only after the instincts and intellect have been resurrected and transfigured on the mount of Arabula.

And here, upon this glorious eminence, from which the world-lifting "Light" becomes universally manifest, we discover another cause of contradictions in human nature. Let us analyze it, if possible, and utilize the results:

Human nature, we must affirm, has in its organization *two* spheres: one physical, the other spiritual. There is, consequently, what might be philosophically termed *a consciousness of the senses*, and of the world of objectivities outside of the senses; and, in the interior life, *a consciousness of God*, and of the infinitude of eternal spiritualities within the spirit of God.

The instincts and the intellect belong to the "consciousness of the senses;" while, to "the consciousness of God" belong the affections and the flower of intuitions, Wisdom.

The intellect, relying solely upon the instincts and the senses, arrives at self-knowledge, and becomes self-sufficient and self-righteous, and—atheistical. Self-knowledge is possible only with the human intellect.

It becomes conscious that it is conscious, but the perpetuity of this consciousness is possible only through *memory*. Any failure in this retentive faculty, any irreparable break in the chain of facts and sensuous experiences which are the property of intellect, is equal to a loss of so much practical mind; and, to the same extent, the individual is incapacitated fo business; being consciously shorn of the available power of self-knowledge. Man's power over the objective world —his skill and achievements in Science, Art, and Mechanics—is determined and proportioned by the qualities and completeness of his self-knowledge. That is to say, he must know that he knows—his intellect must commune with itself, in memory—otherwise he is no more than an animal, knowing merely and simply, without the proud knowledge that he has productive knowledge. Memory makes progression in knowledge possible; not merely the memory of a fact or an event, but the memory of the *thinking*, and of the *conclusions* awakened by the fact or event; thus fortifying the mind with the important consciousness that it is conscious of itself, and therefore potent.

But inasmuch as memory is the only recorder of the facts and events accumulated by means of the senses, it is not certain that the intellect of the individual will continue to grow through life, as does the forest tree; but rather, that, after the sixty-fifth year, the mind will begin to retire insensibly from the senses, and to realize more distinctly than ever before the consciousness of God, and, possibly, obtain glimpses of the future.

This superior consciousness is what metaphysicians call "religion." It takes hold of principles, and in principles alone can the mind achieve absolute growth and development; because a principle contains within itself all the facts and events which are allied to it in the nature of things. Thus, by becoming conscious of a principle, the *essences of all* that has been, is, or may be possible to the operation of that principle, come within the grasp and consciousness of the spirit. The only cement of facts, is Principle. To know by memory the facts, as well as to be interiorly conscious of the principle, is to possess at once both knowledge and wisdom.

Man never realizes God until he becomes conscious of Principles. Justice, Love, Beauty, Truth, Power, have no existence in the intellect, except as one's eyes may look at bright objects "through a glass darkly;" but to the higher spiritual consciousness these Principles are visible, and they are worshiped by this consciousness as the attributes of God. Truth is heard within, like the whisperings of the shell of the Arabian maid in Ghebir—

> "Apply its polished lips to your attentive ear,
> And it remembers its august abodes,
> And murmurs as the ocean murmured there!"

St. Augustine said: "God is nearer, more closely related to us, and therefore more *easily* known by us, than sensible, corporeal things." That is, in other language, man's consciousness of principles is his consciousness of perfection and infinity! And it thence follows that an intelligence without a consciousness of these principles, is without God in the world—is atheistic, selfish, mechanical, and harassed by the limitations of sense, of power, and of gratification—and that such a person is a dangerous force in the family, in society, or in the government. But a *veritable angel presence is that person whose interior nature is conscious that it is conscious of Principles.* One who feels the warmth of love not only, but who also feels the beauty and eternity of love, is in the self-consciousness of God. Or, shall it be said that thus, and thus only, or upon this principle, God is revealed to human nature?

This, finally, is the essence of all life's experience; man's power to have a spiritual consciousness of eternal Principles. This consciousness is a revelation to man of man not only, but also of God to man, with superadded glimmerings of all the infinite progressions and inexhaustible possibilities which are *in* God.

But the age-after-age conflict between the two spheres in human nature—the finite on the side of the body, and of the infinite on the side of the spirit—will account for all the selfishness, brutality, crime, and atheism on the one hand, and for all the religions, vagaries, superstition, supernaturalism, and theism on the other.

But over all and through all is the spirit of omnipotent Truth, and Arabula still sings through angel-lips, "Behold, I bring you glad tidings of great joy, *which shall be unto all people!*"

CHAPTER LIII.

A DISTINCTION WITHOUT ANTAGONISM.

ARABULA'S light, shining through the temple of reason, makes plain and straight the path of reconciliation between man's finite and infinite spheres, *i. e.*, between his instinctively selfish and his intuitively impersonal nature.

The distinction between the intellect or understanding, and the pure reasoning or intuitive wisdom powers, is not teaching that man's nature is organizationally a magazine of incompatibilities. Seen truly, this distinction, while it is a perfect explanation of the inconsistencies in the manifestations of human nature, is not only necessary to a correct analysis of man's mentality, but reveals, at the same time, the profoundly wise duality of his inmost spirit, which is constructed for an immortal career in progression.

By intellect, which is selfish and cold, you obtain knowledge of outside existences and things; and by it, also, you arrive at a state of self-consciousness *distinct* and apart from other existences and things. And this self-consciousness is grounded, externally, in experience through the senses; and, internally, it is powerfully intrenched in the primal fundamental instincts. Selfishness, therefore, is at the very basis of human life—indeed, *selfishness is the foundation of individual and social existence*—and, in order to restrain and redeem this basic principle, men found codes of Morals, and establish systems of Religion and Virtue, and enforce obedience by legislative and military power, and by preaching the terrors of a wrathful God.

Wisdom, which is pure intuitive reason, on the other hand, which is the immortal superstructure reared upon this selfish foundation, is the self-consciousness of God in the spirit. In other words, the sensibilities and sentiments, and aspirations and apprehensions of the superior powers of mind are the voices of Arabula—of God *in*, not outside of, the spirit. The *highest* feeling of Wisdom is a revelation of God; more or less, *all* have this "feeling," crude and vague though it is, and each acknowledges it and each worships it; wisely or otherwisely, according to the growth and education, or the non-growth and ignorance of the individual or people.

The innate feeling of immortality, the innate feeling of boundless ideas, the innate feeling of unchangeable principles, the innate feeling of love toward superior angelic existences, the innate feeling in every human heart, that it is worthy of a better life than that of devotion to animal instinct and selfishness—is the voice of Wisdom. "*I am*," is the language of Wisdom; but the motto of intellect is, "*I think*." No man is sure that he is not a brute, and no man is sure that he will not die and cease utterly like a brute, until he has arisen to the *highest* self-consciousness, which is the unutterably happy and peaceful feeling of perfect oneness, and essential identification with the spirit of God. His spirit then can sing, "I know that my redeemer liveth!" For then he hath knowledge that his "redeemer" is inseparable from his constitution, and will go with him wherever he goes; will judge his acts, condemn his vices, approve his virtues, punish his selfish crimes, pardon his hereditary temptations, burn him in hades, bless him in paradise; and thus, over and over, and from eternity to eternity, perpetually loving, unchangeably just, omniscient in goodness, progressive in power—"his God," pure Spirit, and "his Saviour," pure Truth, the same yesterday, to-day, and forever!

Intellect is the temporary rudimental antagonist of Wisdom. But the highest is supreme sovereign, and in the end brings all opposition in humiliation to its feet. Knowledge, which is the name men give to the acquirements of intellect, is not an eternal property-holder. It is made up of the *memory* of things and experiences outside of the individual—very useful and convenient in passing—whilst Wisdom can truthfully quote the adopted maxim, "*omnia mea mecum porto*" —or, "all that is mine I carry with me."

The teachings of the Wisdom are the teachings of God; and the practice of Wisdom's ways (laws) is obedience to God's commandments. There is no other Religion possible; for this is the consciousness of man's highest attributes attaining to self-consciousness—the intelligence of the redeemed intellect; the living witness in the temple; the voices of the uplifting affections; the philosophical declarations of the intuitions; the light of Arabula in the universe of life; the actual presence of the attributes of the infinite God in the spirit of man!

CHAPTER LIV.

THE USES OF SELFISHNESS.

Under the beautiful guidance and truth-revealing illuminations of Arabula, we have thus far traveled directly toward a knowledge of the true uses of the great first principle of all life, the chief attribute whereof is Selfishness.

This inherent, ever-active instinct is the Mephistophiles that overshadows the glory of human nature. In plants and in animals the existence and exercise of selfishness seem wise and legitimate; and in man not less so, were it not for the fact that he is endowed with a superior consciousness. It is this exalted super-physical, anti-selfish, angelic sensibility, which so vividly separates and distinguishes man from the lower kingdoms of life and organization. At base man is animal—governed by the simple instincts of self-feeding, self-pleasure, self-preservation, and the prolongation of his own life, cost what it may to the life and selfishness of others.

But all this brute-selfishness, remember, is an indispensable ingredient of life at the very basis of human existence. Selfishness is the essential element of growth in the roots of life's tree. Vines, shrubs, vegetables, flowers, trees, animals, were otherwise impossible. Deprived of selfishness, without the instinctive passion for seeking pleasure, they could not exist. They would not eat when hungry, nor drink when thirsty, nor sleep when tired of toil, nor would they mate and multiply each after its kind, because there could be in their constitutions no motive, no impulse, no prime necessity for exertion, no cause for organic existence and development. When you can build a house without a foundation, grow an oak without roots, sow and reap a luxuriant harvest without soil, raise men and women without first having baby-boys and baby-girls, *then*, but not before, can you have a world without centripetal forces, a circumference without a center, animals without self-preserving and self-gratifying instincts, and a human family without units, without individuals, without senses, without intelligence, and without selfishness.

But it has been seen, in the light of the indwelling witness, that man, unlike the animal, has the feeling of an *infinite* life in his superior consciousness. He can, through this spiritual sensibility, put himself in the place of another, or he can think of himself as though he was outside of himself and another individual, and thus he can identify and blend his *real* existence with the existence of the whole. In this realm of higher consciousness man becomes, both in qualities and quantities, in property as in amount, a higher and superior order of being. Here is revealed the impersonal ideas, or those truths which have universal application. Here, and only here, he sees the divine Principles—Love, Justice, Truth, Beauty, Power, Perfection, Eternity, Infinity. If these attributes were not in the essences of man's higher endowments—or, stronger, if these principles were not as essentially in man as they are essentially without him, in the infinite heart of Mother-Nature and in the sensorium of Father-God—he could not, by any possibility, either *feel* their presence or intellectually perceive their application. In persons of low development—who are yet on the plane of pure, simple, brutal, instinctive selfish life—these Ideas, these Truths, these Principles, this feeling of God, this yearning for Immortality, are unknown. Whilst in minds of the higher development, whose selfishness and intelligence are resurrected and consecrated to higher uses, these Ideas, Truths, Principles, Feelings, Yearnings, are as familiar as flowers in the gardens or stars in the firmament.

"Self-love but serves the virtuous mind to wake,"
As the small pebble stirs the peaceful lake."

Man's selfish instincts demonstrate his origin. They lie at the foundation of his indestructible superstructure, and contain a vast repository of trustworthy biographical sketches, showing that, in the departments of physiology and life, the human family "was born of poor, but respectable parents"—surnamed, in the records of the oldest and only true Bible, "Minerals," "Vegetables," "Animals," and their "Elements."

On the other hand, man's unselfish, fraternal, magnanimous, infinity-feeling principles of mind, demonstrate his Destiny. They prove that the human family is, in the departments of intention and spirit, organized for progression without end, and for promotion in all that is God-like, celestial, and absolutely perfect.

CHAPTER LV.

PATENT MEDICINES FOR SINS.

MEN of higher moral developments, but who are not yet sufficiently balanced in mentality to be wise and large in their views and conduct, originate and elaborate various remedies for the cure of selfishness, sins, crimes, and wretchedness. But for one "prevention" system, there are one hundred plans of "cure," five hundred schemes of "palliation," a thousand machines for "restraint" through fear, and a million-horse-power mill of brimstone "punishment" and eternal misery.

Man's superior consciousness, which enables him to project himself into an objective and abstract existence, is the father of anthropomorphism. And this anti-progressive conception of God is the father of many arbitrary schemes of rewards and punishments. It proceeds on the principle that man's will is free to act, and that it does act, at variance with the decrees of the anthropomorphic God. Reason, affections, the power of willing, the freedom of action, they assert, are powers given to man, whereby he may elect to live and die in the Lord, or to live and die in the devil.

But are not these moralists, religionists, and metaphysicians blind to the fact that *will* is but the effect and the servant of feeling? The will of a tiger reflects the feelings of a tiger. Motives in man vary with his moods; and these, for the most part, are determined by circumstances without or by conditions within. The anthropomorphic God, however, is unable to take knowledge of constitutional differences, and will not look at palliating considerations in man's surroundings. At this point the doctors prescribe; and the first patent medicine recommended is "Faith."

Faith, by some moralists and metaphysicians, is supposed to be an *act* of will; on the same principle that the mind, by the projection of its higher self-consciousness, can construct a personal God. But do you not perceive that the feeling of faith is the effect of an antecedent feeling? If the *object* of your faith is outside of your private, selfish, lower consciousness, it must be, at the same time, *within* the realm of your unselfish, public, and spiritual consciousness; because it is impossible that you should have feelings without causes, or faith in an object which is totally foreign to the inherent sympathies and aspirations of your spirit. The moment you attempt to believe any thing, or to repose faith in an object, which contradicts nature within you or nature without you, that moment you depart from the righteous ways of truth, and become an unreasoning, dogmatic supernaturalist, perhaps a religious fanatic, and certainly a *hypocrite*.

Faith, in order to act as a curative medicine for the sins of selfishness, "must be well shaken before taken." Believe in the impossible, and behold! your life does not improve. And why not? Because you do not feed the roots of your mind with truth. The morality that rests upon faith in the righteousness of a foreign object, which is not part of the unchangeable laws of your own superior nature, is *immoral;* because its first acts are treachery and surrender, and because its second acts, worse than the first, are inhumanity and tyranny.

The impossibility of separating man's faith from the causes of feeling, which causes ante-date or predominate the power of willing, renders all faith in a supernatural religion absurd. The theology of the Roman Catholic Church is founded upon anthropomorphism, and the religion of the various Protestant churches is founded upon a supernatural Christ-ism; but the world's history, to say nothing of its present condition, proves that the patent medicines, manufactured and faithfully administered by these soul-physicians, do not cure mankind of selfishness and its resultant evils. The Catholic ideal is to become "God-like;" the Protestant ideal, to become "Christ-like;" and the two establishments, and the lives and conduct of the peoples who support them, show the error, yea, the *immorality*, of their ideals and plans.

And why immoral? Because these religious systems start with the theory that man's nature is radically wrong, needing reconstructing, and must be practically *blotted out* before he can be "saved" and the world "redeemed."

In the blessed and sacred light of Arabula, on the other hand, we read that the true ideal for man is not to attempt to be like God nor yet like Christ, but to be *healthfully and harmonially* A MAN! God cannot be manifested in the flesh upon any other principle. The glorious majesty of Divine Wisdom becomes visible in the harmonial glory of *a whole human being*. Such holiness (wholeness) is supremely beautiful. And this is your Ideal—that is, if you are rational and truthful and natural; but if you profess "faith" in an object irrational and beyond the possibilities of human nature, and *rely* upon such "faith to make you whole," then prepare your heart for disappointment and despair. You are guilty of *treachery* to the light and love and laws of your higher consciousness; guilty of *surrendering* the holiest parts of your spirit to the devouring beasts of superstition; guilty of *inhumanity*, in joining a party that blasphemes and disgraces and perverts human nature; guilty of *tyranny*, by aiding the theological foes of mankind in their efforts to force the millions out of Nature's ways, which are the pleasant paths of God.

The reconstruction of human nature is an idle dream. The plan is perfect, and the pattern is before all men, in the superior consciousness with which all are more or less sensible; and to attempt a different plan and pattern is to offend the divine order, the punishment for which is sure mortification and ultimate despair. To the religionist it is a final atheism and hopelessness with regard to mankind; to the sensualist, it is an insupportable weariness and the cause of suicide.

Let all who seek to reorganize Society take warning; let all Communists, who would build a social state without *meum et tuum*, beware; let those who work to harmonize Labor and Capital take heed; for the Omniscient goodness hath ordained that man's primal principle of Selfishness shall have and shall enjoy its legitimate rights as much, and as *surely*, as any other principle in his constitution. Any social system, any political party, any religious plan, not in harmony with man's *whole* nature, will meet with obstacles, failures, disappointments, and final overthrow. One part of man's nature cannot be sent to war with another part. The whole must be duly and reverently recognized. Selfishness, the centripetal force, and philanthropy, the centrifugal tendency, must be fully provided for in your new social system. Call thou not unclean, untamable, or wicked, any thing which the Lord God hath made.

CHAPTER LVI.

APPLICATION OF PRINCIPLES TO LIFE.

THOSE who have read of the "Battle between the Spirit and its Circumstances"* will remember that the spirit of man is situated in the midst of many concentric circles of fashioning influences—of primitive, constructive, impelling, shaping, misshaping, educating, miseducating "circumstances;" that man is the "center-stance" stationed at the pivotal center of the several concentric circles; that his outermost circle is the external coating of the earth with its invisible atmosphere; next, the heat of the sun, and its light, and all the rays that come from the star sources, enter into the most external primitive sphere of man—using the word "man" in the general, comprehensive sense; the next circle of circumstances is social, or societary, the result of combinations of persons and of institutions, customs, and laws which come out of such combinations, touching all parts of the human, nervous system, whereby mankind are shaped or misshaped, are made or unmade, are driven forward in a straight track to success or are switched off into defeat, and sent back to the target-stations of society; the third circle of circumstances may be termed the phrenological—showing that the brain organs which a

* See the discourse referred to in a volume by the author entitled "Morning Lectures."

man inherits are not himself, or, rather, his spirit is not to be forever identified with his case of brain-tools and instruments, although, for the present life, they compose the positive circle of circumstances which the internal spirit and character are obliged to recognize, employ, and contend with, in their progress from birth onward and heavenward; but the most primitive circle of circumstances is the physiological—the first direct influence proceeding from what men have inherited—the primal fortune or misfortune of the pre-natal life, bringing to each both the form and the functions of his body, including the combination of temperaments, fixing for a lifetime the relation of the internal organs to each other, and measurably determining whether they perform their functions vigorously or indifferently, perfectly or slovenly, whether they be fast or slow, whether healthy or freighted with the seeds of disease and misery. Thus all involuntarily enter into the first circle of circumstances—into the physiological organs and conditions—with which the babe is obliged to contend on its way up the road toward manhood and the future. The babe desires to eat and drink, to be nursed and caressed, to be fed, to be let alone, and to sleep; and thus all its plays, attractions, inclinations, and dispositions, spring primarily out of that circle of circumstances which is called "physiological."

The inmost point of consciousness, remember—at the very center of the individual life—is the MAN. This pivotal consciousness of the internal and eternal individuality, is what we call "spirit," which is the *highest* of man, and is, consequently, the very last to be heard from. There are multitudes of persons, in all communities, who seem not yet to have heard from the highest God-consciousness with which each is everlastingly endowed.

Therefore a distinction should be made between "force" of the vitality and the "power" of the inmost essence or spirit. Force comes out from motion, life, sensation, and from so much of the intelligence as naturally blossoms out of these primal principles which live in man in common with the animal world. Vital or primal human "force" suffers reaction commensurate with the energies of its puttings forth; action and reaction among man's vital or primal "forces" are nearly equal; and a human mind, to conquer its many and various circumstances, must rise superior to force and become "a power," which is the first manifestation of the inmost spirit. Power is silent. It rises superior to force, which always goes to battle, being the source of discord, of anger, of war, and of every passion that afflicts, distorts, and mars the human race.

Advancing, rising up from within, power comes forth and takes the ascendant, and the individual is lifted out of the discords of its circumstances into a regal stratum of spirit consciousness—imparting to the mind a magic power to let war and strife, whether of the body or in society, whether in the nation or in the kitchen, pass by and not disturb the profound depths of that inner life which touches infinity on every side.

Such minds, as I have illustrated throughout this volume, have what may be truly called a deep "religious experience." It comes from the presence, and low sweet voice, of Arabula. It is within every one's reach. Only learn the origin, nature, and number of the circumstances which environ you, and the side-influences which you are called upon to overcome and vanquish, not by violently cutting them asunder—not wildly and madly, as an infuriated animal butts its head against an enemy that is blocking its way—but by spreading "the wings of your spirit," and soaring in hope, in thought, in aspiration, and in power, *above* the frictions, and tumults, and contentions which environ you, many of which you may have inherited from father and mother, and their progenitors.

In this way a man becomes "reformed" from the center to the outmost circle of his circumstances. It is the newest new birth, and the shortest road to the kingdom of heaven. All this beautiful reformation and regeneration is possible long "before you die." It is not necessary to wade through any ministerial "quackeries" to attain to *one*ness with Nature and God. The pure, the beautiful, the powerful principle of inmost life, is illimitable. When the spirit's power rises up from its inmost—when it expands above force and war, both private and public—it sees itself to be "a conqueror" in the midst of its material surroundings. This is that high power which the martyr feels, lifting his soul into unison with God and angels, when his body is environed with the consuming flames. This is the power which, for a moment, the poet feels when lifted by his highest afflatus. And so Byron said—

> "I live not in myself, but I become
> Portion of that around me; and to me
> High mountains are a *feeling*."

A high utterance of the identity of the inner life with the sublimest endowments—an exalted moment, when the "power" of the heart was felt to be *one* with the silent and grandest manifestations of God and Nature in the physical globe.

Cannot you arrive at this condition? Suppose you adopt the principle of Liberty. Can you not contemplate Liberty as a "great mountain?" Can it not become to you "a feeling?" If so, then, you *love* it. If you love it, it becomes *sacred;* and whatever is sacred to you, you are *consecrated to* with all your soul and spirit. When you are truly consecrated to *a principle*, the kingdom of heaven is very near to you, and you are very near to that, and it is no longer necessary that you should hire ministers to steer you along the road to a salvation from the consequences of sin. Independent of pulpit quackeries, you are put into *sympathy* with the Divine Spirit, which is the never-failing fountain of all eternal PRINCIPLES. And when the mind rises up into sympathy with even *one* of the eternal Principles which dwell in the living central heart of the universe, its spirit-pulses quickly harmonize with the inmost beat of the Infinite; and such a mind is responsive day and night—faithful, loyal, always saved, always silent, ever hopeful, never despairing. Emerson said:—

"Devils despair; Gods forever hope."

Individuals in all times and countries have these exalted spiritual experiences—these fine thoughts and heavenly emotions—these sublime, ennobling, immortal aspirations. I take it for granted that many of my readers have identified themselves with something which is not theological, not creedal, nor educational—something deeper, diviner, sublimer than all—which was the first "revelation" to intuition and reason that all are "immortal beings."

Kind reader, do not you cling to a Principle that surges out into the sublime realities of infinitude? If you would draw your inspiration from the ocean of infinitude, you must first be "loyal" to at least *one* of its many central principles. Use, Justice, Power, Beauty, Love, Truth, Fraternity, Wisdom, Liberty: take *one* of these. Take *truth*, take *kindness*, take *love*, take *charity*, take *justice*, take some plain patriotic *sentiment*. Be faithful to some Principle in which you have faith. Become perfect in that *one*, although you be defective in all other principles; for so long as you are truly *loyal* to *one* of them, so long and to the same extent will you receive testimony that you are deathless at the center of consciousness. The power of the spirit is something different from the "force of the will." The vitalic force of will is self-exhaustive. "It uses itself up." The person who does every thing by force will look in the face like a beast when maddened. The stubborn-headed, willful character, when angry, bellows like a bull; he roars like a lion—that is, when the will borrows all its available force from the animal elements which the soul (the intermediate sphere) has inherited from the lower kingdoms of earth. Each one, therefore, should become, so to speak, a spiritual Van Amburgh. Men should go into their organic cages, and, with spirit power, say to the different animal, turbulent forces, "Down!" Spirit within is a Daniel, amid lions that dared not array their forces and appetites against him. "Get thee behind me, Satan," is the command of Spirit.

It is a voice from the seat of "power" amid the passions and appetites of selfishness.

Now apply all these examples and reasonings to the human will, which we may call the mind's vital force. What do you suppose is the limit of Will? It would be difficult, I think, to place any boundary to the ultimate sphere of its action. Force, from the soul, is limited. It commits suicide frequently. At the very climax of outward success, "men of force" drop down into every kind of bankruptcy; they tumble headlong from the pinnacle where it would seem they were to be victorious. But the Spirit's power never loses, never faints; it always gains, for it is a part of omnipotence. Verily, man's spirit has revealed proofs that Will has an attribute of "power" which enables its possessor after death to rise up bodily, and thus to come into sympathy with great magnetic rivers which flow through space from the Golden Belt to the Earth, to Mars, to Jupiter, to Saturn, and to the clusters of smaller planets between all these and the sun, including Venus and Mercury, and thus, also, to correspondingly inhabited planets (to other and more distant earths) revolving around other and more immense suns, belonging to that great assemblage of constellations which constitute the Milky Way.*

But there is a far more *practical* view of our principles of spiritual power and progression. Arabula carries the torch of celestial sunshine into the labyrinths of intellectual darkness, into the obscurest fields of materialistic science, and shows "loyal natures" how to

* For explanation, see the author's work, entitled, "A Stellar Key to the Summer Land."

master and mold *matter*, and how to augment the material prosperities of the day and hour. In these fields we meet Liebig, Dove, Oerstedt, Ehrenberg, Tyndal, Youmans, Ashburner, and many others equally eminent—all profound and enthusiastic believers in scientific and philosophical knowledge, as the great stepping-stone to a world's advancement. They exalt scientific above all scholastic education; they think infinitely more of chemical than of classical knowledge. The learned humanists, among whom stand conspicuous Ulrich von Hutten, Reuchlin, Erasmus, &c., by enlightening the darkness of ignorance and the fanatical prejudices of their time, prepared Germany for the Reformation. "But," says an observing writer, "our time and country are different. Our material and industrious progress has no parallel. The means of their development accord with the genius of our people. The practical nature, habits, and modes of thought, peculiar to the American people, are not destined to govern the world by the revolutionary influence of profound philosophical speculations, or by the overwhelming power of a martial despotism. We are people of figures and facts. Our relative geographical situation, natural resources, climate, in short, the working up of our material wealth is to be the source of our national greatness. The most feasible mode of accomplishing the object referred to is by the intellectual emancipation of the people by a mental culture adapted to their natural proclivities and their true 'manifest destiny.'

"Providence does not always lead mankind with easy steps. Sometimes the spirit of the time moves so rapidly and vehemently that the globe seems to tremble from pole to pole. Within the space of a single generation we witness the appearance of more discoveries and inventions than we are able to enumerate. We live in an epoch infinitely more prolific in useful inventions than that in which Guttenberg came to enlighten the world. The most ingenious machines, admirable for their power, velocity, and delicacy, produce effects so wonderful as to make men despair; the power of steam is applied, by an infinite variety of mechanical contrivances, to annihilate distance and time, and render the impossible among the easiest of things feasible; mountains, rivers, gulfs are traversed with the speed of the hurricane. By the mysterious agency of electricity thought is flashed from continent to continent, ere we can say 'it lightens;' the quiet ray of the sun becomes our most expert and accurate painter. All things not absurd become possible. These manifestations of the human mind may triumph side by side with the most wonderful works of time. Institutions designed to operate in such a sphere, to open wide the avenues of wealth, power, and intellectual omnipotence over the material elements of nature, are mostly of the profoundest considerations and the noblest efforts of the world's benefactors."

But from this it should not be inferred that *material* knowledge and *selfish* progression are totally antagonistic to the development of an interior life in the individual. The truth is, it is impossible for the whole to advance materially without promoting and enriching, indirectly, all the dependent parts; even as true intellectual culture leads, sooner or later, to more interior and spiritual growth of character.

CHAPTER LVII.

FINAL VIEWS OF PRINCIPLES.

MAN, viewed in the light of Arabula, is the repository of the germs of all divine principles. Every property of matter, in the outlying universe, finds its respondent and counterpart in man. That which in matter is chemical affinity and attraction, in the human spirit is love and sympathy. The correspondence is perfect. The world of mind is clothed and harmoniously dressed with a world of matter. Man's spirit is composed of all principles which, in their totality and infinite organization, is called God. This identity, of the essentials of man's inmost with the principles of the infinite spirit, is the basis of his immortality, and the cause of his tendency for endless progression.

The footprints of Arabula are visible on all "the sands of Time."

The Greeks believed in the existence of a Dæman (a guardian intelligence) in the heavens, which could speak to the "Reason" in men. This is the "Logos" of which something is divulged in the beginning of John's Gospel. He affirms that this Dæman was the "Logos" which *was* God; in other words, the Reason of the Universe and the Supreme Intelligence of the Universe, are *one and the same*. The life of the Spiritual Universe—the "Logos," or God—became "Light" in the spirits of men.

Thus the essences of infinite life flowed into finite consciousness in the human organism, and thereby became "the true Light, which lighteth every man that cometh into the world." Did Plutarch learn this doctrine from the Christians? Did Marcus Aurelius first read this idea in John's spiritualistic gospel? Nay; from Intuition and Reason, and not from written authorities, did the Grecian Spiritualists learn of the impersonal "Logos" resident in the life of every man. John, in his beautifully pure gospel, admitted the harmonial view of man, as did Jesus and Plato and Socrates, teaching that the "Logos"—*i. e.*, the essentials of the life of the Universe, God—"was made flesh," or was clothed in material organs and forms, "and dwelt" in the visible realm, "full of grace and truth."

But neither Plato nor John were fully up to the view presented from the stand-point of Arabula.

Plato, while teaching that the human soul is an emanation from the infinite Divinity, and thus admitting the essential affinity between man and God; yet, in his logical reasoning, he was compelled to run the individual through various transmigrational ordeals, and finally, when perfectly pure, to annihilate him by a process of absorption. John, on the other hand, taught the immortality of every man, but introduced a sectarian mystery, contrary to the fixed principles of Nature, by teaching the dogma that the "Logos" was manifested in one individual. Nature brings to "light," by perpetually recurring manifestations and examples, the fact that the Divine life is incarnated—is made "flesh" and human—every time a child is born! The harmonial view of this subject is anti-Platonic in that it makes the individual immortal, and is anti-John in that it demonstrates the universality of the "incarnation."

Associated with this doctrine of *incarnation*, as a kind of correlate, is the doctrine of *salvation*. That something in the human universe is "vitally out of order," is the conviction of both heathen and Christians; and the question arises on all sides, "What is it?" and "How is it to be remedied?"

The greatest pre-Christian philosophers substantially said: "We must strive to bring the God that is within us into harmony with the God that is within the Universe." This was their effort. The God within was believed to be estranged from the God without; and the conflict between mankind and the Divinity (they said) would continue till the God without is found and inseparably allied to the God within. The Christians, on the other hand, said in substance: "The God of the Universe is the same as the God in you, but He is striving to bring you into harmony with himself." The heathen, therefore, strive as strangers to *find* God, and thus attain "Heavenly rest;" the Christians behold God striving to attract man unto himself, to crown him with "eternal life and peace."

There is a vast gulf between these teachings and the harmonial view of progressive principles, which is—

Finite man, in the properties and possessions of his spirit, is a miniature of the Infinite. Growth, endless improvement, progress in all directions, throughout everlasting ages, *is the central law of his being*. Let us reaffirm that the attributes of the human spirit are the repository of the seed-grain of an eternal development. He stands at the center of an infinite radius. He is made and endowed by Father (God), and by Mother (Nature), with immortal powers of individual growth. He is constructed on the infinite plan—"in its image and likeness"—not in form, but in the *essentials* of his being. The law of progression regards and endows all men equally and impartially. There is perfect harmony between endowments and responsibilities. Obligations are commensurate with powers possessed. All men are born alike, not equal. All men are equally dependent and independent; but no two individuals are on the same plane of growth, having exactly similar wants and needs at the same time; all go to the Fountain to be filled and inspired, but each with *his own measure* which holds more, or less, or different, than that of every other at the inexhaustible source.

In man's physical structure are found all the primates of the globe, or, rather, all the proximates of metallic and non-metallic substances; in man they come forth as the ultimate particles and refined principles of matter. It cannot be true that all minerals are poisonous, because all minerals are found, in their ultimate (finest) state, in the fluids and solids of the human composition. Oxygen is everywhere present in man's body; so is phosphorus in his bones, blood, and brain; hydrogen is in all the fluids, and some of the solids; carbon is in all the secretions and excretions; iron is an essential of the blood; soda is in his muscles; silex is found in the hair and nails; magnesia exists in blood and brain; lime is abundant in the bones; albumen and fibrin; and sulphur, and the several associate metals; also the acids and alkalies—acetic, uric, oxalic, benzoic, potassium, &c., demonstrating, as perfectly as science can establish any discovery or proposition, that MAN'S BODY IS THE ULTIMATE of all mineral, vegetable, and animal properties and organizations of the globe.

Man, therefore, is the *final*, because he is the *highest* physical organism possible. The same rule applies to his mental structure and inmost possessions. We find him the final finite embodiment of the infinite Love and Wisdom. He is a *child* in this world. Wars, cruelties, evils, injustices, sins, diseases, miseries—these are the effects of undevelopment. His salvation from hell-punishment is progression, growth, unfoldment. His growth is both automatic (unconscious), and conscious (or volitional); and thus *each man* is inevitably and forever *a party* to that which may enter into his experience, either good or evil. Man is a type of the infinite Universe. Bailey, the author of Festus, saw the initials of this correspondence when he wrote—

> "Earth is the symbol of humanity,
> Water the spirit, stars the truths of heaven;
> All animals are living hieroglyphs:
> The dashing dog, the stealthy-stepping cat,
> Hawk, bull—all that exists—*mean something more*
> To the true eye than their shapes show."

Man's spirit *destitute* of the essential principles of Justice, Truth, Science, Philosophy, Love, Wisdom? Impossible! If mankind were "strangers" to these center-most principles, man could not acquire any permanent knowledge concerning them. Once more I affirm that every man's intuitions are filled with the seed-grain of all principles. Agriculturists never attempt to raise harvests on soils destitute of the essential properties of which their grain is constituted.

Man's mind takes to music, to mathematics, to science, to philosophy, to poetry, to spirituality, and to the realities of eternal life, because *his mind is the repository of all principles*, in a germinal state, of which all immutable truth is composed: Thus—

The harmonial view is apparent. Men existed before bibles and churches! Prelates, bishops, priests, and preachers are only men. They may be wise or otherwise; they may be honest or impostors; they may draw intelligence from heaven or from their own selfishness and ambition. The bishops who "rejected" the apocryphal books, and who adopted as inspired the books now called "holy," were no more qualified as *authority* than would be the same number of merchants, mechanics, or lecturers on Spiritualism. *Authority is invested in the primal principles of the individual spirit.* "The internal witness" is final, "the still small voice" is absolute; the language of intuition is beyond the mistakes of worthy translators; the verdict of Reason is "the voice of God in the garden."

In the Harmonial Age, when Arabula's light shall shine through all things, there will be no constitutional authority on religious questions. Neither can infallibility of teaching be expected from any individual; because man is a progressive being, increasingly toiling between the world of "Ideas" within and the outlying universe of "Things;" and as no one mind can, according to these principles, perceive and comprehend *all truth*, not even in one line of his boundless realm, so no one person can, with any justice or reason, ever assume to be "authority" above his fellows in spirituality and divine principles; although it is true now, and it will everlastingly continue to be true, that some minds, by largeness of capacity, immense susceptibilities, and corresponding industry, may possess more knowledge of and be higher developed in science, philosophy, and spiritual principles, than others who give these subjects little or no attention.

And thus we have among us at all times "teachers," "writers," "mediums," "orators," and "masters," qualified to address mankind, to teach the masses, and reveal in clear light the pleasant and peaceful path of wisdom.

CHAPTER LVIII.

THE RELIGIOUS VALUE OF SPIRITUALISM.

The fanaticisms and follies of many, in the ranks of a new Religious movement, first attract attention. For example: Superficial minds couple the "extremes" of fanatics with what they have "heard" of the manifestations called spiritual. A totally false "opinion" is thus set up in society. The real genius of Spiritualism, meanwhile, is becoming more and more apparent to unprejudiced investigators.

It is the first religion that takes "facts" for its foundation; the first religion that rears its temples of thought on the immutable principles of philosophy; the first religion that sees a Mother, as well as a Father, in God; the first religion that has demonstrably "brought life and immortality to light;" the first religion that has overcome death and the horrors of the grave; the first religion that has sounded the gospel of Freedom equally to woman and man, to young and old, to lord and serf; it is the first religion that has satisfactorily explained the phenomena of matter and mind, in and out of man; it is the first religion that "is to the manor born," and congenial to the true children of Nature; and it is the first religion to free mankind from slavery to creeds and dogmatisms, and to *give the individual wholly to himself!*

Spiritualism, consequently, is the enemy of *conformity.* It teaches that it is better for a man to think for himself, even if he think wrongly, than to conform to the tyranny of social selfishness and to the dictum of ecclesiastical shams. The ape-epoch among men is passing away. "Where the spirit of the Lord is, *there* is liberty" TO THE INDIVIDUAL.

It is probable, yea, it is certain, that "individualism" will also have its follies and fanaticisms. It may lead to *isolation* in some persons; in others, to selfish acts of pride and tyranny; and it may, for a period, set up a barrier to associative efforts, for the progress of the multitude; but these errors will correct themselves, while the *positive benefits* of individualism will come out clearer and clearer, like the golden sun from behind the clouds.

Opposition to every new phase in religious development is natural. The world is full of the tragedies of antagonism to benefactors. Socrates taught the Athenians (who believed in polytheism) the simple "idea" of a Supreme Being; they put him to death. Jesus taught the Jews (great believers in Moses and the Prophets) the "idea" of higher revelations from God; they put him to death. The people of Ethiopia cut St. Matthew into pieces with a sword, because he advocated the doctrines of the Nazarene. Mark, the next named in the Testament, was dragged through the streets of Alexandria, in Egypt, and subsequently died in great agony. Luke, because he *would* teach the "blasphemies" of Jesus, was hung on an olive-tree in Greece. The beloved John, for his religious heresy, died at Ephesus only after he had escaped from a caldron of boiling oil. James, the great, was beheaded at Jerusalem, while the lesser James was thrown headlong from a pinnacle of the temple. Philip was hanged by the neck against a pillar in the streets of Hieropolis. Bartholomew was flayed alive. Andrew was bound to a cross for his heresy, and thus addressed his persecutors till he expired. A sharp spear was run through the body of Thomas. Simon was crucified, as was the Nazarene before him; and Matthias was first stoned and then beheaded. Galileo, a disciple of Copernicus, came near losing his life for teaching the revolution of the planets. Descartes taught the philosophy of "innate ideas." For this the University of Paris denounced him as an atheist, and ordered that all his books should be burned! Dr. Harvey was treated with scorn, deprived of his practice, and driven into exile, because he discovered and taught the circulation of the blood! Dr. Jenner was violently denounced and threatened with disgrace, because he advocated vaccination as a means of mitigating the violence of small-pox! Columbus, Fulton, Fitch, all suffered by the opposition to their several discoveries and reforms. Fulton was laughed at and neglected by the "respectable" and "intelligent" of his day. The ungrateful Frenchmen let Fourier die in extreme indigence. Examples of folly, prejudice, hatred, condemnation and crucifixion of pioneers in any thing absolutely *new*, need not be multiplied. From an outward standpoint this opposition seems "a cross too heavy to be borne—"

> "But truth *shall conquer* at the last,
> For round and round we run,
> And ever the right comes uppermost,
> And ever is justice done."

Spiritualism, then, viewed from the Harmonial stand-point, is the last, and therefore the best, development of the sublime relations between mankind and the next higher sphere of existence. To the opponent only, its outward manifestations are incomprehensible; rappings on a piece of furniture, "signifying nothing." But to us who live with the "Light," those same sounds are the musical beatings of the tides of an infinite sea against the forms that cover the shores of a material world. Yea, to us they are freighted with the mystic loveliness of deathless guardians who inhabit the firmamental spheres; and with uplifted hearts we hail the voices of our loved "departed," whom the benighted mourn as "dead," for we behold in them the *absolute certainty* that whatever is human is immortal.

This, truly, is the grandest religion ever bestowed upon mankind. Every mind under these blessings should aim to become intelligent, self-poised, well-balanced, intuitive, independent, reasonable, charitable, just, noble, and progressive in all high directions. GROWTH is the central law of our being and the object of all exertion, as it will be the result of all experience. Such a mind is the firmest supporter of education. It will, through growth, "overcome evil with good," and straighten the crooked ways of error and injustice. These labors and efforts receive the benedictions of angel intelligences, as good deeds inevitably attract the admiration and co-operation of the generous, intelligent, and noble of every age and country.

CHAPTER LIX.

LIVING FOR OTHERS.

God and Nature are one, the Earth is one, and the human family is one; therefore, nothing lives, because nothing can live, for itself alone. But Arabula dwelleth only in the consciousness of those who, lovingly and willingly, live and work for the progression and benefit of the whole. All work for all by the immutable laws of divine necessity, but how blessed to make this necessity our *choice!*

We, who live in this very hour, exist only as the successors and heirs of the millions and millions departed, who, long ago, lived and struggled through pain and wretchedness to exist and be happy in this world. But all selfish natures, while they have fleeting excitements and sensuous pleasures, are never truly happy. The God-feeling goes out of the spirit when selfishness grasps the scepter of passion. Do what you will, find any company, witness any miracle, take any medicine the diplomatized physicians of Church or State offer you; but unless you live to benefit *others*, as well as yourself, there is no happiness for you, and you can have no positive feeling of God's presence.

One day I walked abroad with Arabula; and I saw that the word "Good" was written upon the constitution of every thing. Sometimes, one of the middle letters was omitted in the orthography, and then the word was, "God." We walked together arm-in-arm through many of the fields of infinite goodness and infinite Wisdom. And behold! every thing and every condition was *good.* The darkest night was as good as the brightest day. Death was as good as life; pain as good as pleasure. Selfishness, yea, even selfishness, was good! It lives honestly in the five senses; it walls in the land; it sows and reaps; it builds houses; it gets married; it cultivates the sciences; it plants gardens; it cuts down forests; it builds roads; it accumulates comforts; it develops works of arts; it multiplies the species; it prolongs individual life; and lastly, according to a natural law, *all it does for itself it leaves to those who come after;* and so the world's material growth is promoted as much by savage selfishness on the one hand, as by benevolence and self-sacrifice on the other. But, Oh, remember: *Only those who lovingly and willingly live to benefit the world find true happiness in the bosom of Nature and God.*

The gladdening consciousness of God can become a guest of every human mind. This, and only this, is your savior. It will defend you against the strong temptations of instinctive passion, and the subtler and more deceitful perils of intellectual atheism and false ambition. This is the divine Life and the divine Light within the vail of the temple. It reveals to you what you may hope and expect from, and look for and find in, others. There is a happiness in it which the unresurrected intellect is not competent either to grasp, analyze, or discern. It is the holy and sanctifying presence of USE, JUSTICE, POWER, BEAUTY, LOVE, WISDOM, TRUTH. Oh exceedingly beautiful! exceeding grand, uplifting, and abiding, is this consciousness of God! It is altogether clairvoyant, and looking through the externals of all life, it sees the saving love, the essentially divine, the perpetually harmonial and everlasting truth, in the very inmost soul of things. Oh reader! open your higher powers, and welcome to your heart a full revelation of THE DIVINE GUEST.

THE END.

LIST OF THE WORKS OF

ANDREW JACKSON DAVIS,

IN THE ORDER OF THEIR PUBLICATION.

	Price.	Post.
NATURE'S DIVINE REVELATIONS	$3.50	50
A CHART. (In Sheets)	1.00	
PHILOSOPHY OF SPECIAL PROVIDENCES	0.20	
GREAT HARMONIA. Vol. I.—The Physician	1.50	20
GREAT HARMONIA. Vol. II.—The Teacher	1.50	20
PHILOSOPHY OF SPIRITUAL INTERCOURSE. Paper, 60 cts. Cloth	1.00	16
GREAT HARMONIA. Vol. III.—The Seer	1.50	20
APPROACHING CRISIS	0.75	08
HARMONIAL MAN. Paper, 40 cts. Cloth	0.75	12
PRESENT AGE, AND INNER LIFE	2.00	24
FREE THOUGHTS CONCERNING RELIGION	0.20	
GREAT HARMONIA. Vol. IV.—Reformer	1.50	20
THE PENETRALIA	1.75	24
MAGIC STAFF. An Autobiography	1.75	24
HISTORY AND PHILOSOPHY OF EVIL. Paper, 40 cts. Cloth	0.75	12
GREAT HARMONIA. Vol. V.—The Thinker	1.50	20
HARBINGER OF HEALTH	1.50	20
ANSWERS TO EVER-RECURRING QUESTIONS	1.50	20
MORNING LECTURES	1.75	20
MANUAL FOR CHILDREN'S LYCEUMS. Cloth, 80 cts. Gilt and Leather	1.00	08
PROGRESSIVE LYCEUM MANUAL. Cloth. (Abridged edition)	0.44	04
DEATH AND THE AFTER-LIFE. Paper, 35 cts. Cloth	0.50	08
THE ARABULA, OR DIVINE GUEST	1.50	20
A STELLAR KEY TO THE SUMMER LAND	1.00	16

Cost of the Complete Works of A. J. Davis.

Complete works of A. J. Davis, comprising twenty volumes, seventeen cloth, three in paper. Nature's Divine Revelations, 30th edition, just out. 5 vols., Great Harmonia, each complete—*Physician*, *Teacher*, *Seer*, *Reformer* and *Thinker*. Magic Staff, an Autobiography of the Author. Penetralia; Harbinger of Health, Answers to Ever-Recurring Questions, Morning Lectures (20 discourses), History and Philosophy of Evil, Philosophy of Spirit Intercourse, Philosophy of Special Providences, Harmonial Man, Free Thoughts Concerning Religion, Present Age and Inner Life, Approaching Crisis, Death and After Life, Children's Progressive Lyceum Manual, Arabula or Divine Guest, Stellar Key to the Summer Land—full set, $26, sent by mail or express as soon as ordered.

WILLIAM WHITE & CO.,

158 WASHINGTON STREET, BOSTON, MASS.,

544 BROADWAY, NEW YORK.

PROSPECTUS

der

von dem amerikanischen Seher und Verkündiger der
"Harmonischen Philosophie"

ANDREW JACKSON DAVIS

in der

Reihenfolge ihrer Veröffentlichung in Nord-Amerika erschienenen und mit Autorisation ihres Verfassers

eines Theils von

dem im Jahre 1858 verstorbenen

Präsidenten der Kaiserlich Leopoldinisch-Carolinischen Akademie der Naturforscher zu Breslau,

Professor Dr. Christian Gottfried Nees von Esenbeck,

und andern Theils von

dessen Mitarbeiter und Herausgeber

Gregor Constantin Wittig,

aus dem Englischen in's Deutsche übersetzten Werke.

These volumes, as fast as translated into the German language, will be forwarded to America, and can be obtained at the offices of

WILLIAM WHITE & CO.,

158 WASHINGTON STREET, BOSTON, MASS., OR,

544 BROADWAY, NEW YORK.

NOW READY AND FOR SALE.

THE HARMONIA, 4th vol., ***"THE REFORMER."***

ALSO

THE MAGIC STAFF, an Autobiography.

Price of each, $2.75. Postage, 32 cts.

www.ingramcontent.com/pod-product-compliance
Lightning Source LLC
LaVergne TN
LVHW020102110826
845151LV00001B/46

* 9 7 8 1 4 2 5 5 4 4 2 8 7 *